The Testing of Hearts

D1137742

The Testing of Hearts

A Pilgrim's Journal

Donald Nicholl

Lamp Press

Marshall Morgan and Scott
Lamp Press
34 – 42 Cleveland Street, London, W1P 5FB. U.K.

Copyright © 1989 Donald Nicholl
First published in 1989 by Marshall Morgan and Scott Publications Ltd
Part of the Marshall Pickering Holdings Group

British Library Cataloguing in Publication Data
Nicholl, D.
    Testing of hearts,
    1. Christian theology
    I. Title
    230

    ISBN 0-551-01904-2

Text Set in 11/12pt. Times by Selectmove Ltd.
Printed in Great Britain by Courier International, Colchester, Essex.

For silver, the crucible
for gold, the furnace
for the testing of hearts,
Jerusalem.

(adapted from Proverbs 17.3)

This book has been written
in gratitude for all those
who shared testing of hearts with me
in Jerusalem,
both those whom I tested
and those who tested me,
especially
the staff and scholars of
Tantur,
and the Maryknollers,
who
made all the difference.

Contents

Introduction

Anyone who starts to read the Introduction to a book naturally expects that it will enable a reader to grasp more easily what the book is all about. Let it be said immediately, therefore, that the present book, as the title indicates, is about the testing of hearts in three concentric spheres. The outermost of these spheres embraces all the peoples who live in the Holy Land that is centred on Jerusalem; the next sphere is defined by the Ecumenical Institute for Theological Research at Tantur, situated on the road between Jerusalem and Bethlehem; the innermost sphere is the heart of the author of this book, who was Rector of the Tantur Institute from 1981 until 1985.

A word about each of these spheres seems desirable. Much of what appears in this book concerning the peoples who live in the Holy Land was originally composed for a series of 'Letters from Jerusalem' which I regularly wrote for the *Tablet*. My intention in those letters, an intention maintained here also, was not to deal with the political issues which tend to obsess commentators on the Holy Land, but rather to touch upon the struggle going on in the hearts of ordinary people for a decent, human, dignified and peaceful life. Already in 1976–7, when I was a scholar at Tantur, I was amazed to discover that almost nobody in authority seemed to pay heed to the aspirations and sufferings of the ordinary people, whether Jew or Arab, Moslem or Christian. Knesset politicians, Arab rulers, US diplomats, the PLO leaders and Christian hierarchs all appeared to move in a stratospheric realm far removed from the day-to-day grind of life in, say, Beit Shemesh, the Musrara or Hebron. It took the *intifada* of 1987 to bring such people down to earth.

As regards the Institute at Tantur, it is helpful to know

that the inspiration to found it came out of the Second Vatican Council. On 17th October, 1963, the observers appointed to the Council met with Pope Paul VI in the Pope's library and there agreed to establish an institute where Christian scholars of every tradition might live together and work towards establishing Christian unity. The site finally chosen for the institute, Tantur, was at that time under Jordanian control. Nowadays, according to international law, it is just inside the Occupied Territories; according to the Israelis, however, it is just inside Israel proper. Although it was originally hoped that all churches would contribute to the Institute's finances, in the event the financial burden has been borne almost entirely by the Catholic University of Notre Dame, Indiana. Not surprisingly, therefore, the splendid building of the Institute reflects an American conception of architecture. And when I first set eyes upon it in 1976 I spontaneously characterised it in my mind as a Crusader castle. I then asked myself whether the Institute might not therefore have inherited the mentality of a Crusader – that is, an inclination to look down from the heights of Tantur upon the concerns of the local people. Be that as it may, since the inhabitants of Tantur enjoy a far more comfortable life physically than do the local people, the struggle for them was not about basic needs but how to live in communion with one another in spite of the traditional tensions between their diverse religious, national, racial and class backgrounds.

More interior yet was the struggle in the third sphere, in the heart of the Rector of Tantur. For a Rector of Tantur it is inevitable that his position will act as a prism which intensifies the hopes and hatreds from all sides to which he is exposed and which will burn his heart.

Since it is possible to distinguish clearly the three spheres named above it would have been convenient both for the author and for the reader to have divided the book into three separate sections. What decided me against such a format was a conversation I once had with the late

Sir Maurice Powicke. Sir Maurice was speaking rather sadly, and with some irritation, at the failure of certain reviewers to understand his recently published book *Thirteenth Century England*. He said that what many reviewers seemed to have anticipated from his pen was a series of chapters each of which would have neatly summed up a particular aspect of English life during that century – one chapter on home policy, for instance, and another on foreign policy followed by others on social movements and religious life; completing the book would have been a chapter on art, architecture and literature. 'The only snag with that format', Sir Maurice said, 'is that life is not like that. On the day, for example, when King Henry III was dealing with the architects responsible for rebuilding Westminster Abbey he was also attending to the troubles in France, making decisions about ecclesiastical appointments and the raising of armies. As historians we do, of course, have to draw out certain threads so that their significance is not obscured by mere chronology. But we must never leave the impression that they were not interwoven with everything else. That would be a falsification. Life is not like that.'

Sir Maurice's words kept coming back to me when I began to think of writing a book focused upon the years that my wife and I had spent in the Holy Land. The easiest course would have been to have developed a series of reflections under such headings as 'community', 'Eucharist', 'encounters with Arabs and Jews', 'peace spirituality', and the like. Yet to have done so would have left a false impression since it was precisely the concatenation of events, their density, which constituted the peculiar flavour of our life at Tantur.

What I mean may be illustrated by just one example that is to be found in its chronological order.

On a certain afternoon I had invited a German biblical scholar, Professor Jeremias, to come to my apartment to discuss matters of mutual interest over a cup of tea. We had not long entered upon our discussion when we heard a noisy argument taking place in the corridor outside the apartment door. On opening the door I found myself facing two angry Arab shepherds who were shouting at each other, disputing which of them was entitled to pasture his sheep on our land and appealing to me to judge between them. I realised immediately that the best way to prevent mayhem around the Institute was to invite them into the apartment and to sit them down, in the hope that the unfamiliar surroundings would awe them into silence. No sooner had I done so, however, when a message came from our reception desk to say that the Cardinal Archbishop of Toulouse had just arrived, unannounced, with his secretary; and he would like to come down straight away to introduce himself.

Ringing the changes upon a German biblical scholar, a French cardinal and Arab shepherds, as I then had to do, was not, admittedly, an everyday occurrence; but something of the kind certainly was. Which is why I decided that the most authentic way to give an account conveying the lessons of those years would be to base it upon the detailed journal which I kept throughout the period. The phrase 'base it upon' needs stressing since my original journal contains many entries so brief as to be unintelligible to anyone but myself without some elaboration; and there are other entries, naturally, which are of no interest to anyone but myself.

It was, nevertheless, only with considerable hesitation that I eventually opted for the journal form since experience has shown that it has many disadvantages and often gives rise to deep misunderstanding. One need only call to mind, for instance, the shock and even outrage expressed by many Swedes upon the publication of Dag Hammarskjold's *Wägmarken* in 1963. Numbers of them felt betrayed at discovering in *Wägmarken* that their much admired representative of Sweden before world opinion, the Secretary General of the United Nations himself, had all the time been leading a hidden life of self-scrutiny based upon the teaching of medieval mystics, who in the minds of

4

modern secularised Swedes symbolised dark age ignorance and neurosis.

Yet that reaction on the part of many Swedes ought not to have been surprising for anyone who remembered the storm provoked in England by the publication in 1838–9 of Hurrel Froude's *Remains*. These were in large part extracts from the young Froude's private diaries and recorded spiritual and ascetic practices undertaken by him such as even his close friends had not suspected to lie behind his handsome appearance and lively manner. As with *Wägmarken*, so with the *Remains*, their publication led many to deem their author a neurotic, pious prig. Yet anyone who tries, as Froude did, to record honestly the testing that he and his companions have been undergoing will inevitably concentrate on their struggles and failures from which they hope to learn. They will leave it to others to list whatever triumphs there may have been.

And though I am not quite so unbalanced as to suggest comparison with either Hammarskjold or Froude nevertheless I do realise that by choosing the same journal form as they employed I run the danger of similar incomprehension.

One example may explain that danger, especially as it illustrates incomprehension on the part even of the journal writer – that is, myself.

Being the *episcopus* (the Greek word *espiskopein* means 'to oversee') of the Ecumenical Institute, part of my duty was to keep an eye upon all the members of the community so as to detect early any signs of unhappiness or dissatisfaction. And towards the end of one term I did, in fact, imagine that distinct signs of dissatisfaction were appearing in several members. The first was a Jesuit priest who had spent many years in various of his Society's houses; and amongst the others was a Protestant married couple. After detecting the signs of their dissatisfaction I began to worry over what to do about the matter before the term came to an end. However, several days before the term did end both the Jesuit in question and the married couple made

5

a point of coming to tell me that their stay at Tantur had proved to be 'the best experience of community' that they had ever enjoyed in the whole of their lives. That such a comment might have been made upon Tantur at that time would have been quite incomprehensible to any reader of my journal, including myself, since it was full of forebodings, problems and failures.

However, there is one great advantage about a journal which is quite irreplaceable. The advantage is that the entries in it, far from being 'emotions recollected in tranquillity', do record the emotions, feelings and thoughts experienced in the actual turmoil of making decisions, facing obstacles and encountering joy and truth. The turmoil is very similar to that experienced by a married couple during those hectic years when they are still struggling with their own sexual relationship, with earning a living for themselves and trying to control their turbulent children, as compared with that period years later when they can now look back with some detachment upon their middle years and can afford a description of them that is much more smooth than they were in reality.

A further advantage of the journal form is that it makes demands of the reader which, if the writing is reasonably well done, are legitimate in the sense that they help him to unearth truths which he could not have discovered had he not been subjected to those demands. In this Introduction, for example, it would have been simple to have provided a brief biography of the writer with an account of his interest, of how he came to find himself in the Holy Land and what subjects the reader may expect to learn about. Instead I have paid heed to the admonition given by Eduardo Galeano when he said, 'Reading should not be an act of consumption. The reader is the creator and completes what is written. The act of reading completes the act of writing.' In the light of Galeano's admonition a *Prelude* to the years in the Holy Land has been given which contains a few extracts from my journal previous to my going to Jerusalem in 1981, and which may be seen, in an oblique, unwitting manner, to foreshadow some of the testing that was to come.

One further remark. Nearly all descriptions that I have read of Christian communities – or, indeed, of other kinds of community, if it comes to that – fall into one of two categories. Either they reflect the disillusion of the author, whose unreal expectations of his companions had been compounded by his own lack of self-criticism; or else they are cosmeticised descriptions intended to advertise the virtues of a specifically Christian community, to say nothing of the wisdom and tolerance of the author. What I miss in virtually all descriptions of community are the nitty-gritty details, those irritations over seemingly small matters which are often more difficult to deal with than big ideological differences. I hope that at least some sense of the nitty-gritty emerges from the following pages.

In order for that to happen, of course, an honest journal must record certain conflicts; but when it has been essential to do so I have disguised the identities of people involved as well as I could – though the identity and character of the journalist himself is obviously beyond disguise.

Finally, after finishing with my journal I had intended to add an Epilogue in order to bring it up to date. With that purpose in mind my wife and I spent some time during November of 1988 visiting many places and many friends all over the Holy Land. But when I came to collect my impressions and thoughts after returning to England I realised that although there have been great changes since November 1987 at the political level, nevertheless those changes will be superficial and will not bring peace unless the peoples of Jerusalem submit to that testing of hearts which is even more searching than the crucible and the furnace. For that reason I am ready to leave as the final word the last of my letters to the *Tablet*, which appeared at Easter, 1985.

Prelude

'I must not turn this into poetry.' That is the sentence which has been dinning itself into my mind as I have sat by the bedside of my dying father for the past several days. He has lain there, propped up against the pillows, his eyes closed, his strong frame shaking as his whole being has panted for breath. Even when we change the catheter attached to his penis, or turn him to ease the pain from his sores, he gives no sign of consciousness, apart from occasionally emitting a deep groan.

Those groans are so deep that each of them sounds as though it must be the final one, all the breath available to him on this earth expended. They warn me that if anything is to be saved from this wreckage of a man it cannot come from outside this room; it cannot come from any subsequent poetry that glosses over the fearful fact that death is now bringing to an end the eighty years of my father's struggle for light against darkness.

And what a struggle that has been throughout the years – the constant effort to survive on this bleak Pennine hilltop where tonight the snow is swirling against the windows and the freezing wind outside is blowing it into deep drifts, leaving the road along the village to the moors impassable. And how typical it is that in my father's involuntary groans no trace of self-pity is to be heard, any more than there was in his last words to me before he drifted down the road into oblivion.

We did manage to speak a few halting sentences to

9

one another the day after I arrived back from California. Late on Monday evening he said very clearly and firmly, his voice full of that lilting wonder with which he has always greeted life, 'The human frame, lad! Isn't it a marvel?' In view of the fact that his own strong frame was at that very moment breaking up I could not help reflecting how generous and noble was Dad's response. Nor could I help smiling at his words, so characteristic of one who had always been given to philosophising. He continued to philosophise even to the end, when a few minutes later he pronounced his last upon this world: 'It's all a great mystery. Nobody can fathom it.'

10th February 1979. Claremount

To-night the wind is fiercer than ever, and one can readily believe what people say: there is no high ground between the Ural mountains in Russia and this bare Pennine ridge that might shelter us against the bone-chilling blasts from Siberia. So it demanded a real effort on the part of the young Anglican vicar this evening to struggle through the deep snowdrifts from his warm home to this barely-heated house. Sometimes it feels as if the wind is wuthering through the walls as though they are made of nothing but rice paper.

All the same, we, every one of us – the vicar, my mother, my sister and myself – felt a real glow of warmth as we knelt together around Dad's bed and said the 'Our Father'. And we were grateful when the young vicar said he hoped to come again tomorrow and celebrate Holy Communion here, in this tiny bedroom. For a moment, as he was promising to come, the vicar hesitated when he turned towards me, knowing that I am a Roman Catholic and that it is not customary for Roman Catholics to receive the Eucharist from an Anglican priest.

10

But he need not worry. The man lying there on his death bed – though still thirsting for breath and for life – who is my father, has taught me the meaning of Eucharist more certainly than have any of the theologians whose books I have read or whose sermons I have listened to.

That happened almost fifty years ago, when we lived in an even smaller house, actually inside the yard of the brickyard, opposite the kilns where the workers fired the clay to make drain pipes and toilets – an ironic circumstance, in view of the fact that none of the back-to-back houses on our row themselves had toilets! We had to make do with the earth closets at the end of the row, some twenty yards distant from our own house. That must have made life even harder for Mum and Dad at that time, when it was already hard enough for them, with Dad out of work, because they had to try to nurse me through a bout of pneumonia which was threatening to put an end to me, their seven-year-old son. In fact, I clearly remember one day saying to them, quite calmly, 'I think I'm going to die.' What distress they must have suffered then and subsequently in that tiny bedroom, shared by all four of us, as they listened to me struggling for breath week after week.

But my school teacher, Miss Clayton, sent me a gift of a bunch of grapes, the first I had ever tasted. And from that moment I never looked back. Nor do I ever forget to bless Miss Clayton each time I taste grapes.

Five weeks later I was able to go downstairs. And soon I began to take walks with Dad to get my strength back. Happily it was blackberry time. So Mum sent us off one sunny morning to collect blackberries which would help to feed us for a period when there was little food to be had. As Dad and I were setting out across the flagstones from the brickyard she also gave us an apple apiece for our lunch.

It is not generally known that though the tops of the hills in the Pennines are mostly bare and daunting, nevertheless our valleys in between are often beautifully wooded with oak and elm, ash, elderberry and blackberries. My father made quick pencil sketches of all these trees in the pauses we took to sit down on grassy banks as we walked first towards the upper end of the valley in order to be able to work our return way southwards and finish near to home by late afternoon.

It was a heavenly day and Dad and I were quick to share our delight with one another as first one then the other would come upon a further fresh cluster of the bright black beauties. And I myself was bathed not only in the warmth of the sun but also in the warmth and tenderness of my father whose heart was visibly rejoicing that his son was now restored to him. All the same my strength had not yet fully returned. So by midday it was a tired boy who agreed to his father's suggestion that we should put down our brimming carrier bags and sit on the railway embankment to eat our lunch.

No sooner were we sitting on the coarse grass than I took out my apple and with scarcely a pause for breath proceeded to eat it, every bit of it apart from the pips. All the while I was doing so my father sat watching me, an amused smile on his lips, as he unhurriedly polished his own apple on his shirt.

When he saw that I had spat out the last of the pips he said to me, 'You were right hungry, lad!' 'Yes I was', I heartily agreed. Whereupon my father said, 'Well, would you like half of my apple as well?' 'No, dad,' I answered, almost indignantly, 'You're hungry as well'. My father looked at me, his fine honest eyes filled with love; and speaking in a deep, contented voice he assured me, 'No. I'm not really.'

Of course, I knew that he was. But I also sensed that he had long since mastered his hunger. Strong man that he was, he then took the apple into his hands, which had become cut and calloused over the years through his work, and he very deliberately broke the apple in two. And even now, before my mind's eye, I can see the shining white flesh of the halves of that broken apple, each half

12

resting between the thick muscles of my father's thumb and forefinger. He placed one half into my hands and we ate in silence. This time I ate slowly and deliberately. Something had changed as a result of which the whole world had become a different place: it could never be the same again.

In those days, only a child of seven, I could clearly not have ventured any explanation of that sacred action in which my father had served as the priest. But the course of life since has made me realise how, on that abandoned-looking railway embankment, I had been touched at the centre of my being, in my very substance, at a level far deeper than the consciousness of a seven-year-old could fathom. And nothing would be the same again. That is the effect of communion.

Fifty years later, our roles now reversed, it was I who was serving my father as his body was breaking. And so the young Anglican priest need not worry lest I, a Roman Catholic, might not feel free to share in the Eucharist tomorrow evening. Could anything, in fact, show more clearly how far astray Christians have gone that even the slightest shadow of doubt could be cast on the rightness of my doing so?

For here we are gathered, the four of us: my dying father, my mother brimming with love for him, and my sister solicitous for them both, as well as myself, back home from the far ends of the earth. All their lives the three of them have been devout Christians in the Anglican tradition, faithful in receiving communion each week, saying their prayers at the beginning and at the end of the day, generous in giving from their meagre wages. We four have shared everything with one another for more than fifty years, in sickness and in health, in joy and in sorrow, and now we have reached the moment to share with my father in the breaking of bread on the last stage of his journey.

Could you conceive of anything more monstrous than the suggestion that on this sacred occasion I should stand back from the Lord's Table, separate myself from my beloved family and make a division between us at the very moment when our hearts, my father's especially, are aching for union, for communion? If any such suggestion were to come to me, whether from Pope, bishop or priest, I should not hesitate to tell him, 'If you say I should stand back at this moment, then let me tell you, Pope, that you are far indeed from the mind of our Lord and Saviour, Jesus Christ.'

14th February 1979. Heathrow Airport

six o'clock in the morning

Just before I left home my sister said that she could not understand how I had managed to go on sitting beside my father all the day long and into the night in that cold bedroom and then sleeping for only a few hours on the floor of the room below. There is nothing surprising in that, because you feel you can manage anything when you are serving someone whom you love with all your heart. Nevertheless, sitting as I am doing now on a bench in this almost deserted airport, I have begun to feel utterly bereft and comfortless as I go over in my mind again and again the events of these last weeks and try to discover some meaning in them. Perhaps that is what poetry does for us, and maybe we *are* meant, after all, to try to transform our experience into poetry?

But how can you transform the unrelenting cold, the cold outside on the moors, and within 'a heart cold under a breast of pitiful fear'? You can't run away from it because then it will only pursue you the more relentlessly and bite into you deeper than before. So last Sunday I made a seemingly strange decision that arose unexpectedly from some instinctive source. I determined to go out into the bitter wind through the deep snowdrifts and climb Beacon Hill to the hamlet where as a young man Dad had lived for some years with Grandma Nicholl after his elder brothers had left for the war. From that high point I could look

14

out over Halifax and survey almost all the places where he had spent his life – the school, the mill, the brickyard, the football field, the church and the surrounding streets; and, on the steep slope of the hill, the graveyard where Grandma and the rest of the family are now buried.

As soon as I made the decision to climb the hill I realised that I was doing so as an act of thanksgiving towards Dad and all my ancestors and relatives for the courage that they had shown in living such good lives in the midst of these grim surroundings. Also, I was intent on affirming their faith, and Dad's faith in particular, that beyond the grimness and the cold and the temptation to despair, there lies a meaning in life which even death cannot eliminate.

My mother, I think, did understand at some instinctive level why I was choosing to go out for a few hours on this threatening afternoon when no other human being seemed to be stirring. I'm not sure that the others did. But they nevertheless wished me well when I opened the door and stepped over the threshold as a blast of wind swept down the path and nearly blew me back into the house. They shut the door and hurried back to the warmth of the hearth.

Even though it was quite early afternoon, still the sky was so unbrokenly leaden no one could possibly imagine that somewhere above and beyond that heavy covering there might stand a sun which actually gives out light and warmth. And within a few minutes, after I had walked no more than three or four hundred yards through the village and across the bridge to the bottom of the hill, my feet were wet with snow that had melted inside my boots, and I could feel the cold biting into my hands and fingers, sending freezing shock waves throughout every bone in my body. That is how it has always been for me ever since my childhood in my native Pennines with winter upon us – the cold wind picking on my bones so remorselessly as to leave imprinted on my brain an image of my own skeleton, accurately and clearly defined. And now when I have grown to a height of six feet and six inches, and even thinner – if that were possible – with my blood also thinned out from years in warmer climes, the chill wind has still less difficulty in searching out my bones and striking an imprint of my skeleton.

As I made my way up the hill I kept stumbling and falling into the drifts which were so deep that it would have been useless to seek for the path. Instead, for almost an hour, I kept heading for where I knew the top of the hill to be. It was as well that I did know because several times it was completely obscured by thick curtains of snow.

I kept thinking to myself that if anyone down in Halifax looks up to Beacon Hill and sees this tiny figure darrk against the snow they will conclude there is a madman at large, or a criminal taking advantage of the storm to escape.

Eventually, however, I did reach the very summit of the hill and turned towards the town below so as to face the wind and say farewell to the place on behalf of Dad, who now lay helpless in one of those houses whose shape I could just make out in the white expanse below High Sunderland: never again would he look upon this grim landscape of worn-out industries that had been his life's arena. And as if the place itself was intent upon my not escaping its unrelenting demands the wind blew fiercer than ever as I turned towards the town. It so numbed my brain that I was incapable of making the proper farewell I had intended.

Instead my mind was taken over by one image that sustained itself for the short space of time my face was able to bear the lashing of the wind.

That image was of Grandma Nicholl and Dad on a winter's morning, whilst it was still dark, making their way on foot together down the bank towards the mill at Dean Clough where they both worked. She must have been in her fifties already, several years a widow. Left to bring up four boys on her own in the notorious slum of Charlestown, she had managed it by the simple expedient of working in the mill from six in the morning until five in the evening and then serving as a barmaid in the pub at night. Dad had begun work as a half-timer, also in the mill, at the age of twelve. In later years he would reminisce to me about those early morning journeys with Grandma, remarking what a blessing it was for them to walk together and grow close to one another, whether through talking as they went along or through just being silent with one another. Often they had to struggle along holding each other by the arm because of the strength of the wind.

It was the same wind which now drove me to seek some relief on the lee side of the hill. For a while, as I tramped along, the snow became deeper, and nowhere did I see any tracks to indicate that either man or beast had passed this way. But soon I came to a pair of standing stones that I remembered as marking the beginning of Dark Lane, which leads down into the valley. Dark Lane provided some respite from the freezing wind, but since almost no one uses it these days it also provides pot-holes, broken fences and stray lengths of barbed wire which were now concealed by the snow, as a result of which I several times pitched full length into the drifts.

After about an hour I passed the pit (where Dad's brother, Uncle Isaac, had once worked) and then up past the derelict industrial school where boys used to be sent who had got into trouble. The windows these days have all been smashed and the tiles in the old swimming bath lie scattered around. However, by this time I was beginning to feel warm, not only because of the strenuous plunging around in the snow but also through the warmth that comes from knowing one has carried out the proper ritual, that act which makes some sense out of an apparently meaningless situation, meaningless beyond redemption. Nor did it take me long, once I was on the paved road, to walk the remaining two miles, again without meeting another soul, that brought me home, where there was a hot meal waiting for me.

That night, at half-past nine, I was due to set out on my journey back to California and we had been hoping that my eldest daughter, Mary, might be able to drive up from Shropshire so as to take over from me at my father's bedside. Yet with every hour it was getting more and more unlikely that she would do so, in view of the warnings on the radio that even the main roads over the Pennines were virtually impassable and should only be attempted in extreme emergencies. The news saddened me because it would have been a great comfort to me to have seen Mary just then, not having seen her for a long time. But what will be, will be. And by nine-thirty she had still not arrived whilst the snow was coming down in thicker flakes than ever. So I said my last good-bye to Dad; and then to Mum and the rest, and I set out alongside the garden wall leading to the village street. There, through the curtain of white flakes, I saw approaching the headlights of a car which was moving ever so slowly, as if trying to find a grip upon the shifting snow.

When I came abreast of the car it stopped, and suddenly my beloved Mary's face became visible through the car window. 'Hello, Dad', she said in her soft voice as she stepped out into the storm, and she put her arms around me and kissed me. For a minute we stood there holding one another, knowing that there was no time to go back to the house and talk. With the wind screaming around us, the snow gathering on Mary's fur cap and the car engine throbbing away the world seemed to have become a wild nightmare of a place in which the two of us were left orphaned, exposed to every force of terror known to man or demons.

Within a minute we had parted, and already as I struggled on against the wind my meeting with Mary had acquired a fictional quality, as if it were a scene from Pasternak's novel *Dr Zhivago,* as if our desolate hilltop had become another Varykino with a different sort of wolf howling around us.

But the railway station in Halifax, when I finally reached it, was real enough, in all conscience – or surreal enough – to drive every hint of poetry out of my head. It was like

18

the house of the dead – no human being to be seen, only ghosts of what had once been the junction for a prosperous community. The grimy sign-boards, the broken benches, the platform lamps of which only half gave light, the waiting room with its dead cinders in the fireplace and gaps in the door through which the wind whistled, all of these once shining artefacts now witnessed to the neglect and despair which had overtaken the culture of this Pennine township.

And the same message of despair was spelled out to me once more as I sat almost alone in a scruffy carriage whilst the train made its way slowly through the frozen countryside, past chapels that had once been centres of life but were now empty shells, past factories and warehouses that were now neither dead nor alive, not standing up yet only half fallen down.

So it was in accordance with all these silent messages that in Leeds, when the train for London drew in, it turned out that only those carriages fitted with sleepers were heated. The handful of us without sleeper bookings at this midnight hour would be spending the night shivering in the semi-darkness.

And yet by comparison our discomfort seemed as nothing when a few hours later, stretching our stiffened limbs, we stumbled across King's Cross Station, because there, dozing on benches or hanging around the public lavatories, some of them seeking solace in cigarettes and others in strange contortions with each other, was such a haunting group of derelicts as you would rarely come across by day. Most of them looked starved, their eyes bulging with hunger; their clothes were worn thin, no protection against the winter's night; and whenever they moved their limbs seemed to be sighing that they had long since come to the end – and beyond the end – of the road.

So if my daughter Mary and I had seemed to be characters in the story of Zhivago, these poor wretches appeared rather to have come out of the storm scene in *King Lear*. As I travelled on the first tube train of the morning towards

Heathrow airport the image of them before my mind's eye was all I needed to push me into a state of frozen despair. And that is how I felt as I wandered around the halls of Heathrow, which were almost entirely empty and echoing hollowly at the sound of my own footsteps. Where I was supposed to go to wait for a stand-by place on a Pan Am flight to San Francisco, I had no idea. Nor was there anyone about of whom I might enquire. And if it came to that, I was so tired from all those nights by my father's side, whom I would never see again, that I felt too disorientated to search for anyone.

That was when I saw a young woman come round a corner some thirty yards away. She was a rather dumpy person, bespectacled, with short hair of a nondescript brown colour. But as she approached that undistinguished appearance of hers mattered less to me than the fact that she was wearing a uniform, a uniform that held promise that its wearer knew about airways.

So I moved over to my left to intercept her, and I asked her if she knew where I was supposed to go in order to secure a stand-by place on a Pan Am flight to San Francisco. Though she was clearly in a hurry she stopped to listen to me, and then looked kindly at me as she answered that she was sorry but she didn't know.

And then something happened. Whether it was some note of sadness in my voice that she picked up or whether she saw something in my face that moved her – whatever it was, she had been touched. Perhaps that is why she in turn touched my sleeve and said, 'Wait a minute, my love. I think I may be able to help you. Please come with me.' And at that she led me across the hall towards a window on which she tapped. Soon a man appeared to whom she explained my need, and he straightaway assured me that if I were to wait outside his window for a quarter of an hour he would assign me a place on the flight to San Francisco.

The young woman who had come to my aid turned towards me and smiled. 'There you are', she said. 'Have a safe journey.' I bowed towards her and thanked her for her kindness.

1st September, 1985. Rostherne, Staffordshire

It is never easy to convey in writing the significance which certain seemingly trivial events or actions assume in a person's life. To an outsider that casual encounter on a deserted Heathrow between an unusually tall, bearded man wearing a duffle coat and a dumpy woman airport worker could hardly have seemed of any importance in the life of either the man or the woman. They had never met before and they have never met since – not knowingly, at least, since neither knew the other's name and almost certainly would not recognise the other's face. Indeed, it is doubtful whether the woman even remembers the incident since she has probably dealt with thousands of such passengers subsequently who are no more than a blur in her mind.

But the man, myself, will never forget how his numbed heart was melted by the warmth in the woman's voice when, though a total stranger to him, she said, 'my love'. I have wondered since if she often says 'my love' to total strangers or whether it was the Spirit of God which inspired her to do so that winter morning. And is she a believer? The answer to that, I shall never know, any more than she can have the remotest idea what significance her generous, though modest, gesture has come to assume in my own life.

What further fascinates me about the whole incident is the hint it provides of how the web of human relationships may well be more determined by such 'small deeds', accomplished each day by millions of unknown people, rather than by the decisions and acts of those who imagine themselves to be the controllers of human destiny.

The great virtue of such deeds, small in the eyes of the world but great in the sight of God, is that they cannot be contrived. They cannot be planned; for if they were planned they would be no more than exercises in manipulating other people. And none of us can have the faintest idea of the reverberations for good that they may produce throughout the world wherever the good news of hope is being spread. It always fills me with wonder, for instance, when I think of those words spoken to Jesus by the centurion at Capernaum, 'Lord, I am not worthy that you should enter under my roof but only say the word and my servant will be healed.' When he pronounced those words the centurion cannot have known that they would reverberate in the hearts of millions of human beings over the centuries and over the face of the whole earth at the most sacred moments of their lives, when they receive the sacrament of communion – in their childhood, at their marriages and in their last moments as death approaches.

Nor again can that peasant serf on the Dostoevsky estate, Marei, have ever imagined that he would be remembered and blessed throughout the world for that moment of *umilenie,* that melting of his heart by grace of the Holy Spirit which the great Russian novelist has recorded for all time.

Dostoevsky tells us how on Easter Day, 1852, when he was serving as a political prisoner in Siberia, he was so disgusted by the drunkenness and violence of his fellow-prisoners that he climbed on to his bunk and turned his back upon the hell of a barrack room. For a long time he nursed his loathing of the other prisoners until there suddenly arose within him the memory of an incident which he had completely forgotten from twenty years past.

As a child of nine he had one day been wandering alone across an open field on their estate when he thought he heard a wolf approaching. In his terror he ran towards the lonely figure of Marei, the serf who was ploughing the field. Marei quickly comforted the boy, stroking him on the cheek and murmuring, 'Don't be frightened, my dear. Christ be with thee. Cross thyself.'

'But I did not cross myself,' writes Dostoevsky, 'the

corners of my lips quivered; and, I believe, that was what impressed him most. Slowly he stretched out his thick thumb, with the black nail soiled with earth, and gently touched my trembling lips . . . and he looked at me with a long motherly smile . . .'

And now, twenty years later, it was Marei's soil-blackened thumb that Dostoevsky particularly remembered:

> . . . and if I had been his own son he could not have bestowed upon me a glance full of a more serene love. And yet, who had prompted him? He was a peasant serf, while I was a nobleman's son. No one would find out how he had caressed me and no one would reward him. The meeting was a solitary one, in an open field; and only God, maybe, perceived from above what a profound and enlightened human feeling, what delicate, almost womanly tenderness may fill the heart of some ignorant Russian peasant serf.
>
> And when I climbed down off my bunk and gazed around I felt I could behold these unfortunate men with a wholly different outlook, for suddenly, by some miracle, all the hatred and anger had completely vanished from my heart.

27th March, 1980. The Hermitage,

Big Sur, California

Monks and nuns often seem to establish themselves in quiet, beautiful places, which can lead one to ask them, 'out of the moiling street with its swelter and its sin, who has given you this sweet and given your brothers dust to eat? When does their wage come in?' And yet, however critical I sometimes feel about monasteries and hermitages I have to recognise, whenever I spend a few days here, that I am glad there are such places as this – an oasis of sanity and peace to remind us that the world of noise and words and money and power and sex can never satisfy the longings of the human heart.

It is quite remarkable how soon after arriving here I always feel the whole of my being to be changing, even within only a few hours. I sit on a bench at the edge of the tiny garden fronting my small cell and look out over the Pacific Ocean some two thousand feet below. Behind me the wooded mountain rises to a height of five thousand feet. And everywhere there is a profound silence which seems all the easier to breathe in by virtue of the regular songs and cries of the birds which nest in the steep gulches on either side. The warm sun relaxes all the muscles in my body and my lungs take in deeper draughts of air than they ever imagined possible. And it is pure air, so sparkling that one understands why air is sometimes said to be like wine. The whole of my being, my body, my mind and my spirit, slips into a rhythm so perfect that if only I could sustain it for ever I would be in paradise.

For there is something paradisal about those of the hermits who have not allowed the rhythm of monastic life to put them to sleep. That is what also endows them with such unusual sensitivity to the feelings of their fellow creatures. One such person is Fr Bede, the eighty-year-old Englishman who entered the hermitage almost forty years ago. He is now incredibly bent but still manages faithfully to cultivate the garden and to celebrate Mass with complete absorption. Yesterday he moved me to tears by unexpectedly coming over to me and saying that he had heard of my father's death; and would I allow him to celebrate Mass this morning for my father's sake? What moved me so deeply is that he and I have never spoken more than a few words to one another. But at some very deep level he has been exquisitely aware of myself and my needs. And during the Mass at which he presided I was made aware of a need within myself so deep down that only a touch of God could have brought it to light.

I need to go home, to return to England and live there so as to be with my mother when she is dying. The grace of being with my father in his last days now makes clear to me that there is nothing more important for a son or daughter than to be present at the dying of their mother and father. In the strictest sense of the word that is a unique occasion. It can never be repeated and if one fails to be present at it through choice or through heedlessness then the burden of that failure can never be lifted.

22nd July, 1980. Santa Cruz, California

What a blessed release, and relief, it would be if a messenger from the Lord were to appear and say to me, 'Once you are back in England, for the rest of your life, you are not required to utter any word of criticism of any institution or any individual. You need rebuke no one. You are henceforth relieved of that obligation. From now on you may live as Father Sergius lived, who gave his name to Tolstoy's novella: doing menial tasks, teaching Scripture to children, eating simple food, in quietness and peace.'

But that is not what the messengers are saying. They have been saying, 'Don't imagine that you are meant, like a *sannyasi*, to "get beyond" all earthly tasks whilst you are still in the body. Your longing for utter purity, simplicity and peace itself needs to be purified by the tensions of finding shelter, earning your bread and your clothing and raising your voice on behalf of the dumb. Not until the very end will you be relieved of those tensions.'

27th July, 1980. Spode House, England

If someone had staged it they couldn't have plotted a better illustration of the need for inter-faith dialogue than Sister Imelda provided this afternoon.

During the course of the conference which I gave I must have quoted Buddhist teachers on several occasions with evident enthusiasm. That seemed not to have pleased Sister Imelda, because as soon as the chairman opened the floor for discussion she immediately popped up and, somewhat archly, put to me the question, 'You seem to

25

have a high regard for Buddhists, so perhaps you can explain to me why, although they constantly speak of "compassion", they do not seem to understand what we mean by "love"?' Though I realised it might sting her I felt that I would be resisting providence if I did not reply by recounting what had happened to me only a few days earlier in San Francisco.

There I had been requested by the Roshi of the Zen Buddhists to give a talk to about thirty of his pupils on *Prayer of the Heart in the Christian tradition*. This I had done to the best of my ability, facing row upon row of Zen Buddhists, all sitting attentively in the lotus position. When I had finished speaking the Roshi called for questions, and, much to my surprise – since Buddhists are supposed to be passionless – there was an unmistakable note of aggression in the voice of the young man who asked the first question. He demanded, 'Why is it that Christians are always talking about love but do not seem to understand compassion?'

19th, June 1981. Rostherne

Often I have to laugh at myself for my habit of wanting to communicate with virtually everyone under the sun when I read what they say or watch the way they are behaving. But sometimes my impulsiveness can surprisingly turn out to be rewarding, as it did today in the Israeli Embassy in London.

On the surface my impulse to write to the Israeli Ambassador on account of his letter to *The Times* of December 24th last year was strange. After all, his letter contained no arguments that one has not already heard thousands of times from Israeli propagandists; but there was something about it that moved me. Perhaps it was the fact that the letter appeared on the eve of Christmas and I was saddened to think that our Jewish brethren are excluded from the joyous celebration of the birth of the Jew, Jesus. Even more significant, I think, was an echo that

26

could be heard beneath the Ambassador's argumentative sentences, a cry from the heart lest the fears of Jews should once more go unheeded.

For several weeks I looked in *The Times* for some response to Shlomo Argov's letter, but none appeared. So after three or four months I myself decided to write in order to assure the good man that his *cri de coeur* had not gone entirely unheard; but also to ask him to explain to those of us who feel committed to the Jewish people, how we may yet be free to criticise the policy of the State of Israel (just as we criticise other states, especially our own) without fear that we shall be condemned as anti-Semites.

Unfortunately from my point of view, the Ambassador had just been subjected to a terrible grilling by the British media in recent weeks, so when we met today he was too excitable to deal calmly with my question. In fact I never raised it during our hour-long meeting. Instead he poured out torrents of words denouncing a British television programme about Israel entitled *Hanging Fire*. Much of his criticism was justified, though I demurred at his demand that the producers of the programme should be put in jail. But one thing he said about Israel was so fundamental that anyone venturing an opinion on that State should never forget it.

His own family not being a particularly religious one, he said, their longing to escape from exile and persecution and live in a state of their own had not been inspired by religious tradition. Rather, what his family hoped for, above all, was to live in a country of their own, like all other human beings, in order that gradually the memory of all those thousands of years of persecution would be eroded and the ancient wounds would be healed. Whereas instead, he continued in an agonised voice, just the opposite had happened. 'When we started living in the Land we discovered that absolutely everyone else there, everyone whom we met, had a similar history to our own; so that far from the dreadful memories being eroded and the ancient wounds healed, everything reminded us of our terrible past and every encounter called attention to our wounds.'

When I heard those words from Shlomo Argov's lips I recognised on the basis of my own sojourns in Israel how true and fundamental his words were. The ingathering of the Jewish people has heightened their sense of isolation and for them the State of Israel has acted like a burning prism, intensifying the remembrance of their suffering.

My interview with the Ambassador left me puzzling over another conundrum as I walked away from the Embassy down Kensington High Street. How is it that there are certain people you cannot take to, although they are altogether polite and correct in their behaviour, and their viewpoint is close to your own; whilst there are other people of whom you can hardly say the same, and yet you like them – even sometimes when they are rogues? Well, Shlomo Argov is anything but a rogue; all the same he is explosive and unreasonable on some questions, but I really did take to the man. He has a good heart.

10th July, 1981. Rostherne.

'I would never go there now', said a friend of mine when I met her for the first time in many years and told her that I was going to live in Jerusalem. 'It would be like going to live in Naboth's vineyard.' In spite of being slow on the uptake even I realised that by Naboth's vineyard she was referring to the land of Palestine and that she was casting present-day Israel for the role of Ahab. My friend was carrying out a typical rabbinic exegetical practice by taking a biblical story as paradigmatic for the state of contemporary relations between Arabs and Jews.

For my own part I do not find that particular exegetical practice to be very illuminating generally; and indeed on many occasions its use has proved positively dangerous, having been invoked to justify robbery and slaughter on a large scale. All the same my friend's remark brought me up sharply and set me wondering what precise role I myself might be cast for in the drama of Naboth's vineyard. I could never, for instance, imagine any event that would convince me to don the mantle of Elijah the Tishbite who went to the King of Israel and declared, 'Yahweh says this: you have committed murder; now you usurp as well. For this – and Yahweh says this – in the place where the dogs licked the blood of Naboth, the dogs will lick your blood too.' And I fervently hoped, of course, that I was not destined to share the fate of Ahab's son, Jehoram – he upon whom Jehu drew his bow and sent an arrow between his shoulder blades which came out through his heart; then Jehu had his body thrown into the field of Naboth, at the same time calling upon the blood of Naboth and the blood of his sons. There has, in all conscience, I thought, been altogether far too much blood spilt already in this neck of the woods, from the day of Cain and Abel until today, without any sojourner adding to it even directly, whether by thought or by word or by deed.

So now, in my third sojourn in the land, I thank God for the instruction that he gave me years ago, before I arrived for the first time. And it is significant, I believe, that he gave the instruction, not through the Peoples of the Book, but through the peaceable and tolerant Taoists.

My instruction came in the form of a story. This story tells of a scholar who was about to leave his native town on a journey of many years. Before setting out he went along to say farewell to his friend, the town butcher; and in the course of doing so he noticed the butcher's chopper. It was shining and spotless, its blade incredibly sharp. After admiring it at some length the scholar bade his friend farewell and then set out on his travels, which were to take him all of twenty-five years. Upon returning once more to his native town and settling in home again the scholar went to visit his butcher friend. After they had greeted one another with due ceremony, the scholar chanced to notice a chopper on the butcher's bench, just as shining and spotless as the one he had noticed twenty-five years previously. And when he tested the blade it was just as incredibly sharp. 'It amazes me', he said to his friend, 'that you are able to secure a supply of such wonderful choppers, year after year, and that you can keep the blade so sharp in spite of all the meat that you chop with them.' 'It is quite simple', the butcher replied. 'That chopper is none other than the same chopper which you saw twenty-five years ago, and I have never needed to sharpen it since then, in spite of all the meat that I chop with it each day. You see, in every piece of meat, in between the various parts, there is always an infinitely small space, a way *(Tao)*, and if the blade is sufficiently fine, the chopper can actually go along that way between the parts, without spilling any blood or getting stained or becoming blunt.'

In the Taoist story God was saying, 'Go through it all without harming anyone, without spilling blood or yourself becoming stained or blunt.' And I continue to think still that the Taoist story offers a better paradigm than the Naboth story for anyone who is going to spend some time in the Holy Land.

But even my Taoist story cannot be regarded as a completely satisfactory paradigm. Certainly it brings out the need for detachment in a memorable fashion, but it does not do justice to the demand for commitment asked of one in Jerusalem.

And 'demand' is the right word to use here because Jerusalem is the most demanding of cities to live in – not in the same way as Calcutta is or New York, but in the much more subtle sense that here you are called upon to exercise the virtue of justice every minute of the day, or so it seems. Nor is this exercise of justice required of you simply in your deeds or in your words. In deeds or in words it is comparatively easy. Far more demanding is the fact that you are called to make a secure dwelling for justice in the deepest point of your heart, in the *guha,* as the Hindu sacred scriptures name it, 'the cave of the heart'. For in this mysterious city of Jerusalem you can not only see men's deeds and hear their words, you can actually feel their heartbeats and sense what is going on in

30

their hearts – and they in yours. Which is why, perhaps, this is the city of lies: men pile one lie upon another in a desperate, futile attempt to heap lies so thick that the truth relentlessly demanded of them by this holy city shall remain hidden.

How then, can one reveal to oneself those lies that in this city prevent justice from securing a dwelling in the cave of one's heart? Is there any sign available to indicate when one's heart is becoming corrupted? These were questions that I anxiously put to myself during the months when I was preparing to live once more in Jerusalem. And an answer was given more apposite than that of Naboth's vineyard or even of the Taoist chopper.

It is simple. If your immediate spontaneous reaction – if the movement of your heart – upon hearing of some tragedy, is an ideological one rather than a human one, then your heart has become corrupted, and you should leave straight away and go on pilgrimage until it is cleansed. Suppose you hear, for instance, that scores of civilians have been killed in an air raid upon PLO headquarters in Beirut, and your immediate reactions is, 'Well, what else do they expect if they share quarters with terrorists?' In that case your reaction is not a human one but an ideological one. Your ideology may even be correct; but if it is primary then you have lost your heart of flesh and set up in its place an idol of stone.

I quoted this example to a high-placed Israeli official, and when I noticed how his facial muscles twitched I realised that he was grieved by what had been revealed to him in the cave of his heart. A good man, nevertheless; and he grieved. More saddening was my encounter with a Marxist whom I know. After describing to him the sign of discernment that I had been given, I proposed a different illustration as a test, an incident in Haifa bus station. There a bomb planted by the PLO killed a number of innocent citizens. Again, I said, if one's instant reaction is to sigh, 'Well, such things are only to be expected if they are oppressing another people', then an ideology has

31

turned one's heart to stone. However, my Marxist brother seemed not to be grieved, as my Israeli brother had been, by what had revealed itself in the cave of his own heart. Instead he attacked me sharply for being obscurantist, for not recognising that ideas also 'have life'.

Granted that ideas 'have life' in a metaphorical sense; but it is also true that they can kill compassion, and when compassion dies, what is there left in the cave of the heart except an idol of stone? And though such petrifaction is saddening when it happens to people in any city of the world, whether in Belfast or San Salvador or Washington, there seems something peculiarly tragic about its happening in Jerusalem, this holy city so improbably situated high in the hill country of Judea, a provincial city which nevertheless remains the cave in the heart of the world. It is a cave full of stone idols.

26th August, 1981. Rostherne

Packing up once again! How many scores of times Dorothy and I have done this in the last fifteen years. Every time it is like a little death, especially the task of putting my books into cardboard boxes once more. As I was doing so today it was like seeing my life pass before me all over again in my books, which represent various aspects of my life's journey: 1935, *Stalky and Co.*, my first school prize; 1940, another school prize, *The Destiny of Man* by the Russian thinker, Nicolas Berdyaev; 1944, *The Complete Works of St. John of the Cross,* given to me by Dorothy for my birthday. Oh! the fragility of human life and aspirations! Seeing and handling those series of Celtic books and Russian books and books about church history and many others also made me feel miserably how little I have to show for all those years of learning and reading – *Holiness,*[1] for instance, seems very small fruit for all that endeavour. Also, how quickly it seems empty as soon as it is brought face to face with suffering. Suffering strips away all our pretentiousness.

'How long must this go on, Archpriest?', Dorothy said to me this morning in a self-mocking voice as she painfully straightened up after filling yet another cardboard box. She was referring to our in-joke that our destiny is duplicating the story of the seventeenth-century Russian priest Avvakum and his wife Markovna. Avvakum, his wife and children spent many years being dragged around Siberia in the train of the soldier-adventurer, Pashkov. One day, as they were tramping along the icy roads, Dame Avvakum – and not for the first time – stumbled and fell. This time, almost too weary to get up again, she cried out to her husband, 'How long must this go on, Archpriest?' He answered, 'Until our very death, Markovna!' And she replied, with a sigh, 'Let us, then, plod on, Petrovich.'

So to Dorothy's similar question I gave Avvakum's reply, 'Until our very death, Markovna!' To which she replied with feigned resignation, 'Let us, then, plod on, Archpriest.'

A Pilgrim's Journal

30th August, 1981. Tantur. (Letter to the Tablet)

Yesterday sunrise was more splendid than ever. Usually these days, when the sun rises beyond the mountains of Moab east of us, it instantly appears like a clean disk, clearly outlined over the sharp horizon of the mountains. It can be quite literally breathtaking. You hold your breath as you see the sun slowly rise – first the brilliant tip of light and then the rest of that golden ball. Some days ago, when only half of it was visible, yet all golden, it seemed for a moment as though the very Dome of the Rock had been lifted by the hand of God from the Temple Mount in Jerusalem five miles north of us and gently set down upon that mountain range in Moab, just beyond the Dead Sea. But then the rest of the sun's globe ascended and you realised that the Dome of the Rock upon the mountain was just a mirage. Except that for a moment, yet enduring still in one's memory, it was not just a mirage. In such moments one begins to understand how in this land people can believe that everything is possible.

Yesterday, however, was different again because lying upon the mountains was a low bank of purple clouds, and the first rays of the sun lit up the clouds' edges in hues of red and gold and silver – until eventually the sun emerged fully above the purple bank. And for an instant, from where I stood on the roof of Tantur, looking through a gap between the bare hills of the Judean desert, I could just make out a sliver of light which I knew to be the waters of the Dead Sea.

What more beautiful spot could you dream of as a place to practise your morning yoga than the high, flat and spacious roof of this Ecumenical Institute with its superlative views. Eastwards, as I have said, lies the Judean desert, there where Bishop Pike of San Francisco perished ten years ago. South-eastwards the Herodian is visible, unnaturally flat-topped, the mound within which Herod the Great built his palace and to which his body was later transported with such pomp and ceremony across the desert from Jericho. As your eyes scan towards the south, towards the Shepherds' Fields at Beit Sahur and the church of the Nativity at Bethlehem you can hardly avoid the contrast between the worldly and successful Herod and the under-privileged child of Bethlehem, who finished up on the gallows. The world never learns. Perhaps, indeed, that is the very definition of the world: that which never learns.

Somehow Herod seems very remote now and Jesus very close, since in the clear morning air you feel as if you could stretch out your hand and touch Bethlehem with its endless jumble of churches and convents and bell towers that nestle in the hills around. To say nothing of the mosques that have sprung up in recent years, especially in the ancient town of Beit Jala, which for centuries had been wholly Christian but today houses many Muslim refugees with their numerous children. As to the nature of their faith I can hardly remain in doubt because every morning at about quarter past four the voice of the muezzin, many times amplified by loud speakers, comes billowing in through our apartment window to assure us that God is great, that he is one, that he has no son and that prayer is better than sleep.

Beit Jala lies south and west of Tantur, leaving the western and northern bowl of the hills to the dominating, fortress-like stretch of apartment blocks which is the modern Israeli settlement of Gilo, where many Jews from the Soviet Union are now housed and where no one seems to know what the population will eventually number – some say 10,000, some even more.

I have never heard anyone describe Gilo as beautiful, and yet from our magic roof I have even experienced the beauty of Gilo. That was on the day of Yom Kippur, the Jewish Day of Atonement, when this present Jerusalem took on a touch of the heavenly Jerusalem. Across all the roads around the city hurdles were put up in order to stop traffic going into and out of the holy city on that day of awe. They were set up outside our own enclosure walls since we are just at the point where the Bethlehem road crosses the boundary of Jerusalem. By the dawn of Yom Kippur all traffic within Jerusalem had stopped; Israeli radio and television had gone silent; the air itself was uncannily still that day. Something totally unique in the modern world had happened: the noise and bustle and tension of a great modern city had been stilled, not because of a disaster such as war or an earthquake but simply in obedience to the command of God. It was truly awesome – a touch of the eternal *shabbat* of God. And Gilo also took on a look of great peace, its stone apartments no longer forbidding but mellow and quiet in the early morning sun, beautiful.

The air was so still that a few minutes later when the muezzin was calling to the Muslim faithful of the Temple Mount in Jerusalem I could hear not only his cry but, very faintly, the deep groan of the answering faithful, like the swell of the sea. Soon they were followed by the gentle, modest sound of the Christian church bells in Bethlehem, Beit Jala and Beit Sahur.

Lastly, but most important of all, came the birds. Every morning one hears the smaller ones chattering in the pine trees that sway above the four-foot-high wall encompassing our roof. They sustain their chatter for about a quarter of an hour and then suddenly, as if in obedience to some great conductor, they all go silent on the instant. Afterwards, within a few minutes, one hears the whirring of the wings of bigger birds – wild pigeons, I think – which fly past in formations of forty and fifty. Winging in from Jerusalem in the north they head for the hills towards Hebron in the south and then swing eastwards round the bowl of the hills

37

before turning north to speed a second time over our roof.

In a land beset by political divisions and strident theological quarrels those birds are such a blessing: in their flight they pass with ease over the boundaries between Arab and Israeli territory. Amidst the often wearisome talk of God which is my lot they witness to his presence not by words but by their simple existence.

7th September, 1981. Tantur

Though this is not the first time in my life that I have succeeded to an office in some institution and had to spend many hours working through the files of the institution so as to familiarise myself with its operation, yet never before have I come across records, memoranda and letters so fissiparous as those deposited here. The impression they are leaving upon me is that from its very beginning this Institute has served as an almost perfect screen upon which men and women from far and near have been enabled freely to project their own schemes, desires and dreams. And then, when those schemes and desires have proved impossible to fulfil in the actual, as opposed to their dreamland Tantur, it seems that their positive projections have suddenly got switched on to the negative and consequently appear upon the screen in the form of frustrations and criticisms.

Some notables scholars, for instance, have dreamed of this place as an ideal spot to which they and their friends could retire, and gather about themselves a group of younger men selected to scurry around the Institute's marvellous library collecting materials which the elders then use in the production of their magisterial works. Others have wished to make Tantur into the highest institute for Arabic Studies in the Middle East.

A further result of reading through the files is that I am now beginning to understand some of the runic sayings passed on to me in recent months. 'I was the one who in the early days saved Tantur from the pushy Jews' was one of the sayings which completely baffled me, since the rune-sayer is himself a Jew – though not to be numbered, apparently, amongst the pushy sort! Similarly, it was an Anglican who in a lowered voice warned me, 'The Anglicans are trying to use Tantur as a back door to get into Jerusalem after foolishly abandoning their archbishopric there.'

There is more in all this than meets the eye, as the prescient detective in Victorian melodrama used to say; more, certainly, than my eye can discern.

But one feature of this organisation I have picked up, I am pleased to say. I have been able to do so in virtue of my experience in the University at Santa Cruz where I was at first extremely puzzled as to why intelligent faculty members should choose to spend so much time and energy writing memoranda and quite frequently sending me summaries of conversations about university business which we had only just held. At the end of my first year in Santa Cruz all was revealed! Those faculty members who contributed least to the teaching and the general well-being of the university were frequently the ones whose files were the bulkiest, filled with memoranda and summaries bearing witness – often false witness – to their industry. On the basis of this testimony they were in a position to claim promotion or pay rises. The exercise, so one of my colleagues explained, is endemic in American academia and is called, in an appropriately inelegant phrase, 'covering your arse with paper'.

That distasteful practice, both a symptom and a cause of distrust, seems not unknown in this place and, by a supreme irony, has infected what must be the very heart of any Christian community, the Eucharist: that *koinonia,* to use the Greek word, which means both communion and community, a sign that what in the end makes community is the sacred meal.

Sadly, and not for the first time in Christian history, it is precisely the act by which it is hoped to create the perfect community that seems to have precipitated most division here at Tantur. Communion/community is the *reason d'être* of the Institute, and if we slacken our efforts towards communion/community then nothing else we achieve will be of any lasting significance. So it is essential for me to get my own head as clear as possible on this issue of Eucharist before the scholars arrive and the arguments begin.

Here is how I see things as a result both of reading the files and of speaking with those who have been living here of recent years.

It is painful merely to listen to people living here as they give vent to their pain at having been expected to attend a Eucharist in which not all those present are permitted to receive the sacrament of the altar. This pain, which is felt on all sides, suffuses the atmosphere of the Institute – not always very perceptibly, of course, but nevertheless it is apt to surface quite suddenly at the most unexpected moments: – at meal times, for example, or in the children's playground or the laundry. In the expression of pain which I hear there is often, as I recognise, an egotistic note: my pain is greater than his pain, and therefore he should concede that my theological position is more genuine than his theological position. All the same these good people are for the most part giving expression not merely to personal pain but even more to a common agony that is felt by the whole Christian community throughout the world. What intensified both the pain and the agony is that here Orthodox, Baptists, Quakers, Mennonites, Lutherans, Anglicans, Melkites, Methodists, Congregationalists, Presbyterians, members of the Church of Christ and Catholics are all living next to one another, skin to skin, as it were, sharing everything, minute by minute, hour by hour, day by day, for a long period. There is no escape! And this, I imagine, makes the experience at Tantur different from the ecumenical experience anywhere else in the wide world: nowhere else does such a wide variety of Christians live so much on top of one another and for such a sustained period as here.

There is a further source of the pain being experienced here of which the sufferers themselves may not be aware – or, at least, they may be aware of it at some level of their being below consciousness, but they are suppressing it. That element is one of anger against the guidelines for eucharistic practice at Tantur laid down by our international Advisory Council. What, in particular, causes the anger is the guidelines' insistence that there shall never be more than one Eucharist celebrated at Tantur on any day and that all scholars are expected to attend the one and only Eucharist on a Sunday, the celebrant to be nominated each week by the Rector, whose duty it is to give each ordained minister the opportunity to celebrate in turn. It is further specified that the celebrant is expected to adhere to the rubrics of his own tradition (with the implication, presumably, that he is not to start fashioning a liturgy according to his own personal whims or according to what he takes to be the special circumstances of Tantur).

In my own judgement these guidelines are perfectly sensible but I can understand why they have got under the skin of so many members of the community. As always when communication is attempted one can hardly exaggerate the crucial importance of words, of idiom, of language. And the language of our guidelines is sober, measured, precise English, the idiom of the Anglican tradition. I could hardly have foreseen that it would be criticised as 'cold and juridical', but since that same criticism is urged by both Baptists and Catholics we must pay attention to it. And I think that I have found the clue to this unusual accord amongst Baptists and Catholics: the Baptists and Catholics in question are all Americans, and it is the American in them which looks for more warmth and emotion when speaking of the Lord's Supper; their national idiom, being more rhetorical, demands something of a *fervorino*.

I must try to explain to the dissidents that it was precisely on account of the passions and hot words generated between Protestants and Catholics by the Eucharist that the Advisory Council devised such a sober and measured statement, in the hope that the very choice of language might help to cool passions. The upshot, perhaps, will persuade the Council to accept an axiom that is fundamental to this enterprise; that is, *you can't win*. You can't win quite simply because the contradictions within Christianity over Eucharist have arisen from the history of the whole Christian Church and cannot be resoved except by the whole Church. Only a reckless fantasy could claim that this Institute is capable of resolving those contradictions. To demand that we should do so is plain foolish.

The Advisory Council themselves need also to recognise the presence of suppressed anger against them for the way in which they fly in here once a year for two or three days, lay down laws that the scholars have to observe and then fly out again, not to appear for another year. The reaction of the scholars reminds me of our reactions as young soldiers during the war, when we were confronted with orders drawn up by pundits in Delhi which we would have to carry out but the demands of which we believed made no impact upon the pundits' own lives.

The soldiers in this case are the four or five Benedictine monks of Montserrat who have been living here for ten years already, ever since the foundation of the place. And, as is the fate of common soldiers, they bear the burden and heat of the day whilst others are giving orders and making grand speeches, oblivious of what pains the common soldier has to bear in silence. No one, for instance, seems to realise the quite elementary fact that every Sunday when a Protestant is the chosen celebrant here the Benedictines obey the Advisory Council guidelines by attending the celebration and thereby they have to miss the Mass to which they are obligated as Roman Catholics. At the same time they follow the rubrics of the Catholic Church by not receiving communion at the hands of a Protestant minister. In doing so they seem constantly to incur the wrath of many Protestants who attribute the monks' abstention to personal narrowmindedness.

The mutual pain is made all the more acute on account of the fact that these monks, being Catalan, speak little English, and so their position is never fully explained. Moreover they are all blessed with the monastic virtue of discretion and are therefore reticent about the restraints from all sides under which they live. Whether they could ever satisfactorily explain the weightiest of these restraints to the scholars who come here I very much doubt. Even the most sensitive and perceptive of the scholars are hardly here long enough to appreciate the weight which attaches hereabouts to the Orthodox church and, supremely, to the Orthodox Patriarch of Jerusalem. Yet it is above all in view of unity with the Orthodox that the Benedictines were called to Tantur. Our monks are constantly working, in season and out of season, to assuage the traditional hostility felt by the Orthodox towards the other churches whom they regard as 'invaders'. In spite of the warm personal friendship that the monks have steadily cultivated with both Orthodox clergy and laity, we at Tantur need only put one foot wrong in Orthodox eyes for years of patient work by the monks to be brought to nought. The Orthodox hierarchy are particularly suspicious of the Free Churches whom they accuse of proselytising, of stealing members from the Orthodox flock. And their suspicions are returned in good measure by a number of Western scholars who do not conceal their contempt for a church which they regard as superstitious, priest-ridden, archaic and unevangelical.

When currents of suspicion are running so strongly and so deep almost any issue can give rise to open polemics and even serve as a pretext for holy warfare; and the Lord's Supper in Christian history is not just any issue; it is *the* issue. Predictably, therefore, soon after the establishment of the Institute the rumour ran around Jerusalem that Tantur fostered the practice of intercommunion, by which all members of the community, no matter what their ecclesiastical tradition, whether Quaker or Anglican, Lutheran or Catholic, were urged to partake of the Eucharist, even though their beliefs about what is happening at the Eucharist are quite irreconcilable. That was enough for the Orthodox Patriarch to forbid Orthodox to come to Tantur, a prohibition to which some Tantur supporters responded with a shrug of *je m'en fiche*, but which for the Benedictines was a body blow – their hope of a reconciliation with the Orthodox seemed to have been dashed from the beginning by the heedlessness of others. No wonder that they have cringed whenever the issue of 'intercommunion' has been approached in a cavalier fashion, or that they have discreetly let it be known they will leave Tantur if any Rector practises 'intercommunion'.

Nor, as may be imagined, did it please the Vatican some time later when an article written by an Anglican who stayed at Tantur was published in a prominent Catholic journal praising the Institute for its policy of 'open communion'. The Vatican riposte arrived during the period years ago when I was myself a scholar here. Which of us, indeed, who were present in chapel that Sunday morning when it was read out will ever forget it? As the reader droned on through one severe paragraph after another, each couched in Vatican jargon, you could feel a chill wind blow through the chapel and the bones and hearts of all the worshippers freezing.

I had always considered that an indispensible quality of every living body is warmth, and I concluded that any community which claims to be the Body of Christ must likewise be characterised by warmth: the relations between the member have to be warm. If that is true then we were not the Body of Christ when that bone-chilling Vatican statment was read out.

Yet in the end it is perhaps neither the Vatican nor the Orthodox nor the Advisory Council which has laid the heaviest burden on our eucharistic gatherings but certain

Americans. At least you know where you stand with the former three authorities, but the lack of consistency, the unpredictability amongst American priests and ministers inevitably sets certain other peoples' teeth on edge. One week, for instance, a celebrant priest or minister will announce that all those are invited to receive communion who are baptised Christians, and then another week later a priest or minister from the same tradition as the first will issue a much more restrictive invitation. This is particularly true of the Catholic priests. Many of them come from American university campuses which are often genuinely liberal and enlightened but where sometimes it seems as though 'anything goes'. They, in the eyes of our Protestant scholars, tend to be 'good guys' whereas those who stick to the official guidelines are classed as 'reactionary' and 'narrow-minded'. The impact which this inconsistency has upon priests from the Third World is particularly grievous. Granted the condition of their countries and their own training they are bewildered and pained at being pilloried as unenlightened and reactionary.

It is certainly not going to be easy disentangling all these issues so that we can live together at peace, especially since I suspect that one of the main difficulties is rooted so deeply in such a sensitive area that it is hidden by taboo. For just as Catholicism in, say, Scotland is strongly Calvinist and in Latin America strongly Indian, so in the USA it is markedly Protestant: US Catholics do not spontaneously think of the Church as a divinely established organ of salvation with a hierarchy that must be obeyed and a tradition that must be revered. In accordance with good democratic traditions they have a tendency to think of the Church as a countinuing town meeting at which the members present can at any given moment change everything that has been decided in the past. That is a perfectly defensible concept of a church but it happens not to be the Catholic one, according to which it is the Church which makes its members and not the members who make the Church. Confusion results when Catholics act upon one concept whilst professing something different.

Reading about these matters in the files and listening to the permanent residents discussing them convinces me that on the first Sunday of our year we must not attempt to celebrate the Eucharist. Before doing so everyone must have the opportunity to say, in a leisurely atmosphere and at full length, what Eucharist means to them, as well as to listen and discover what it means to the others who are to constitute our community. When we do eventually enter the chapel to celebrate there must be no debates going on inside our heads. Rather we must enter with clean hearts, hearts turned towards God, not towards our own arguments.

26th September, 1981. Tantur

This evening I am feeling very happy with the mood that the community has achieved as a result of many hours spent in discussing the Eucharist – or the Lord's Supper, to adopt the usage of our Baptist friends, who pertinently reminded us that to them the very word 'Eucharist' has a strange sound. Even in our language we must be careful not to impose our own habits upon others.

What has struck all of us, I think, is how near the mark Karl Rahner is when he says that 'faith as it is actually experienced today is the same in the different churches amongst average Christians', and that 'the major Christian Churches of today could unite, even institutionally: their sense of faith presents no insuperable obstacle.'

At the same time we all recognise that only a minority of people in the various churches have so far realised the truth of Rahner's statement. And so it would be irresponsible of us at Tantur to say, 'The people who do not agree with Rahner and us are just ignorant and reactionary. We who constitute the community at Tantur will go ahead and act as though the churches are institutionally united and will thereby advance the cause of Christian unity. The rest will have to catch up with us.' On the contrary, we are here as *representatives* of the different Christian churches; if we turn Tantur into an *ecclesiola,* a little church on its own, we thereby turn ourselves into members of a tiny new sect and cease to have any influence within our own churches, because we no longer represent them.

It is at this point that St Paul's admonition to the Corinthians is most appropriate: 'You say, "Is my freedom to be called into question by another man's conscience? We are free to do anything." Yes, but is everything good for us? Does everything help the building up of the community?'

These words of St Pauls' must constantly guide our behaviour, especially in view of our Orthodox brethren whose whole historical experience has been different from that of the West. Until now the Reformation, the Renaissance and the Industrial Revolution, which have so shaped Western theology, have scarcely had any influence upon Orhtodox theology, and so their theologians come to these questions with a very different mind-set from ourselves, and it is both wrong and foolish of us when we dismiss their hesitations as 'anachronistic'. They may, in this instance, be the 'weaker brethren' whom St Paul is constantly urging us not to offend with our 'liberalism'. And perhaps we should even ask ourselves whether we may not have something to learn from them, since 'God has chosen the weak ones' to teach the clever ones.

Yet when all is said and done, we do not want to remain stuck in our present positions, and so today we decided to emphasise certain aspects of the eucharistic liturgy which will to some extent assuage the pain of division and symbolise our longing for full communion.

In the course of our discussion, for instance, someone pointed out that it is a symptom of superstition and of a mind given to magic to imagine that the Eucharist 'takes place' in the very split second when the priest pronounces the words of consecration over the bread and wine on the altar. So we should not fall into the habit induced by such a misconception of treating all the other rituals of the eucharistic ceremony as secondary. After all Jesus said that what he leaves to us is peace and that peace comes to us in many ways which are symbolised in the ritual kiss of peace. We resolved, therefore, to accord the ritual kiss of peace the devotion which it requires and not to perform it perfunctorily, as happens in so many churches. Since our congregation usually numbers no more than fifty it is easy enough for each of us to give the kiss of peace to every other member of the congregation, and to do it in an unhurried fashion. Which means that the celebrant must not start any subsequent prayer until everyone has greeted everyone else.

That resolve about our Sunday celebration seemed to be wholeheartedly accepted but I am not so confident that the same is true of my own suggestion. Though it was accepted eventually, that may have been, I fear, because it was the Rector who proposed it. In an attempt to temper the sense of being excluded which must afflict all of us at one time or another when we cannot receive the Sacrament of the altar I proposed that we adopt an Orthodox practice which I have found consoling when I have attended the Russian Orthodox liturgy at which, obviously, I am not permitted to receive the sacred species. But on those occasions I have received the *prosphora,* the blessed bread which is distributed to everyone present. In taking the *prosphora* not only have I been brought closer to all my fellow worshippers but I have done so in the faith that Christ does not need permission from anyone to be truly present in any form he chooses and if he chooses to be so present in the form of the *prosphora* then I am doubly grateful.

In future, therefore, at the end of our Eucharist here there will be *prosphora* for everyone as they are leaving the chapel.

Yet on reflection I am beginning to get slightly queasy about what I have done. Remembering the facial expressions and body movements of one or two scholars during the discussion I fear that some of them are going to regard

48

the *prosphora* as a rather contrived device to try to conceal the truth that they are being treated as second-class citizens. We can only hope and pray that it will come right!

And I think it may do so, because you really could sense that we are all of one heart in believing that it is a nonsense for Christians to keep insisting on the importance in our lives of the Eucharist, the *koinonia,* and then to spend the rest of the week in petty quarrels and egotistic tantrums that undermine community, that very *koinonia* about which we make such a fuss on Sundays. Our lives throughout the week should manifest the *koinonia* which we enjoyed on Sunday, the first day of the week, and they should in that way prepare us for yet deeper *koinonia* on the coming Sunday.

Just when chair legs were being scraped on the floor as a sign that everyone thought our discussion, had finished I introduced a rule about which I had consulted nobody. I left it until last because I wanted to emphasise that there are certain matters beyond discussion. The rule is that nobody is to raise for discussion, or to gossip about, the reason why anyone did or did not go to receive communion. If someone chooses to explain why they did or did not, that is a different matter; but it is quite intolerable that the most intimate relationship of any creature, their relationship with their Creator, should be subject to speculation on the part of anyone.

29th October, 1981. Tantur

At last I have done what I have intended to do from almost the first day that I arrived at Tantur. That day was the very last of the year 1976, when I came here as a scholar. The Rector at that time, Dr Walter Wegner, very kindly gave me a tour of the Institute, in the course of which we walked together on our open, flat roof. As we were examining the landscape westwards my eye lit upon a stone shack situated beside an old quarry some fifty yards outside the high, protective walls of Tantur.

'Is there someone living there?', I asked Dr Wegner. 'Yes,' he said, 'an Arab woman and her children.' At which reply there came into my head, unbidden and spontaneous, the words 'Dives and Lazarus'. Already, at a subliminal level of my mind, I must have been troubled at the contrast between the triumphalist style of Tantur and the poverty at our very gate; and I must have further felt in my bones the parallel between our position and that of the rich man, Dives, gazing down on poor Lazarus, symbolised by our Arab neighbour.

Having previously read a list of the projects that Tantur scholars were engaged upon I was in a position to enquire, 'Is there not one of this year's scholars working on the meaning of the Beatitudes?' 'Yes, there is, a Benedictine Sister', replied the Rector. His reply left me musing to myself, 'I wonder if she has ever gone over to the Arab woman in order to find out from someone who is poor what it feels like to be in the Kingdom, as is promised in the Beatitude, "Blessed are the poor"?'

My question on the roof has pointed itself at me ever since we came back to Tantur two months ago. So I was very happy this morning when my Arab friend, Geries Khoury, agreed to accompany Dorothy and myself over to our feminine Lazarus in order to act as translator for us. Since today is the Muslim feast, *Id al Ras al Sena al Hegira,* we hoped it would not seem patronising for us to take sweets and fruit across to the lady in the shack whom from the vantage point of our roof I had observed hanging out her washing and doing her cooking at an outside oven in all kinds of weather.

I need not have worried about seeming to patronise her. There are some people so strong that you would come a cropper if you tried to do so. After all, as her sister-in-law who happened to be visiting her explained, our Lazarus had lived in that shack for twenty-five years and for the

50

last fourteen years she had been a widow, her husband having been blown to pieces in 1967 by an Israeli land mine as he was tending his sheep on the adjacent land. Since that date she has brought up four boys and two girls in that one-roomed shack where there is neither electricity nor running water. Having heard these stories I then noticed our neighbour's bare feet, gripping the earth so confidently, each of her toes regularly spaced, as she prepared for us cups of coffee so strong and so highly sugared that I felt as though they were knocking my brain against the top of my skull.

Women such as these, I mused to myself, could eat pompous Western men of position and power for breakfast, partly because they have endured so much but partly also because of their Islamic formation – witness the sister-in-law's unhesitating words this morning as soon as she understood why we had come. With no preliminaries whatsoever she simply said, 'When we die – and we shall all be brought to death soon – the only thing that will count for anything will be our good deeds.' That instant reference to life beyond death and to the day of judgement is so typically Muslim. For a Muslim the path is straight.

6th November, 1981. Tantur

God is a great puzzler. Today's puzzle left me quite incapable of working out in what way our meeting with Mother Teresa has changed my attitude towards her.

I truly don't think that I have idolised her in the past, though certainly she has proved a tremendous influence on my life as she has on the lives of millions of other people. Nevertheless, I have sensed a karmic connection between us ever since our first meeting fifteen years ago. On that occasion, in Southall, she was being introduced to four or five of us in a quiet drawing room. Coming to me last of all she paused, looked at me with those all-encompassing eyes of hers and then said, 'We have met before, haven't we?' When I said not she thought for a moment as if searching

51

in her memory, and then said, 'I seem to recognise your face.'

Granted my temperament, her remark was enough to make me believe that in some dimension of time and space we had indeed met, and that she, being more sensitive than myself, was recognising me from a previous existence. It also stilled at source any hesitations I might have conjured up as reason for refusing when she suggested that I might teach her novices church history. When I agreed to do so she calmly accepted my offer without bothering to discover that it would mean travelling down from Northern England one Saturday each month just for a two-hour session!

In Jerusalem today Mother Teresa once again filled me with wonder. She did something apparently trivial, but her manner of doing it provided an unforgettable lesson. Dorothy and I were standing on the cobbled street in the Old City which leads to the Bab el Jadid. We had just spent an hour or so with Mother Teresa and two of her Sisters, all three of whom were now beside us waiting for their van to pick them up and take them to Gaza. Up the street there came wandering in twos and threes a group of pilgrims – Italians, I would guess from their appearance and gestures. When they came to within a few yards of us one of the pilgrims looked up, immediately recognised Mother Teresa and quickly started nudging her companions, drawing their attention to this world-famous figure.

At first the pilgrims, caught unawares, were rather confused, not knowing quite how to respond to this occasion – whether to pass by as if they had not recognised her or to fall on their knees and ask her blessing. However, one of their number relieved the confusion by going up to Mother Teresa and handing her some money for her work, a gesture that was followed by the others before they all went on their way in wonderment.

What remains quite unforgettable was the manner in which Mother Teresa received the pilgrims' offerings. It was perfectly done, such an act as persuades devout Jews to cry. 'I go to my teacher not in order to learn Torah from him but to see how he laces and unlaces his felt boots', or 'I learn Torah from the very limbs of my teacher.' Mother Teresa's action was perfect in the sense that she simply took each offering, thanked the pilgrim and then, not even looking at the money that had been pressed into her hand, she passed it on straightaway to the Sister beside her. If her manner had been in the very slightest degree more casual it could have seemed brusque, even ungracious. On the other hand, if she had responded any whit more fulsomely she might well have left the pilgrim filled with pride at having made an offering to this holy woman. As it was Mother Teresa's action struck a perfect line between brusqueness and fulsomeness, much as a great singer strikes the perfect note – or a great cricketer hits the ball, absolutely in the centre.

Another aspect of that incident which made a powerful impression on me as I reflected on it was that you cannot act in that fashion by taking thought, by deliberately intending at a particular moment, for instance, to strike a perfect line or a perfect note. An action, if it is to be perfect, has to be spontaneous. It can only come about, in a human being, as a result of unremitting training directed towards some other end beyond the immediate one. In this case it was Mother Teresa's life-long struggle towards the love of Christ which gave birth to that action which taught me so much.

Nevertheless, what I find so intriguing about our encounter with Mother Teresa today was that, far from dazzling me it had the opposite effect. Because during the hour of conversation before we had emerged into the street not only had she said a number of things which I realised to be uninformed or simplistic but I also noticed that none of her Sisters uttered a single word spontaneously in her presence. As a result I have to recognise that our encounter today 'demythologised' Mother Teresa for me. That does not mean I am disillusioned in the bad sense of the word, because I feel that my respect for her is even deeper and more real than before. In a sense I feel more at ease in her presence but I can't quite work out why that is so, beyond saying that my encounter with Mother Teresa today 'demythologised' her to me.

24th November, 1981. Tantur

There must be many lessons about community to be derived from the ups and downs in the mood of the *piccolo mondo* of Tantur this day.

Soon after breakfast I received pouting protests against the notice I had posted which announced that Fr Carlos Alvarez's colloquium, *Healing in St Matthew's Gospel*, would be given in Spanish since Carlos speaks very little English. Spanish, admittedly, is not one of the three official languages of the Institute and so my notice afforded one or two scholars the opportunity to wax indignant about such a departure from the rules of the Institute. I was not altogether surprised, knowing that in any group of academics in any part of the world one always comes across certain characters who at the drop of a hat will draw themselves up in indignation, adopt a wise mien and announce that they 'foresee difficulties' – as though foreseeing difficulties is their speciality and a sign of their superior wisdom. The difficulty, they said, is that 'We are thereby setting a precedent.' And then, 'What is to happen when, say, some Polish scholar wishes to give his colloquium in Polish? Shall we all be expected to listen to Polish for an hour?'

On reflection I realise that I should not have treated the protests so cavalierly as I did. After pointing out that we had already agreed to translate Carlos' Spanish into English as best we could, I added, rather casually and impishly, that no doubt we could probably manage to translate Polish if necessary, or even Serbo-Croat at a pinch. (Will I never learn that the English habit of teasing should be strictly confined to transactions amongst English people? – and not with all of them, either!)

In the event, however, Carlos' colloquium proved to be a memorable occasion which no one enjoyed more than the protestors from earlier in the day.

What happened was that Carlos would speak a phrase, or a sentence, or even sometimes a whole paragraph in Spanish, and would then look towards Brother Bartomeu or myself to translate. One or the other of us would do so, though quite often we both began at the same time and collided with each other in mid-sentence, and sometimes certain of the scholars would break in with their unsolicited suggestions, hoping, presumably, that their knowledge of English might make up for their ignorance of Spanish. As a result the conduct of Carlos' symposium was not such as would have commended itself to a session of the American Academy of Sciences. At times it was hilarious, and at times it was riotous, especially when everyone in the room seemed to be prompting Bartomeu and myself, or when he and I concertinaed our sentences. Yet it proved to be a wonderful couple of hours; because no one was pretending to an expertise which he did not possess, and because everyone in the room was drawn into a common task. So no one got huffy or stood on their dignity when their proposed translations were queried or criticised or even laughed out of court. In fact an atmosphere of celebration was generated which grew more exhilarating as the scholars came to realise that with good will a group of human beings can accomplish much more when working together than they ever imagined possible.

At the same time what saved the day was the quality of Carlos' presentation at both the academic and the human level. His rare combination of academic rigour and human feeling must surely be due to the fact that Carlos spends half his days as the inspirer of a base community in one of the poorest areas of Bogota and for the rest of his time teaches in the university – due to also to the fact that he leads an extremely disciplined life of prayer and austerity. That is why he was able to take us through the texts of St Matthew centred on healing in a rigorous scholarly fashion yet with such conviction that we began to feel ourselves being healed in some extraordinary way by the very texts which we were meticulously analysing. As a result, when Carlos brought his presentation to a close everyone sat for quite a time in silence, the atmosphere of the seminar room being permeated by a deep sense of peace.

And then something happened which I found really strange and disconcerting. As if at the tap of a conductor's wand all of the scholars simultaneously closed their Bibles, shut their notebooks, pushed back their chairs and stood up to leave the room. It was as though they were saying in unison, 'That was an excellent seminar. I now have it filed away in my notebook, ready to take out again when next I have to lecture on Matthew. Now, what is the next item on the programme?'

I found such a pattern of behaviour on the part of the scholars to be really amazing: its implicit message seemed to be that nothing remarkable had occurred during the two preceding hours which might give us pause for thought before we carried on with our various routines. This reaction, or, rather, lack of it, is so symptomatic of the professional deformation endemic in academic communities that I asked them all please to come back and sit down, and then to discuss whether it was good enough after such an extraordinary experience simply to sidle off as though nothing had happened. Had we not just learnt how the Gospel, according to St Matthew, had healed both individuals and communities in centuries gone by? And had we ourselves not now received a touch of that healing? Ought we not to respond to that touch by seeking healing for whatever wounds there might be within our own community at Tantur here and now?

Happily, the scholars immediately realised what I was getting at and they urged me to call a gathering for healing which would include not only scholars but also their spouses and other adult members of the community. Though they maintained that it was my responsibility to preside over such an occasion they also agreed that Carlos should be invited to initiate and lead our search for healing. We were all of one accord, moreover, that we should direct our attention to what St Paul calls 'the deep things of God', and not upon surface issues such as the preferred time for dinner or the cost of field trips and so forth.

28th November, 1981. Tantur

Talk about sailing between the rock of Charybdis and the monster Scylla – or perhaps, more exactly, between Martin Luther and Ronald Reagan!

That is a bit hard on Martin Luther because Lutheran Pastor Wehrmann's invitation to deliver a sermon in Jerusalem's Erlöserkirche was wholly prompted by motives of friendship and in the end proved to be 'a happy fault'. After all, it was quite reasonable of him to assume that since all previous Rectors of Tantur had been ordained ministers, then I must also be ordained; and since he knew I am married then I could not be a Roman Catholic, because all ordained Roman Catholics are unmarried. Hence there was no obstacle in his mind when he asked me if I could preach a sermon in German at the Erlöserkirche on 1st November.

He asked me out of friendship and I agreed out of friendship; but neither of us realised at the time what we were letting ourselves in for – not, that is, until some weeks later when he asked me what Scripture readings I had chosen for that day – so that he could then announce them in the church bulletin. As soon as I pointed out to him the Scriptural passages I had chosen his brow furrowed and he enquired further in some puzzlement, 'Then what is to be the theme of your sermon, Donald?' 'What else', I replied, 'would a Roman Catholic preach about on All Saints' Day other than reverence for the saints?'

At which his puzzlement turned to alarm and he said, 'That would be a very strange sermon for a Lutheran

57

congregation on Reformation Sunday! I didn't know that you were a Roman Catholic.'

And then it was my turn to be embarrassed as he continued, 'I had hoped you would concelebrate with me, and would take round the chalice at communion.'

Once more I was back in the labyrinth which Christians have constructed for one another around the issue of Eucharist. Certainly I could not concelebrate since I was not ordained, but would it not offend my Lutheran friend if I said that in obedience to Catholic discipline I could not take round the chalice at communion and – even more offensive – I could not receive communion at a Lutheran Eucharist?

For several days after our conversation, and for some sleepless nights as well, I wrestled with these issues, knowing that if I chose a way that would not offend the Lutherans I would thereby offend others – Jerusalem is such a gossipy place; and Reformation Sunday is a big occasion at which non-Lutherans are present, and church people are such a gossipy crowd that some of them were bound to take scandal no matter what I did.

How I wished that those ecclesiastics who formulate the disciplinary rules were themselves more frequently thrust into exposed positions, and did not spend their lives like army generals, issuing commands to the troops whilst they themselves are protected by whole phalanxes of subordinates who dare not say boo to a goose.

In the end it was not as bad as I had feared because my Lutheran friends turned out to be a most sympathetic congregation. But the Reaganite Scylla a few days later proved a different kettle of fish, if I may use such a mixture of metaphor of such a monster.

Why I should have again been asked to preach in the Erlöserkirche within three weeks of Reformation Sunday I can hardly guess. Since the occasion was American Thanksgiving Day the reason may again have been a case of mistaken identity: Rectors of Tantur have been Americans, so the present Rector is American: therefore he is eligible to speak on Thanksgiving. Or perhaps it is simply that I am fated to confront Reagan, albeit indirectly, since I had already found myself publicly opposing his policies twice during my time in California when he was Governor.

'Third time unlucky', I thought to myself, as I sat in one of the seats of honour, and listened to the US Consul General in Jerusalem reading out President Reagan's Thanksgiving message to the packed congregation in the Erlöserkirche, a congregation composed not only of Christians but also of American Jews and American atheists, indeed of all sorts of Americans, apart from blacks.

From where I was sitting during the address I could see that many of the congregation were very content with Reagan's message, chauvinistic though it may have sounded to alien ears. And for the opening ten minutes of my own address I could sense the same content with what I was saying. I was speaking about how much the world owes, and how much I personally owe, to the American people in their pilgrimage as a nation. In particular I declared my conviction that if democracy were to go under in the US then democracy would perish throughout the rest of the world.

For the same reason, I continued, all who look to the US for democratic leadership are distressed at having to recall that the United States has also taken the lead in the development and deployment of nuclear weapons which threaten to destroy the whole of the human family and possibly all other living creatures as well. Moreover, when we proclaim the danger to the world of a 'Communist bomb' or an 'Islamic bomb' we should always bear in mind that there has already been a 'Christian bomb', the one dropped on Hiroshima by a country which claims to be Christian. Nor should we forget that those airmen taking part in the mission also took part, before they did so, in a service of worship conducted by a Lutheran pastor.

By this time the atmosphere in certain areas of the Erlöserkirche had changed from the earlier mood of contentment with my praise of the US to one of hostility against me for reminding them of matters that they wished to forget. In particular, there was one lady sitting only a few yards in front of me, very fat and lavishly dressed, from whose shoulders I could almost see the steam rising, so angry was she at what I was saying.

No sooner was the service over than she strode up to me looking like thunder and castigated me for speaking about politics at a time when people had come together 'to praise the Lord'. That phrase, 'praise the Lord', confirmed my intuition about her: she is, indeed, a very rich charismatic, one of those who constantly use the phrase as a thought-stopper, as a pious way of avoiding disturbing thoughts – which they usually describe as 'politics'!

She was not the only one, of course. From a similar stable there came a Protestant minister who felt I had abused the hospitality of Americans by speaking harshly of America on a day that was meant for rejoicing and not for dwelling upon the troubles of the world. When the American Consul General himself accosted me at the reception afterwards he was more genial and diplomatic, though as a good diplomat he knows how to make double-edged remarks. He said, 'We will not take your green card away from you'; and then, after a pause, 'at least, not yet.'

1st December, 1981 Tantur

Doesn't it bring you up with a jolt sometimes when a incident or a remark reveals to you how you appear to other people?

This morning I called together the senior permanent members of the Institute and reminded them that for several months now, on Tuesday mornings, I had left myself free of engagements so that any of them who wished could come to my office and talk to me about their worries and hopes and needs. 'Today,' I said, 'having listened to all of you for three months, I myself now wish to say a word. It will not take long – no more than twenty minutes.' And so for twenty minutes I outlined what I took to be the virtues and defects of everyday life in the Institute, with some indications of changes that need to be made.

Later in the day I learnt that one of those present, an Arab, whispered to another Arab as soon as they had left my office, 'We are back again under the British Mandate.' Amusing as others may have found the observation, I have to confess that it brought me up with a jolt. Can it really be true that I give the appearance of belonging to the same stable as those colonialists from whom I have always tried to distance myself?

4th December, 1981. Tantur

How grateful I am to Carlos for the manner (not only spiritually but also psychologically skilful) in which he conducted the healing meeting for the community this evening. Probably such skill in psychological dealings is anyhow a function of spiritual sensitivity – I am thinking of how Carlos quietly but authoritatively ensured that our meeting began at the time arranged and how he impressed upon us all, without actually saying anything, that we were going to finish in good time and that we were not going to drift on and on into what Americans call a 'bull-session'. The effect of his quiet insistence was to have everyone alert and concentrating on the matter in hand; they were on their best behaviour, not slouching around as people everywhere tend to do at evening meetings. This in turn produced a sense of common purpose in which each of us was listening for the needs of others and showing our readiness to bear one another's burdens. I do believe that many misunderstandings were overcome and I could see the dawning of relief on many faces as one knot after another of pain and anxiety within

the community was unravelled. Indeed you could see
something more than relief; you could on many faces
see radiant peace by the time I brought the meeting to an end by praying Bishop Appleton's beautiful
prayer:

> Grant, O Lord, that each day before we enter the
> little death of sleep, we may undergo the little
> judgement of the past day, so that every wrong
> deed may be forgiven and every unholy thought set
> right. Let nothing go down into the depths of our
> being which has not been forgiven and sanctified.
> Then we shall be ready for our final birth into
> eternity and look forward with love and hope to
> standing before thee, who art both judge and sav-
> iour, holy judge and loving saviour. (*Journey for a
> Soul, p.229.*)

5th December, 1981. Tantur

Carlos surprised me this morning, when I spoke to him
about last night's meeting, by being much less sanguine
over it than I had been. In particular he said that in
spite of some good things that emerged it was obvious
to him that many of those present at the meeting had
come to Tantur with much heavy matter of unforgiveness
and resentment lodged inside them from previous experience. That heavy matter is now blocking the flow of life
and love within the community; and the worst of it is
that it is precisely those who talk most about community-
building who block the flow because they are the ones
least aware of the matter of unforgiveness that they are
carrying around with them, like a lead ball attached to
their waists.

I have great respect for Carlos' insight, which reminded
me of the observation made by Dietrich Bonhoeffer that
whenever someone came along full of talk about the need
to 'build community' then he could be pretty sure that such

a person would prove disruptive of whatever community (not ideal but real) had already been established.

Those comments by Carlos and Bonhoeffer certainly accord with my own experience both here and in the USA. So many of those in California who preached the 'need for community' had themselves failed to live at peace in the basic community of their own family and went around trailing their failure behind them. But because it was behind them they never turned round and noticed it. In consequence they took no responsibility for their own feelings of discontent but instead blamed them on to others. Perhaps there is an essential connection between the refusal of responsibility and the tendency to blame other people.

Also, in the light of what Carlos said, I can clearly see the answer to a puzzle that has been nagging at my mind for some time about this community at Tantur. That is, how do you account for the difference – which anyone with even half an eye can recognise – between the quality of the presence here of the Benedictine monks and that of all the rest of us? For long enough I have been conscious of such a difference but have never been able to put my finger on it.

The answer has to be that the Benedictines came here out of one hundred per cent obedience to their community in Montserrat and so they brought with them no hidden agenda – not, at least, in their relation to Tantur. In contrast all the rest of us have come here with some hidden agenda; for some of us it may only constitute about five per cent of our motivation for coming whilst for others it may represent almost one hundred per cent. But no matter how small the percentage may be in any of our cases still it does in some degree flaw our presence here and constantly gives rise to difficulties: it makes members of the community frustrated and angry with one another, when the hidden agenda of one person clashes with the hidden agenda of another person. Not surprisingly, therefore, it is precisely those people who have hidden their agendas so deep that they no longer believe they have any who are for ever causing dissension.

9th December, 1981. Tantur

What a character Mother Teresa is! The story told to us this morning by Sister Damien is so typical.

Because she is nowadays in such great demand Mother Teresa no longer has the time to write letters to the Sisters in every one of their houses across the globe, so instead she speaks her messages on to a cassette and copies of it are then sent to all their many houses. But in the Gaza house, because they did not possess a cassette player nor money enough to buy one, they were unable for many months to discover what Mother Teresa was saying to them. Eventually, however, some friends in Jerusalem bought them a cassette player so that they could listen to Mother's messages.

Unfortunately for them Mother Teresa came to visit Gaza soon afterwards and noticed the gleaming cassette player on a table. She asked who it belonged to and when the Sisters said it was theirs, a gift, Mother Teresa grew stern. 'Then you must give it back', she said. 'To own a cassette player is contrary to our vow of poverty.' When it was timorously pointed out to her that the player was only used for listening to her message (with the implication, presumably, that they did not go in for pop music) she put an end to all discussion by saying, 'Our vow of poverty is more important than my messages.'

And when later the donors of the offending cassette player protested that there was no need to be so literal-minded Mother Teresa countered by saying, 'If they will do that whilst I am still alive, what will they get up to when I am dead?'

It is also the case, probably, that Mother Teresa was offended by the very slightest contrast, however innocent, between the lifestyle of the Sisters and that of their Arab neighbours in Gaza. Because one of the Sisters has told us that in many ways there is even deeper misery in Gaza than in Calcutta. And I can believe it after having visited a number of Arab houses today. One such house will haunt me, I am sure, for the rest of my life.

The house is at the very end of a long dirt-track and consists of one room. At least half of the room is taken up by a heap of straw that is there apparently to feed the family donkey which was standing patiently in a corner. The family consisted of father, mother and their daughter, some twenty years old, though she might well have been their grand-daughter, so aged-looking were the parents. Until six weeks ago there had been a second daughter, but she had died from skin cancer which my well have been caused by the miserable state of the house. And judging from the eyes of the surviving sister, shining with unnatural brilliance, it will not be long before she follows along the way of death. Although that event will undoubtedly be a tragedy for the household I was left with the strange feeling that it would be an equal tragedy if the donkey were to die, because the donkey is for them more essential to the household than the daughter. Harsh as that thought may seem it is at least plausible in view of the fact that the only water available to them for all their needs (washing, cooking and watering their little vegetable patch) has to be carried a distance of one kilometre: and that task belongs to the donkey. We were told by the father that there is no prospect of a more convenient water supply because the Israeli occupying authorities here, as on the West Bank, refuse to allow Arabs to sink wells.

What shattered me, however, really making my bones shake, was the moment when the mother declared that she was going to kill one of their five chickens in order to provide a meal for us. Luckily we all agreed spontaneously and immediately on a white lie to say that we had already eaten. But as we came away my mind was still trembling at encountering such a depth of hospitality from these utterly poor people: they have absolutely nothing in this world save some straw, a donkey and five chickens; and yet they would gladly have presented us with one of those precious chickens.

14th January, 1982. Tantur

It was late in the afternoon by the time I made my way into the new church, which is now nearing completion. It is most majestic, a whole cosmos of finished stone. There was no one else in the church except that in one of the far chapels, almost camouflaged in stone dust which floated in the atmosphere and also lay like a grey blanket upon him, there sat an aged Arab stone mason. Holding the heavy mallet, his arm was rising and falling in a mechanical fashion, almost as though it no longer belonged to him but had been hired out. As I walked slowly around the numerous chapels, noticing the fine mosaics, I kept watching him at his work; the mallet seemed to be getting heavier all the time and his arm wearier. I felt nigh on frantic for him as I thought of all that dust getting into his lungs and mouth and ears and nose every day of his life. When eventually I came to his chapel I said to him in Arabic, 'You seem tired'; he replied by placing his mallet down and raising his hands towards heaven, as if calling Allah to witness; he whispered hoarsely, 'I am very tired.' Like many Arab workers, he has a lot of dependants to support.

As I moved on I began to examine the hundred of chisel marks on each of those thousands of magnificent stones that make up the church. Running my fingers along the grooves left by the chisels I saw in each of them the stroke of the mallet made by poor, weary men such as my friend in the corner. Then I thought, as I was going along the corridor where the tourists were buying their picture post-cards and souvenirs, 'Things can't go on like this much longer. This order of things must soon pass away, under which rich visitors like ourselves have

66

these magnificent spaces adorned for our contemplation by those who have to work from dawn until dusk simply in order to put bread into their mouths and the mouths of their children.' Because you always know, whatever land you are in, who it is in that land who bears the burden of history. All you need to do is to travel on the buses between five and six o'clock in the morning and look at your fellow passengers. They are the ones who are carrying society on their backs, whether you are in Rotherham or Pittsburg or Bombay. Here in the Holy Land it is the Arabs. And they are in no way 'romantic'. Take away their keffiyehs from around their heads and you can see quite clearly that by middle age their bodies are just as broken as the bodies of those being jolted along in the first buses in Rotherham, Pittsburg or Bombay.

10th February, 1982. Tantur

Where angels fear to tread it is precisely fools who will rush in. On Friday afternoon, during the colloquium, a Protestant minister suddenly broke the rule which has until now done so much to keep the atmosphere around our eucharistic discussions clean. In open session he not only challenged Ned Jackson, a Roman Catholic priest, to explain why he does not go to communion if a Protestant is the celebrant, but when Ned sent out many signals to indicate that he did not wish to discuss the matter in the presence of twenty people, the Protestant scholar kept pressing his question. For a moment I thought I should be forced to intervene with a really stern rebuke but fortunately Ned, whose neck by this time was rapidly turning red, did the job for me by exclaiming angrily, 'You are out of order.'

That put a stop to the unpleasantness for the moment; and I gather than many of the scholars afterwards gave Ned a word of support. But I was not altogether surprised this morning when he came into my office and asked me to remove his name from the list of those who have accepted the invitation to celebrate the community Eucharist on a pre-arranged Sunday this term. 'I couldn't celebrate', he said, 'knowing that there are people present who are so critical of my eucharistic practice.'

Though not surprised at Ned's request I was saddened, not only because he is such a kindly fellow, but because I am not at all sure what to do about his inquisitor.

23rd February, 1982. Tantur

Yesterday morning I came across an article in the *National Catholic Reporter* for the 26th November, 1981, which troubled me greatly. The author of the article asserted that a lot of the money which makes the University of Notre Dame so wealthy comes from the coffers of a billionaire called Ludwig and that Ludwig makes his money by exploiting Indians of the Amazon and destroying the land upon which they depend for their livelihood. Since, in turn, much of the money for Tantur comes from Notre Dame we are now faced with a serious moral dilemma: are all of us here, so comfortably established, living on the backs and on the skins of Amazonian Indians? And if so, should we not leave as soon as possible?

Throughout the whole of yesterday that question was running through my mind in spite of the day being so busy as seeming not to permit even one chink of space for the question to pop through. But it did so continuously.

In the morning Dorothy and I went to visit the stricken Roumanian Archimandrite Vasileus in the hospital on French Hill, taking him a cake which Dorothy had baked for his birthday. Vasileus' room was bathed in a wonderful sense of peace which both Dorothy and I remarked upon afterwards. It was due, we did not doubt, to the two beautiful Roumanian nuns who are nursing Vasileus, night and day. One or other of them is present in the room at every minute, usually sitting there in a corner, quiet, still and radiant with prayer, watching all the time for any sign of need on Vasileus' part, ready to move across to his bed calmly and completely composed. These two nuns have imbued me with a quite different awareness of what nursing is really supposed to be.

At lunch time we were plunged into a completely other world. We were entertaining as our guests at Tantur about a hundred members of the Jerusalem Committee, an international group of wealthy and influential figures assembled by Teddy Kollek in order to help him make Jerusalem into the beautiful city of his dreams. I also suspect that Kollek, wily politician that he is, finds that the Jerusalem Committee's standing comes in useful for him sometimes when he faces opposition from the central government people, who are not so enlightened as he is.

Many of the Committee are what the Americans call 'fat cats'. One of them was sitting next to me at lunch, a millionaire Socialist. Through misinterpreting one of my remarks he obviously concluded that I am by background a member of the British establishment, for which reason he gave me a lecture on the sufferings of the English poor in the nineteen-thirties. I thought of my native village in the thirties, looked at the suit he was wearing which must have cost as much as my monthly salary, and said nothing. However, I did permit myself a wry smile as I stood watching him drive away, the sole passenger in an extraordinarily luxurious chauffeur-driven car.

By contrast I had a pleasant chat with Conor Cruise O'Brien, who was surprised and delighted to discover that I had read some of the poems in Irish written by his wife, Maire Mhac an tSaoi. He was so taken by the attractions of Tantur that he suggested he might like to come and stay here in order to write his next book. Knowing his reputation hereabouts as a scourge of the Arabs I was a bit alarmed at the thought of what effect his presence might have. However, when I earnestly enquired what kind of theological research he was engaged upon he dropped the matter.

No sooner had the Jerusalem Committee departed than I found myself presiding over a colloquium given by one of our scholars, Daniel Philipps. He was extremely crotchety during the discussion.

From the colloquium we went immediately and thankfully to evening prayers. Waiting for us outside our chapel were some forty Yugoslav priests who are on pilgrimage. They were such a wonderful tonic. Everything about them – their open faces, their rough dress, their manly voices and ready smiles, their complete unpretentiousness – all these characteristics told you that these men were worker priests, not as a result of some theory or experiment but by nature and through the situation of the church in their homeland. And their singing seemed to come from another world, especially when those deep, masculine voices were joined in tender, traditional folk hymns to the Mother of God. After the last of the hymns all of us continued standing in silence, immersed in the beauty of the occasion.

Then, suddenly, the silence was broken by the leader of the Yugoslav group, a professor of theology, who stepped to the centre of the chapel and began to speak. I was expecting him simply to say a few words of thanks to us for inviting them to join us in our evening prayers. But instead he launched at full throttle into an astonishing lecture, delivered in excellent French, on the theme of unity and its relationship to *différentiation, non-identité, diversité* and *altérité*. It was a scintillating *tour de force* which led us though Parmenides, Plato, Plotinus, Scotus Erigena, Nicholas of Cusa, Hegel and Heidegger. There was no reason for him not to speak in French since French is one of the official languages of the institute; nor was he to know that in practice the institute is becoming monoglot through the predominance of language-lazy Anglo-Saxons. But by plunging *in medias res* the good professor had caught us all on the wrong foot.

However, our people quickly recovered their balance and composed themselves, self-consciously reverent, ready to endure two or three minutes of incomprehension and bewilderment. But as the minutes passed by with no pause in the breathless flow of erudite philosophy in a foreign language you could see the bodies beginning to sag, their eyes growing wider in disbelief. Since I was standing facing them all and could notice how the expressions on their faces and their knees pleaded that this torture might end soon I almost disgraced myself by bursting into laughter.

At least the professor's long discourse did give me an excuse to make my own reply very brief and to thank him sincerely for an address which did, in fact, explicate the philosophical concept of unity so expertly as to make it unexpectedly relevant to the task of Christian unity.

Nevertheless, below all these diverse and demanding tasks which engaged my attention through the day there murmured an undercurrent of worry: are all of us at Tantur, and particularly myself as Rector, living on the backs of exploited Amazonian Indians?

So in spite of feeling distinctly weary I was actually looking forward to the 'Carlos'* that we were due to hold after supper because it held out to me the hope that I could share my worry and seek the help of my brethren.

In the event what happened at the 'Carlos' was both revealing and symbolic. For although I do believe that most of the community take seriously the injunction 'bear ye one another's burdens' and so fulfil the law of Christ, I am afraid that their voices were never heard. Because no sooner had I expressed my concern over the Ludwig story than one scholar jumped into the discussion and told me, in the flip-sided manner of a Job's comforter, that it is really misguided of me to go on worrying about such matters. 'Even if the *National Catholic Reporter* story is true,'[2] he said, 'you cannot possibly be so scrupulous about

* The name attached by this time to any healing gathering, after Fr Carlos Alvarez.

71

where money is coming from – in the modern world each of us is involved in similar financial networks every day of our lives.'

On the surface, the man seemed to be consoling me, and even, so to speak, absolving me. But that was only on the surface. In fact he came near to mocking me for my naïveté. And he certainly was making light of my burden. And once he had dismissed that matter in such a cavalier fashion there was no way that anyone else could then bring the 'Carlos' round to centring upon trying to heal wounds in the community.

The course of the evening was fittingly symbolised in the one decision taken: each Wednesday evening we are to lay on a 'happy hour'. The 'happy hour' is a rite of Academia according to which members of the university faculty gather during the period preceding the evening meal in order to drink and gossip. 'Happy', it usually is not.

28th February, 1982. Tantur

For more than a week now I have been trying to discover the root, or roots, of the impurity within me that caused me to behave so badly towards Antoine Foucauld. It is a sign, perhaps, of how very deep the impurity is rooted that I was quite unaware of having offended him until he came to see me. As soon as he began to speak I realised that this good man was having to exert himself strenuously in order to control the anger that he felt towards me. He accused me of having 'banalised' the talk he gave two weeks ago by the way I had presided over it and he felt that I owed him an apology. What saddened me even more was that he interpreted my behaviour as a sign that I have little personal regard for him and his intellectual work. Since the opposite is true, and I respect him highly, I have to ask myself: How does one manage to give such a false impression?

The surface reason is obvious enough: my mind was preoccupied by the expectation of a telephone call from the US, from HQ, as a result of which I would learn whether money was going to be made available to pay our staff this month, next Friday being the pay day. The adrenalin had therefore been flowing fast all day as I prepared for a possible show-down with HQ over the issue, so that when the call did come some ten minutes into Antoine's talk I was on a real high of aggression. Then, as it happened, there was no battle with HQ. They were sad that we are spending so much but realise that if there is no money for the Arab staff next week I may have a rebellion on my hands.

My expectation of battle having been frustrated, when I returned once more to the lecture room to preside over the discussion, the adrenalin in my system was still bubbling yet I was at the same time sighing with relief. So I let it all out in provocative questions, ill-considered parallels and wisecracks, which must have both mystified and infuriated Antoine.

But below that surface explanation there is a deeper and, I imagine, a complex series of reasons, for my offensive behaviour.

Strictly speaking, of course, one ought always to be able to switch one's attention from one subject to another, or from one person to another, with no emotional carry over from one subject or person into the realm of the other. Certainly that is an ideal to be worked towards, but to be realistic one has to acknowledge that almost no one achieves such a blessed ideal. And whilst working towards the ideal one has to pin-point other possible changes in behaviour patterns that may at least mitigate one's failures.

But if I have to make a guess at the root cause of my behaviour I would put it down to my constant desire to protect people, a desire which is itself rooted in a reluctance to share my concerns and anxieties with them, a reluctance which in its turn is rooted in a lack of trust. In other words, if only I had told the scholars about the money shortage that was looming before us then I would not have felt so isolated, tense and embattled. And they might well have suggested to me that I had no obligation to preside over the lecture in the afternoon and should feel free to deal with the thorny question of the money. Then this unpleasant episode would never have occurred.

On the other hand, knowing what gossips some of the scholars are, I am pretty sure that within a few days rumours would be circulating in Jerusalem that Tantur is on the verge of bankruptcy. After which tradesmen would start to demand immediate payment for their goods, intending scholars would be writing to ask if the Institute is going to be open next year, and so on. That would be much more disastrous than my contretemps with Antoine, which we were able to clear up within the confines of my office without involving people in Jerusalem, Chicago, London and Rome!

There is here a real problem about institutions. For institutions to be real communities there needs to be the very widest possible sharing of information and feelings. In an ideal community everyone completely trusts every other member. In fact there has never been such a community. Even in the honeymoon period of the Christian Church, for instance, we know that 'there was grumbling on the part of those who spoke Greek against those who spoke Hebrew'. And, unfortunately, the barrier against complete trust is fixed and located according to the capacity for trust of the least trustworthy member of the institution or community. That is why monasteries tend to be good communities capable of lasting for centuries whilst hotels are non-communities which spring up and vanish like mushrooms: monasteries examine carefully the trustworthiness of those wishing to enter, whereas hotels only ask for your credit card.

Tantur is a monster of an institution, something between a monastery and a hotel. In trying to form a community within it you are bound to win some and to lose some. But I must learn to push the barrier of trust as far out as possible, and at least a little bit further than is strictly advised by my 'loner' temperament.

6th March, 1982. Tantur, Letter to the Tablet, after visiting Tiberius and Galilee

It was still night when I went out on to the high balcony. The air was almost motionless as though nature itself recognised that today was Sabbath. And the very still-ness of the air and the darkness of the night meant that the lapping of the water on the edges of the lake sounded all the more clearly even on our balcony. I have never heard any lapping of waters so musical and magical as of these waters. 'From all the seas which God created, He chose for Him only the Sea of Kinneret. Why is it called Kinneret? Because the voice of its waves is pleasant as the voice of the harp.' (The word *Kinnor* in Hebrew means harp.)

For a full hour I gazed over the waters of this Sea of Galilee, waiting for dawn to break – though the word 'break' is an inappropriate one to describe the slow, silent way in which the dawn came over the lake and the steep slopes opposite, the Golan Heights. Inevitably I thought of the beginnings of our Lord's ministry beside those very waters. As the dark shape of the Golan Heights emerged and the lake grew pale in the early light a gentle breeze sprang up and I felt again, as I always do in this place, the breath of the Holy Spirit over the face of the deep and the freshness of the message that Jesus brought to mankind. What a contrast between those fresh beginnings, hidden in this remote corner of the Roman Empire, and the noise and strife that has accompanied the spread of the message to the far corners of the earth, to Anchorage in Alaska and Dunedin in New Zealand, to Santiago in Chile, and Kyoto in Japan. What a strange, improbable story! Jesus came to reveal things hidden since before the foundation of the world and what the world does is to shout as loud as it can in order to keep his revelation hidden.

In this quiet spot from which I could now see Mount Hermon rising serenely to the north, snow-covered, as well as the bare heights of Golan to the east, the contrast was striking between the peace, the stillness, the hiddenness of this dawn and all the noise that I knew was being made throughout the world over Golan. Whereas the real Golan was at peace there was another 'Golan' on the lips of radio and television announcers and in the minds of millions of listeners and readers throughout the world, from Manila to Frankfurt and back. This second Golan was like a black, thunderous cloud in the lives of those millions, threatening them with nuclear destruction. This second Golan was a product of their fears and ambitions and lies. The real Golan which they had never seen stood peaceful before me.

Why does the world shout so loud about strife and hide the things that make for peace? This question has exercised me greatly since the day – or rather, the night – when Israeli troops blew up three houses of our neighbours in Beit Sahur just before Christmas. That incident was spoken about and written about in the world press and on television and radio – quite rightly. But there was an incident within the incident that no one has thought to describe which should perhaps be known. It occurred just as the soldiers were preparing to carry out the demolition. A young man who lived in one of the houses, a Christian, spoke courageously and calmly to the soldiers, asking them to consider whether there was not a better way, the way of peace revealed by Jesus whose birth in neighbouring Bethlehem was soon to be celebrated. The young man was gently taken aside by one of the soldiers who whispered to him, 'I agree with you, but don't go on like that or else you will get arrested for trying to convert Jews.' I like to think of that whispered conversation between two young men. It redeemed the bankruptcy of the night.

76

The reason why it is only 'perhaps' that such an incident should be known, however, is on account of the delicate mystery of hiddenness: do you inevitably destroy the hidden things by revealing them? Certainly there can be enormous virtue in keeping things hidden. This was illustrated by yet another incident that arose from the happenings of that night in Beit Sahur.

Soon after the demolitions had taken place I was present when a Jewish professor was being given a rough time about them by some Christian scholars. Though he answered their questions very honestly and bravely nevertheless his defence of the Israeli action seemed lame to them and left them unconvinced. But the next week, by chance, I discovered another side to the story. I happened to be in the company of some friends of that same professor and learnt quite incidentally that in 1948 the professor's whole village had been razed to the ground by Arab soldiers. When I heard that story I could not help thinking that only one person in a thousand, under the barrage of questioning that my professor friend had endured, would have kept silent about that even greater tragedy in his own young life. And I admired the austerity, and what I can only think of as a certain mental chastity, that enabled him to keep that sadness in his life hidden. The professor certainly knows the wonderful Jewish legend according to which our universe depends for its continued existence upon the presence in it of thirty-six just men. But they are hidden. No one knows who they are; they themselves do not know who they are. Yet they are the secret pillars of the universe: without even one of them the universe itself would collapse.

At the same time Jewish tradition does allow that there are certain rare moments when one has a sense of having not so much encountered as glimpsed one of these just men, indirectly, seen his shadow, heard his footfall, felt his breath upon one. We can never be sure; but even the chance that it may be so can redeem a dark situation.

So it was with me when I drove from the lake in the company of two Arab friends, Boulos and Butros. We drove first up the steep, endlessly winding road into Upper Galilee, towards the Holy City of Tsefat. I think of it as the Holy City because of all the places in the Holy Land it is the one that for years I most longed to see. Situated more than 3,000 feet above the lake, Tsefat is the city where the great Jewish mystics congregated in the sixteenth century after fleeing from their Christian persecutors in Spain. When I first saw it from a distance, its white stone houses glistening upon the mountain top, it was utterly ecstatic, and in that brilliant sunshine and pure air it was not difficult to believe that in its streets I might actually meet Rabbi Izhak Luria or Josef Caro or some other of those inspired holy men of the past. Even today, when a swirling mist hid much of the old city and the only holy man around was a meditation teacher from Santa Clara, California, one could still feel the magic of the place. But this morning we were headed beyond Tsefat, to those parts of Upper Galilee from which my Arab Christian friends originated.

I was not prepared for the bitterness of the experi-ence. Previously no one had ever told me the story of how in 1948 Israeli troops had cleared the inhabitants out of these Christian villages allegedly because of the danger from Lebanon, at the same time assuring them that they would soon be allowed to return. Since 1948, however, the villagers' lands had been given to Jewish immigrants and the Christians had not been allowed to return to their homes. So, as we drove by one stretch of beautiful hill country after another, my companions would mutter, 'This is the land of my village' or, 'That is my mother's field' or, 'Here is my uncle's land', all of it now in the possession of Jewish settlements. The longer this went on the more hopeless the world began to appear in my mind's eye. Being an old-fashioned Roman Catholic I did not need reminding of the dictum, *audietur et altera pars* – don't make a judgement until you have heard the other side of the story. Even so, there was no mistaking the bitter wound which my companions had suffered. And it seemed to get worse as we drew near to the ancient Christian village of Kafar Bir'im. You will not find the village marked on your map, and in Zev Vilnay's *Guide to Israel* it is only mentioned (a 'deserted village') in order to call your attention to the ruin of an ancient synagogue of the second or third century. Certainly, the ruin is wonderfully preserved, and nearby is situated what is said to be the grave of Queen Esther. Here was also found the inscription in Hebrew: 'May there be peace in this place, and in all the places of Israel.'

However, after parking our car we did not direct our footsteps along the official path towards the synagogue mentioned in the guide book. Instead we turned left through the wood surrounding the hill top until we came to a church hidden in the trees.

That was when I felt the presence of one of the thirty-six just men at the threshold of the church. Still weary with the misery of the last few hours, I was about to step inside what I thought to be an abandoned church, when all at once I looked into the face of an old man whose white moustache glistened, even as a welcoming smile lit up his face and his eyes glowed with happiness. 'Welcome! welcome', he said, and led us into the church, a Maronite church of which he has constituted himself the guardian. He stays there night and day, sleeping at night on a camp bed in the porch, as if to assure his dear church that it is not after all abandoned.

There were so many of that old man's little gestures which edified me – the grace with which he offered all of us Turkish coffee, the yet greater grace with which he indicated that the money we offered him should go into the church box and not into his pocket; the unfeigned delight that he showed when I revered the picture he had pinned up of St Charbel Maklouf. But what edified me most of all was the courtesy with which he treated two young Jews who stumbled upon the church whilst we were there. They looked pleasant enough young men, but they had not the faintest notion of how to behave in a church. They smoked away, talking loudly and laughed at various of their own observations. If the old guardian had become incensed with them one could scarcely have blamed him. On the contrary, however, he showed them round the church and offered them Turkish coffee (which they accepted) with exactly the same courtesy he had shown to us, his fellow-Christians.

My heart, as I was leaving the church, felt much lighter and the world a better place. After we had said goodbye to the old man, I turned round again as though by a quick backward glance I might discover his secret. But all I saw still was that glistening white moustache, the unfeigned smile and the kindly eyes.

Our next place of call was to be the church belonging to the village of Iqrit, also forcibly evacuated in 1948. My friend Butros especially wished to say some prayers in it out of piety towards his ancestors who had worshipped there. We caught sight of the church when we were already at a distance; and a heart-warming sight it was. Small but beautifully proportioned, it stood on a knoll just above what had once been the village, and it seemed to beckon to us to go there and recite some prayers.

But as we drove up the road we realised that where once the village had been there was now an Israeli military camp encircling the knoll on which the church stood. Nevertheless, we were still hopeful of being able at least to visit the church until we were stopped at the guard post. The soldier on guard with his machine gun was only a young man and he looked frozen, because it was a cold day. He seemed to be glad to see us and even switched off the pop music on his transistor with which he was trying to beguile the hours. At first he seemed puzzled by our request to visit the church but then said he would phone his commanding officer, and he expected it would be all right. Again and again he kept calling on his field telephone to try to secure permission for us, but he seemed never to have any luck. Occasionally he turned to us and explained that he would go on trying, so 'just hang on'. Then he suddenly looked startled as a figure eventually emerged from the unit HQ about 200 yards away, violently waving its arms and jumping up and down like a dancing dervish. We got the message. And he, poor soul, got the message even more explicitly over his intercom. Sadly he came over to us and explained that our visit was forbidden; and there was a look on his chilled face as if to say, 'Sorry, chums. It's a crazy world.'

We thanked him for his efforts and drove away. Butros and Boulos remained silent. They did not even say anything 200 yards further down the road when two Israeli soldiers tried to thumb a lift.

That night I slept in their village. I was awakened around five o'clock by the tramp of men's boots along the village street. The men of the village were all going to catch the buses which take them each morning to work many miles away on construction projects for Jewish settlements. They would return only at nightfall. Meanwhile another people would be cultivating the fields across the valley which had been theirs and their ancestors' for generation upon generation. I thought of their tragedy. And I thought of the tragedy of thousands in the settlements, Jews who had survived the Holocaust or been driven from Morocco or Egypt or Iraq. And I could not sleep.

Then I remembered the young Jewish soldier and his good, innocent face, his warmth and goodwill towards us. And the happy thought struck me that he is one of the thirty-six just men. And that other one, the old Maronite at Kafar Bir'im? He also may be one of the thirty-six. Or perhaps our Jewish brethren would rather describe him as 'a just amongst the Gentiles'. And the other one, the young soldier? We shall call him 'a just among the Jews'!

Then I was able to sleep. The thirty-six are still there. The universe will not be destroyed.

9th March, 1982. Tantur

The trouble with proclaiming ringing truths is that they are likely to fly round, like a misguided boomerang and strike you on the back of your head.

For years now I have been going on about the Lord's injunction that if we come to the altar knowing that one of our brothers has something against us then we must leave our gift at the altar and go and first be reconciled with our brother. In the light of that injunction I have repeatedly underlined the question put by Vincent Donovan, 'One wonders, how often do we really achieve eucharist in our lives?'

That question has now become a burning one for me. Truly it has been burning me up since last Wednesday. Because late on Wednesday evening an almighty, violent quarrel sprang up between two of the scholars, known here as Olaf and Canute. I will not describe the gory details of what took place but simply record that by Thursday morning they were at daggers drawn and each of them was trying to convince their fellow scholars of the justice of their own case.

I think I made a mistake by going to each of them separately on Thursday afternoon, too confident that as good Christians they would quickly forgive one another and be reconciled. That did not allow them a long enough cooling-off period, with the result that when I expressed even a muted plea for a sign of forgiveness the explosive reply I received from each of them said, in effect, 'So you are accusing me of being the guilty one?'

Of course I was not attempting to apportion blame. Yet on looking back I can see why my approaches to Olaf must have irritated and angered him. He interpreted my hunch that he was the one most ready to seek reconciliation as a sign that I thought the obligation to do so was his because

82

he was the more guilty. And I made matters worse two days ago by saying to him, 'How can we in this community celebrate Easter when you two are at enmity with one another?' At which point he went through the ceiling with rage and shouted at me, 'So you are saying that because of me this whole community will be unable to celebrate Easter?'

Although I withdrew at this juncture I have since been going about my duties in something of a daze, wondering what on earth I am to do. All the same Olaf is fundamentally a generous fellow and I believe that my question did lodge in him at some hidden level. Still I cannot imagine what the rest of the community, and the monks especially, are going to say if I announce that I do not believe this community here can properly celebrate Easter Eucharist whilst two of our members are in a condition of such unforgiveness towards one another.

One thing about which I must be particularly careful: that is, not to fall into my lonely-man-on-the-bridge syndrome. As Rector of this place, acquainted with many factors of which almost everyone else is unaware, it is always tempting for me to follow my ingrained habit when facing a difficult decision. That is, I worry about it on my own for a long time and then suddenly announce to all and sundry that I have made up my mind – and that's that!

There are positive gains to be had from that pattern of behaviour which, on looking back, I can see was ingrained in me from my childhood and then reinforced by the British Army's stern and quite justified warning against 'raising alarm and despondency amongst the troops'. That warning echoed the more drastic rule observed by the fierce Vikings that anyone guilty of spreading rumours calculated to cause despondency must be executed. Both Viking and British commanders realised that alarm and despondency is death to a community – and that, in any case, most of our fears eventually prove to be baseless.

On the other hand, if I do follow my natural inclination and gnaw away at the problem on my own for a few weeks and then suddenly tell Fr Adalbert, the Benedictine Prior, that we cannot in good conscience celebrate Easter in this place then I fear he may suffer a heart attack.

14th March, 1982. Tantur

(Sunday)

One advantage, at least, of living in community is that one's estimates of various members of the community are constantly revealed to have been mistaken. Or perhaps it would be more accurate to say that I am for ever being surprised at encountering sides of my colleagues' characters to which I had been blind. My surprise springs from having taken one aspect of a colleague with which I had become familiar to be his overall character when, in fact, it was just one minor facet of his personality,

Sometimes, of course, the surprising revelation may turn out to be unpleasant, as when you are being driven for the first time by a highly cultured, gentle friend and discover that at the wheel of a car he behaves like a berserker, roaring along at 80 m.p.h. and issuing a chorus of curses against every other driver he meets. But this morning provided a most pleasant surprise when we went to the neighbouring Orthodox village of Beit Jala for our Sunday Eucharist as we do fairly regularly at the invitation of the villagers.

I am sorry to have to record that invariably before we are due to go the word seems to pass around mysteriously amongst Free Church brethren that the experience of visiting the Beit Jala Orthodox is not specially edifying. From a Free Church point of view I can understand, of course, that they find the Orthodox service extremely disconcerting. At one level it is highly formal and liturgical, with much bowing and kneeling and crossing of oneself to accompany the processions led by priests who keep vanishing behind the iconastasis and reappearing again to bless the congregation. All the same I was disappointed to discover this morning what a small number of our community had assembled to go to Beit Jala. After all, we had been invited, and I would have thought that anyone who is serious about Christian unity could put up with being a bit disconcerted.

However, my disappointment was completely dispelled by the Millers. The word that had formed in my mind to characterise them is 'dumpish'. The two them look just like the caricature of an American tourist couple beloved of the cartoonists. They look heavy in build, in gait, in speech and in thought. I had never heard either of them utter any sentiment that was not conventional; and the comments they make on theological issues are predictable once you know the particular ecclesiastical tradition out of which they come.

But in spite of the word of discouragement that had gone around previously they both turned up this morning for our Beit Jala visit and really entered into the spirit of it. For instance, whenever we came to a point of the service at which worshippers sit down, I noticed that Anne Miller would very deliberately make sure not to sit with her legs crossed, faithfully remembering my warning that to sit in church with one's legs crossed is regarded by our Beit Jala friends as deeply offensive. Indeed I have known them come across on occasion and slap offending crossed legs. And then, when it came to distribution of the *prosphora,* both Anne and Joe eagerly took the bread and chewed away vigorously – undeterred by the example of their proper English neighbour who declined the *prosphora* rather primly, as if she feared that by eating it she might be turned into an Arab!

The revelation of the day, however, came when I joined Anne and Joe as they were tucking into cakes and coffee in the mayor's parlour after the service. For some obscure reason I felt that I had to apologise to them on behalf of the Orthodox for the fact that out of the whole congregation in the church no more than three members, all of them old ladies, had gone up to the altar steps to receive the sacrament. In the Orthodox Church, I explained, contrary to the practice in their own tradition, it is not customary for virtually all members of the congregation to receive communion.

'That didn't worry me at all', Joe replied. 'In fact, you know, I got the feeling that somehow everyone present received the Risen Lord. I mean, those old stagers, and the young men beside them gathered round their big books, stationed under the pulpit, singing away for a couple of hours and knowing every twist and turn of the liturgy. And then the kids running around with the *prosphora* and the collection bag. No! St Nicholas' really is a people's church. And I believe the Risen Lord came and dwelt in the whole people.'

Ruminating on Joe's words since this morning I realise how that good 'conventional' Protestant has opened my eyes. He is right. The eucharistic current of grace – of the Lord – permeated the whole of the church this morning and not just those three who went up to communion! So though I don't claim to be able to provide a theologically satisfactory account of how it happens, I see more clearly how the Eucharist is not just for one's personal sanctification, nor even for the sanctification of those present in a particular church. The Eucharist is a *cosmic* act, an act by which the redemptive love of Jesus permeates the whole cosmos.

'And in order to know that', as one of my Yiddish friends might exclaim in different circumstances, 'you needed to go to Beit Jala? Oi! Oi!' But it is true, and it took a Protestant to open my eyes.

What is more, not only has Joe Miller opened my eyes; he has also lifted a weight off my shoulders – the burden, that is, of not knowing what path I myself should follow towards receiving communion at our own Sunday Eucharist here in the Institute.

In the first few weeks of my period as Rector I adhered to the practice customary amongst Catholics at ecumenical conferences; that is to say, I received communion when a Catholic celebrated but abstained from doing so when a non-Catholic was the celebrant. But living out that practice, week after week, in spite of its theological rectitude, made me aware that it only heightened the sense of division within the community and gave rise to feelings of anger that you could sense in the chapel as unmistakeably as a foul wind. You could also sense the feeling of relief on the part of some people when they emerged from the chapel after the Eucharist, as if to say, 'Thank God that's over.'

Under the burden of that awareness I decided to follow a different practice. In union with my Protestant brethren I would not receive communion when a Catholic priest was the celebrant; neither would I do so when the celebrant was a Protestant, thereby adhering to the discipline of my own church. This produced the strange situation, therefore, whereby the Rector of an ecumenical institute never received communion at the Sunday Eucharist in the Institute's own chapel!

This evidence of bankruptcy led to a further twist in the labyrinth of paths around the Eucharist. One of the very sweetest members of our community, extremely Protestant and anti-Catholic by background, came to my office recently and very hesitatingly asked if I would mind her raising a matter which was troubling her. No, I assured her, I did not mind. Whereupon she said she had been upset at noticing that I never went to communion, and she was wondering whether I was abstaining as a protest against the reactionary stance of the Benedictine monks!

Since my feelings towards her are warm and affectionate I managed not to react by displaying my distress at the suggestion that anyone would treat the Eucharist as a means of protesting against some policy one disagrees with. But it also became clear, subsequently, that some other members of the community had entertained the same suggestion. Which means that I need to convey obliquely to them my sense of distress at the notion of the Eucharist as an occasion for protest. At the same time I shall be able to pass on Joe Miller's revelation to me that receiving communion is not merely for the good of an individual or even a particular ecclesiastical group but is participation in a cosmic act which benefits the whole of creation. Therefore in receiving communion one is a representative of all creation; and so if one is in a position to receive communion whilst one's friends are for some reason excluded, then, apart from anything else, it is an act of friendship to partake on their behalf. No longer need I abstain.

17th March, 1982. Tantur

Although I am very exhausted, emotionally drained, by the events surrounding Fr Lane's death I feel that I must put some account of those events into my journal so that the memory of him will remain vivid in the years to come.

Having known for some time how sick Fr Lane was I had been negotiating with his superiors to have him recalled either to the US or to Rome, or to some place whatever where he might be better cared for than we can manage here. So I was saddened when it became clear, even to Lane himself, that he would have to go immediately into hospital. At first I tried to persuade him to go to the Hadassah in Jerusalem where they have the very latest medical equipment. But he pleaded with me not to have him sent there – as it is 'cold and soulless' – but to the hospital in Bethlehem. Bethlehem had become home to him by this time and he wanted, above all, to be near his friends, the Christian Brothers, as well as to all his Arab friends. And they would have been nervous about travelling to an Israeli hospital to visit him.

And once he was settled in his room in the French Hospital in Bethlehem Lane was indeed wrapped in consolation as one group of Arabs after another flocked into his room to show their affection for this gentle American priest, and to wish him a speedy recovery. On the other hand, and not for the first time, I found myself having to read the Riot

Act to those Arab friends in order to protect Lane, to prevent them from killing the patient through kindness. They crowded along the corridor outside Lane's room in large numbers, men, women and children, sitting and standing around, loudly chattering except when a hospital official appeared, at which point they would become obediently silent, each hoping to be the one allowed in to see Lane. There is something very touching in the way that Arabs will crowd around a sick person, as though the mere presence of a group of warm human beings will somehow ward off the cold hand of death.

At Tantur, meanwhile, the crisis brought about by Lane's illness generated a wave of generosity and unselfishness fit to melt your heart. There was an immediate response when I proposed to the community that we should set up a twenty-four hour rota to ensure that at least one of us should be present with Lane all the time, whether by his bedside itself or on stand-by outside his room if the nurses or doctors ministering to him needed any help.

There was no lack of volunteers for the rota. Nor was there any lack of them to give the blood which he needed in considerable quantities. And just as one discovered during the war that sometimes it was the most surprising people who came good in an emergency, so now various lesser lights amongst the scholars rose to the occasion marvellously, even anticipating my needs and coming to my aid when they saw me getting exhausted. Also interesting was the fact that Adam and Basil, two of our most grumbly scholars, suddenly seemed to find themselves. They came alive and grew quite cheerful, as though the drama of Lane's illness had provided them with a role in the community which they had previously lacked. Perhaps grumbling is the way in which some quite good people get through life.

The other side of the coin was the undoubted, though scarcely perceptible, dragging of feet on the part of two of the best organised and genuinely research-minded of our scholars. Although those two have actually been the most co-operative in routine administrative matters – their minds being so clear about their goals and their schedules – it may precisely be their capacity for organising their lives neatly around their own egos which makes them reluctant to get involved in anything that seems a threat to their fixed goals. By contrast, some of the scholars who used to spend an inordinate amount of time hanging around the coffee room and constantly grumbling became exemplary members of the community. I expect it is the usual case of swings and roundabouts: you have loss and gain with every type of human being.

Not that the saying about swings and roundabouts can be treated as a general law, because there are some people who are just generous and dependable at all times and seasons. This was proved true of Sister Maria and Brother Maur. In spite of doing her teaching during the day at Bethlehem University this Maryknoll nursing sister, Maria, somehow or other managed as well to tend to Lane throughout the night. Besides keeping us all cheerful she also prevented us clumsy helpers from making any feerful mistakes. In the same way our Benedictine brother, Maur, unobtrusively took on the dead shifts in the middle of the long nights and yet has emerged in time for early Mass in our chapel, showing no signs of strain or tiredness. The example of Maria and Maur has again set me racking my brain trying to sort out my attitude towards professed religious. Perhaps the truth about professed religious is best conveyed by applying to them what Mary McCarthy once said about Roman Catholicism – 'a very good religion for those who take it seriously but a very bad one for those who are half-hearted about it.' When members of religious orders are good they are marvellous, but when they are anything less they are a pain in the neck.

I certainly felt this to be true on the Thursday evening as I was standing in our kitchen handling kettles and cups, preparing coffee for a whole company of scholars and guests whom we had invited to our apartment. In burst an American Sister, uninvited, who accused me of failing to secure the best medical attention for Lane and then shrieked that if he died I would be the one responsible.

In fact that very day and the next day Lane had seemed much better and was himself talking about coming out of hospital soon. But it was not to be.

Saturday was as wild a day as you are ever likely to encounter. The winds blew at gale force from every direction; the dark grey clouds scudded across the stark hilltops in endless succession and the rain lashed mercilessly against the windows and walls of the Institute until there were streams running down over the walls, washing them startlingly clean. Then towards evening the weather became more fearsome still, so that now you could no longer see the hills on account of sheet upon sheet of rain blotting out everything more than a few yards distant. It was one of those evenings when every creature, both man and beast, seeks a dry corner in which to huddle until the storm passes over. So when I said to Dorothy that I thought I might drive along to the hospital in Bethlehem just to make sure that Lane was maintaining his improvement she told me not to be crazy but to wait until morning.

However, my instinct told me that I was meant to go. And so I did. When I drew up at the roadside opposite the hospital the rain was sheeting down so heavily that by the time I had run from the car to the hospital entrance my duffle coat was soaked through. Yet all thought of how wet I had got was driven from my mind as soon as I entered Lane's room, where I found him in a state of wild delirium, with Brother Joe at his side desperately trying to calm him down.

The next few hours were extremely painful since Lane kept demanding to go home and kept attempting to pull out the various tubes attached to him so that he could indeed walk out of the hospital. Knowing that would be fatal Brother Joe and I tried everything we could think of to humour him. At one point we agreed to push Lane along the corridor in his wheelchair, each of us pushing with one hand and with the other holding various pieces of his life-support system. To crown it all we had the bright idea of capitalising on Lane's love of music: we would distract him from his escape plans by singing as we guided his wheelchair up and down the corridors. The only snag in that stratagem was that we knew so few songs in common. As a result we were reduced to singing the first verse of 'The Battle Hymn of the Republic' over and over again until Lane got fed up of our singing and we all burst into laughter at the thought of what an absurd sight the three of us made – Lane sitting in his wheelchair, like some Eastern potentate, and the two of us, wet through, trundling him up and down the corridor, like a couple of incompetent slaves, stumbling over the words of the Battle Hymn.

But the laughter came to an end. After several hours Lane did manage to detach the tubes, not in the event enabling him to walk home but ensuring that his next destination would be the grave.

As I left Lane, who was now sedated, and I climbed into my car, I suddenly realised that for four hours I had been wearing my soaked duffle coat; but so absorbed had I been in the night's drama that I had not managed to take it off or even been aware of it.

The rest of the story – or, at least, the glimmerings of redemption that make the story worth recording – belongs to the Arabs, beginning soon after five o'clock on Monday morning when I reached the hospital and learned that Lane had died just a few minutes earlier. There arrived at the same time Um Ibrahim, the bent old Arab lady whose job it is to clean the rooms in the Institute but who, in fact, manages to clean very few since she is now very old and frail and moves painfully slowly, shuffling along as though her feet are held to the ground by an invisible magnet. She followed after Dorothy and myself, Sister Maria and Fr David Burrell (a Holy Cross priest, like Fr Lane) as we bundled the trolley bearing Lane's body along to the hospital chapel. There we stood by the body and from our prayer books recited the prayers for the dead and the appropriate psalms. We did everything according to the rubrics and with proper dignity, each of us awed in the presence of death.

But then, without seeking anyone's permission and seemingly unconcerned with the judgement of any human being, Um Ibrahim moved forward to a position opposite Lane's feet; and gazing towards a point just above his head, she began to sing a most moving hymn in Arabic, singing not from a book or according to any rubric but freely and spontaneously from her heart. Scant though my Arabic may be, I needed no telling that the hymn, which went on and on and on, was a hymn to the Mother of God, asking her to intercede for eternal blessing upon our dear brother who had just crossed the threshold of death. Um Ibrahim's love for Lane, for Mary the Mother of God, and for all suffering creatures seemed to fill the chapel as one refrain followed another, her voice eventually becoming quieter and quieter until eventually she stopped singing. After a pause she crossed herself, turned round slowly and shuffled out of the chapel, extraordinarily self-contained, as if she knew something beyond the reach of us Western-ers. We, for our part, were aware, without any sense of resentment, that the priest in the early hour of that day had been an unlettered Arab woman.

Not that all Westerners found it easy to bow to Arab sensibility in these ultimate matters. No sooner was Lane dead than I found myself being bombarded with advice by Westerners who flatter themselves on knowing the appropriate Jerusalem manner of burying the dead. One person maintained very firmly that the coffin should be closed, because in this climate the body begins to decay so quickly. Another egregious character recited for me a list of the representatives of local churches and associations who positively must be invited to act as pall-bearers – by the time he had finished I felt as though we would need a computer to work out who should be asked first and how long each should carry the coffin, and so on.

I did notice that no Arabs figured on his list. However, I need not have worried. Our Arab staff, in their affection for Lane, really took over the whole ritual without any fuss. They made it clear to me that it would be more than my life was worth if the coffin were not to be open in the church since that would make it impossible to say good-bye to Lane in Arab fashion. And then, when it came to carrying the coffin from the Dormition Abbey to the cemetery half a mile away, the Arab menfolk simply moved in and took the coffin up without any instructions from anyone. Christians and Muslims, they seemed to know instinctively when to change as bearers – one of them walking behind the coffin would simply move up and tap the shoulder of one of the pall-bearers who would then release his burden to the new bearer. And so the ritual went on, smoothly and quietly, until we entered the cemetery.

At that moment, completely unexpected, we heard the most heavenly sound, the sound of a human voice singing, tender and clear, which seemed to pierce the vault of the blue sky above our heads. For a brief space I could not make out where the voice was coming from and whose voice it was. And then I turned round and saw that the singer who had begun to sing Psalm 130 ('Out of the depths have I cried to thee, O Lord') in Arabic was our own cook, Issa. The gentlest and most self-effacing of men, Issa, the leader of the choir in the Nativity Church at Bethlehem, had timed his cry for God's mercy upon Lane to perfection and was now exercising his authority as liturgist with unwavering confidence.

There is a note of longing in the liturgical singing of all the religious communities of the Middle East which touches you at the very core of your being, whether the tradition be Jewish or Muslim, Armenian or Melkite. The sound of it, sustained over and over again, brings you into touch with the Absolute. Issa's inspired singing this afternoon lifted us into that absolute dimension where we all became present to Lane.

20th March, 1982. Tantur

Whenever someone close to you dies before their time you nearly always start wondering whether you had done enough for them whilst they were still alive. Certainly I have been asking myself whether I had shown sufficient affection to Lane during our time together. The pain of that thought was intensified for me today as I spent many hours going through the articles left in his room to decide what should be done with them. As always on such occasions the whole of the dead person's life is revealed to you at an unexpected depth, and a well of compassion is opened in one's heart at the knowledge of our fragile hopes.

Had I done enough for Lane? Then, as I was sorting out various articles on his besides table I came across a copy of my own book *Holiness*. There was a book-maker placed between pages sixty and sixty-one.

That discovery was a great consolation to me, a sign from Lane that we had become friends during these months together.

21st March, 1982. Tantur

'Whew!' as they used to say in the school story-books. 'That was a close-run thing.'

At Mass this morning I was still worrying – more than ever, I expect – about how we could possibly celebrate Easter in good conscience whilst Olaf and Canute are engaged in cold warfare against one another. Moreover, I realised I had left it very late to share my concern about Easter with the community – perhaps it was already too late to do so. And tension was heightened this morning by the presence of both Olaf and Canute in chapel for the first time in several weeks, which set me wondering whether they would avoid one another when the moment came to exchange the kiss of peace.

What happened, in fact, was a miracle. As soon as the priest had announced the peace dear Olaf (bless his heart) shouted from the side of the chapel where he was standing to the other side where Canute had stationed himself, 'I forgive you, Canute, and I ask your forgiveness!' And as he spoke he strode across the centre of the chapel towards Canute, who then came to meet him. The two of them embraced in the midst of the astonished congregation.

Everyone began to smile as the Holy Breath swept through the chapel and cleansed all our hearts.

I doubt whether anyone quite realises what relief the incident brought to me. It felt as though a heavy weight had literally been lifted off my heart, enabling me to breathe freely and deeply once more. 'Breathe on me, Breath of God', for sure! My very lungs declared their thanks.

23rd March, 1982. Tantur

No wonder that this journal contains nothing for this past week except cryptic abbreviations, times of engagements, names and exclamation marks! Leaving aside all the internal disputes amongst Arabs, scholars and staff it seems as though external relations have entered a delicate stage.

I knew that something was brewing, of course, when Ezer telephoned me ten days ago to invite me for lunch at the Hilton. Never having so far darkened the doors of a Hilton hotel I was very happy to accept, even though I realised that his Ministry was up to something, and that I was not being invited simply by virtue of my scintillating conversation! In any case I like Ezer very much; he is far too nice a person to be in that particular job and would, as they say, 'have risen higher' in officialdom if he had not been such gentleman.

Working out on the basis of the invited company what is afoot nearly always defeats me. The other five at table were three Israelis, a German Lutheran and a visiting Anglican dignitary. The latter baffled me entirely. We had hardly sat down before he told me that he supported Mrs Thatcher's Falklands War and then looked towards me quizzically in that peculiarly English manner as if to say that I, presumably, was not one of those outsiders who disapproved of her policy. It is the bland assumption of the English establishment that we are all 'decent fellows who belong to the same club' which provokes me. So I simply said that it would be surprising if I did support Mrs Thatcher now since I had never previously agreed with anything she has done. Maybe this, in turn, provoked him, because soon after learning that I am a Catholic he commented that 'Basil Hume is very good, of course, but who knows . . . he might be succeeded by an Irishman!' Strangely enough his comment did not so much annoy me as amuse me – it was so damned pompous. I thought to myself, 'Goodness! An Irishman in Westminster Cathedral! A fate worse that death!', and I was tempted to say that a similar remark about a Jew would undoubtedly have brought upon his reverend head the charge of anti-Semitism.

But I let the remark pass out of respect for Ezer, who, in any case, was now burrowing away about his own business, which turned out to be my business. His opening gambit consisted of a very appreciative and quite detailed survey of the articles on life in the Holy Land which I have regularly been publishing in the *Tablet* under the heading 'Letter from Jerusalem'. And then suddenly, in a tone of detached curiosity, he looked at me and said, 'By the way, Donald, did you write that unsigned leader on Israel in the *Tablet* of last month?' So that was what it was all about! The leader, I remembered, was sharply critical of certain Israeli policies.

97

With a little smile at Ezer in which he (bless him) joined, I said quietly, 'No, Ezer, I did not. And, if I ever do publish anything unsigned, rest assured that I shall personally send you a copy – signed!', which was not a bad way of bringing our Hilton lunch to a close.

But that was only the beginning of my encounter with Israeli officialdom this week. On Wednesday I spent several hours, at their request, in a 'getting to know one another' session with two officials, a man and a woman, from a different Ministry. Ostensibly their visit was part of an annual tour of Christian institutions, but as I sat at the desk in my office being grilled – in a civilised manner, admittedly, but grilled nonetheless – I realised what was worrying them: our recent proposal to hold a Muslim–Christian Dialogue Conference.They did not say that in so many words, of course, but their concern was clear; and it saddened me that any sign of friendship between Christians and Muslims is immediately interpreted as a sign of hostility, and even conspiracy, against Jews.

They kept asking when we were going to hold a Jewish–Christian Dialogue Conference here, not seeming to understand that there is no need to put on a special meeting for that purpose since a dialogue of Jews and Christians is going on here the whole time, day in and day out. I wish they could see it as a healthy sign that we do not need to contrive any such a meeting considering that so many Jews come into the Institute all the time, either to work in the library or to give seminars or simply to have meals with us. And all this happens spontaneously because of our personal friendships with Jews – who in many cases studied at the same schools and universities as ourselves and share the same Western Enlightenment background.

By contrast our Muslim brethren come from a world quite unfamiliar to most of us. We speak almost no Arabic, have not travelled much in Muslim lands nor hitherto lived side by side with Muslims; and so we have to undertake quite a campaign to enjoy any sort of communication with them beyond the superficial level.

Contrary to what I would at one time have anticipated, my third encounter with Israeli officialdom this week went much more smoothly. I describe that smoothness as contrary to my earlier expectations because the Israeli official who came in on Thursday was an army colonel and I was brought up with a suspicion of all soldiers above the rank of sergeant. Colonel Nissim is the 'civil' Governor of Bethlehem whom I had really warmed to at two previous short meetings, but I couldn't help being a bit taken aback, as well as amused, at the process by which he now turned up for lunch with his second-in-command, his Arab adviser, a couple of other spare soldiers, all with their guns, and two very attractive women soldiers who are, I imagine, secretaries. Did I invite him? Or did he invite himself?

The answer seems to be neither: I did not precisely invite him, nor did he precisely invite himself; but he and his caravanserai simply appeared at our table through a process of osmosis. The truth behind that seemingly fanciful answer is actually a source of hope for the Middle East because the osmosis in question was achieved by the silent collaboration of our Jewish accountant, Yehuda, and our incomparable Arab business manager, Yusuf Sa'ad. Their collaboration often makes me think that if only the Yehudas and Yusufs who dwell in this land were left unmolested by the Great Powers and external busybodies in general then they would certainly manage to live together in peace. The arrangements they made would not be up to the standards demanded by the hypocrites of the West but at least they would be of a kind that the human beings hereabouts can lives with.

The fact of the matter is that Colonel Nissim, as Governor of Bethlehem, obviously needs to keep an eye on what is going on in this Institute so strategically situated on the hill of Tantur. And I need to have a good line of communication with the Governor for these occasions when members of our staff get arrested, in which case I have to try to make sure that they are not unjustly treated or do not simply vanish for a few weeks, causing heartbreak in their families. And what better way is there of fulfilling both our needs than over a good meal, a glass of wine – and, in the case of the Israelis, endless cigarettes which they light up regularly at the meal table without any by-your-leave? Interestingly enough, I find I do not resent that bad habit in these Israeli soldiers as I would in most people. My explanation to myself is that the habit is just one trait out of the many rough traits characteristic of an army that I think of as genuinely democratic. At least once in talking to Colonel Nissim and commenting on the easy, informal relations between all ranks in the Israeli army I had described it as a 'democratic' army but he had immediately and sagaciously corrected me. 'No! You cannot have a *democratic* army. An army, is inevitably hierarchical. What we have is a popular army, a people's army, and that is why we are so much less formal than other armies.'

There was something else he said today which I shall always treasure. The two of us were standing alone in our library discussing controversial issues very freely when he said, 'It seems to me, professor, that you try as Rector of Tantur to be neutral as between Arabs and Jews, neither on one side nor the other', to which I answered, 'No! I dislike the word "neutral"! It carries a connotation of being unconcerned. What we try to do is to be on both sides, never to lose our sense of compassion for either Arabs or Jews, who are both caught in a situation which is largely not of their own making.'

The vehemence of his reaction surprised me. Vigorously slapping his thigh he exclaimed, 'You are absolutely right! We are all in an *impossible* situation which is not of our own making.' Suddenly I had a glimpse of the man's heart and an inkling of what it must cost a sensitive man to exercise high office in an occupying force: trying to carry out as humanely as possible a policy which is inevitably oppressive.

24th March, 1982. Tantur

In that eerie fashion which seems characteristic of the Middle East a message has percolated up to me from Bethlehem, or, should I say, has been wafted up to me from 'the Arabs in Bethlehem' (whoever they may be). The message is to say, 'What game is the Rector playing? We have thought of him as an honest man who speaks to us from the heart, from a clean heart. But now we hear that he entertains Colonel Nissim and his soldiers at Tantur. Whose side is he on?'

5th April, 1982. Tantur

Every time I think we have now exhausted the list of variations that can be played upon the theme of eucharistic dispute someone comes up with yet another one. The latest comes from a surprising quarter, from a group of our Anglican/Episcopalian priests. Several of them have come and complained that although the Benedictines celebrate Mass every morning there is no provision made for members of other traditions to celebrate on a weekday. I pointed out to them that our present chapel was designed for the founding monastic community, which it was envisaged would include Orthodox and Protestant monks, as well as Catholics. Originally the intention was to build a further enormous ecumenical church for the use of scholars and visitors in the centre of our quadrangle; but the money ran out, so the monks have had to share 'their' chapel with scholars and visitors. If scholars were now to insist upon celebrating on certain days during the week that would involve denying the monks celebration in 'their' chapel on those days, in accordance with our rule that only one eucharistic celebration shall take place on any one day.

That our Anglican brethren showed scant sympathy for the monks in this dilemma was a surprise to me because the Anglican/Episcopalian contingents here have distinguished themselves by their good humour and flexibility, and their readiness to help whenever they have seen me to be in an awkward position. I now realise how their unquestioning assumption that they are the ones who decide ceremonies and fix precedence is so ingrained in the Anglican mentality as a result of being the established church for centuries that they are deeply disturbed at finding themselves on a level with Baptists, Methodists, Quakers, etc. Nevertheless they are justified in their annoyance, especially those who say that celebrating Eucharist each day is for them an essential part of their priestly vocation.

I shall have to work out some *modus vivendi* which is acceptable to them and to the monks yet which does not raise the hackles of either the Advisory Council or the other members of Tantur.

8th April, 1982. A Meditation

Yad Vashem is a touchstone for all time. You cannot prevent this monument from searching out your impurities either by refusing to go near it or, in contrast, by constantly going there. You may try to avoid the self-questioning that Yad Vashem demands of you by staying away from it; or, if you are Jewish, by using it to induce guilt in Gentiles. However, no formula, no matter how brilliant, can settle anyone's account with Yad Vashem, not even that of the Spanish abbot whos said, 'Yad Vashem is a place which all Gentiles should visit, but no Jews.' He meant much the same, of course, as Gladstone did when he declared, 'Let England remember and Ireland forget'. But both the abbot and Gladstone were asking too much of the Jews and Irish respectively in requiring them to forget their peoples' sufferings. Similarly my friend Emmanuel Littmann, himself a concentration camp survivor, is misreading the possibilities for Israel when he maintains that the Israeli government should at least abandon the practice of making it compulsory for all Israeli schoolchildren to visit Yad Vashem. He is right when he points to the danger that the practice will leave generations of Israelis with the self-destructive conviction that the whole world is against them and wishes to destroy them. Nevertheless Jewish children, and maybe even Arab children in Israel, need to encounter some memorial of the annihilation of six million Jews.

There is not, nor could there be, any completely satisfactory way of remembering such an unimaginable catastrophe. But we can all at least be alive to the impurities in us which are unearthed by the attempt to remember it. At the moment I am thinking especially of the danger at Yad Vashem of legitimising the pornography of suffering. The danger of succumbing to pornography in the form of suffering revealed itself to me more than twenty years ago when I used to teach a course on the Holocaust. Surprising as I found it, the fact is that human beings may find surreptitious fascination and pleasure in the depiction of suffering.

And it was at Yad Vashem that I came face to face with that surreptitious pleasure. The occasion was a visit to the memorial that I had arranged for Tantur scholars. As they were slowly and reverently processing through the museum of the Holocaust I wandered away in advance of them, not only because I have visited their museum many times but, even more, because I do not believe that one should got through Yad Vashem as a group. One needs to be alone in that searching examination, unrelieved by the distractions and vulgarity of a crowd.

So I found myself waiting at a corner of the corridor, obliquely opposite to where there hangs a greatly enlarged photograph of a town square in Poland showing the bodies of some half a dozen Jews dangling from a gallows on which in 1943 they had been hanged by the German occupation forces. One feature of this photograph had always sickened me, and that is the expressions on the faces of the Polish townsfolk and peasants who had come to witness the execution: they were fascinated by the spectacle, and thrilled by it.

Just as I was ruminating on these matters a group of American Jews walked round the corner and began to look at the photograph under the instruction of a verbose guide. As I was observing their reactions to the photograph an awful eerie realisation dawned upon me: the expressions on the faces of those American Jews constituted a mirror image of the expressions on the faces of the Poles in the original photograph. The pornography of suffering is not confined to any one people any more than is suffering itself.

Yet maybe there is an area of ourselves which is even more corrupt than the one which allows us surreptitious pleasure in suffering; and that is the area which permits us to use the sufferings of other people for our own nefarious purposes. I shall never forget the disgust that overcame me once when I was walking through Mea Shearim, the area dominated by the Orthodox Jews of Jerusalem, and came across graffiti on a wall proclaiming 'The state of Israel is a betrayal of our six million brethren'. What sort of people have the brazenness to claim for their own ideology the sufferings of millions of their fellows, many of whom were socialists or atheists, some even Christians, and who would never have been accepted in their lifetimes by the Orthodox?

This morning I again felt the same disgust as I had previously experienced at the sight of the graffiti in Mea Shearim, though this time it was occasioned by a very different source, not by an Orthodox Jew but by a very secularised America Jewess who, moreover, had been comfortably ensconced in the US throughout the war. She is a clever woman, as she has shown both by taking possession of a fine house that once belonged to rich Arabs, and by the skilful way she took advantage of our conventional English manners. She cleverly put us into a position where it would have seemed rude on our part to refuse the invitation to visit Yad Vashem with her, although we had mildly indicated that we had already been there.

It was no use. She bundled us out there in a Volkswagen (the irony of which I did not refer to) and then, to my utter astonishment, she left us at the entrance to the museum, saying that she had been round the museum many times, and so would go round to the exit and read a book whilst she waited for us. Once I had recovered from the shock of such *hutzpah* I told Dorothy that I was going to walk quickly through the museum and arrive at the exit before our persecutor got there and see how she reacted. Fortunately Dorothy restrained me and we took a reasonable amount of time going through the museum, though rather too quickly in the subsequent estimation of our unsought guide.

And yet no visit to Yad Vashem is ever superfluous. After my anger at the attempt to manipulate us into feeling guilty as Christians for the Holocaust I said I wanted to spend some time in the Hall of Remembrance, which is incredibly moving and powerful because of the silence, and because of those eternal flames burning before the memorials inscribed with those terrible names: Maidanek, Treblinka, Auschwitz, Sobibor, Belzec, and all the others; the unpretentiousness of that Hall, the simple names the pure flames and, above all, the silence . . . That silence, above all – above all. What, if anything, does God say to us out of that silence?

I don't know if God says anything in the Hall of Remembrance and, if he does, I cannot understand it. But what I do hear through the silence, the simple names and the pure flames, are the voices of those who died in Maidanek, Treblinka, Auschwitz and all those other places of evil. And in the presence of those whose voices out of eternity were now echoing in my heart, even in my very bones, all anger against our guide dissolved and I was

able to behave courteously towards her without any sense
of strain.

10th April, 1982. Letter to the Tablet

'We could do with more Anglicans around here!' These
words, addressed in mock exasperation to my companions
at he lunch table, were occasioned by the fact none of us
had an Anglican prayer book handy and I wanted quickly
to locate an Anglican collect. But, as happens so often with
one's spontaneous and light-hearted words, they began,
some hours later, to take on a really deep significance
for me. In this instance they bore upon the future of the
ecumene. Because as my words continued to echo in my
mind I realised that I have no desire to see a Great Church
of the future that is without Anglicans – and faithful Anglicans at that. And then I realised further that neither would
I feel completely at home in the Great Church of the future
that did not contain my Baptist friends. Moreover if I single out Baptists that is not in order to exclude Methodist
friends, Presbyterians, and others. It is simply that by a
strange turn of events at Tantur during last semester we
were almost all either Catholics or Baptists, more or less
equal in numbers; and during those four months of living,
working and praying together, day in and day out, I came
to appreciate Baptist qualities as never before.

But at first it was something of a shock for me to realise,
and then to accept, that my vision of the ecumenical future
had changed so irreversibly. There always is considerable
shock, of course, when one recognises that one has been
changed at a very deep level of one's being not by taking
thought but imperceptibly, through the reality of God's
demands upon one in the struggles of day-to-day living.
At one time (that is to say, some twenty-five years ago)
I envisaged the shape of the Great Church being more or
less the same as that of our post-Tridentine Church. There
would be a Latin Mass, identical in words throughout the
world. All priests of the Great Church would be celibate.

All its members would subscribe faithfully to the social encyclicals. Everybody would go to Mass on Sunday and to confession about once a month. There would be no Protestant hymns, and the Church of England would return the cathedrals and monasteries which they had stolen at the time of the Reformation.

But if I were to see such a church emerging now it would undoubtedly send my heart down into my boots: because it would imply a denial and rejection of all those traditions amongst Methodists, Quakers, Orthodox, Baptists, Anglicans, Presbyterians, Lutherans, Copts and many others which are manifestly due to the inspiration of God. Somehow or other the Great Church will acknowledge and celebrate that inspiration of God and will rejoice in the manifold and diverse ways that God has spoken to us.

Not, however, that it all becomes easy and smooth once you begin to rejoice in the Baptistness of your Baptist friends or the Orthodoxy of your Orthodox friends. Even within the emerging Great Church there is no doubt that we will continue to suffer unexpected shocks. Take, for instance, my innocent announcement that the seminar theme for the Fall semester at Tantur is to be 'Eucharist and human liberation'. Not for a minute did it occur to me that such a title would prove immediately unattractive to certain scholars who might be considering coming to study at the Ecumenical Institute. Soon, however, my Baptist and Presbyterian friends gently pointed out to me that the very word 'Eucharist' sounds strange to their ears, and they assured me that if I continued to use it many worthy Protestants throughout the world would decide that the seminar was not for them.

Such a difference in terms could, I imagine, have led at one time to strife and enmity. But in these happier days I just said, 'Oops! Sorry!', or words to that effect, and provided an alternative title; that is, 'Worship and Politics'. Not a bad solution, all things considered, when I remember that our seminar leader, Rafael Avila, wrote a book entitled *La eucaristia y sus implicaciones socio-politicos* which was translated by a Baptist minister under the title *Worship and Politics* and published by a Catholic publishing house. It is through such incidents, which crop up every day in an ecumenical community, that we are drawn ever closer to one another in our hearts. Though sometimes these incidents also reveal how far apart we are in other respects. During the course of our discussion of the term 'Eucharist', for example, two of my Protestant friends told me: 'You attach much more importance to eucharist, or communion, than we do. For us it is not central.' When some other Protestants agreed with them I then realised with a certain consternation that whatever else may be true one thing is certainly true: those for whom the Eucharist is not central can scarcely believe the same as we do regarding what is going on at the altar (Lord's Table); if they did believe the same as we do then what goes on at the Lord's Table would be central for them.

This issues of what is central uncovers a further reality about our ecumenical situation which many of us tend to ignore but which the Roman authorities have adhered to firmly. It is that there can be no umbrella formula at the moment to draw all of us into full communion: for some time at least Christians from one tradition will have to commune with Christians from a second tradition in a somewhat different way from the way in which they commune with Christians from a third tradition, but without those differences in any sense implying that one tradition is superior to the other – because the fact is that each has unique, irreplaceable traditions which it is called upon to hand on to the others.

The influx of Anglicans into Tantur this semester, for instance, has suddenly made the lack of full communion between Catholics and Anglicans appear not simply as scandalous and sad but also as quite literally beyond belief. Here we have a group Christians who are really in *Koinonia* one with another. They share their meals together; they share their aspirations and their fears and their intellectual work with one another. They share their very lives. When they pray to God night and morning they use precisely the same words. When a Catholic celebrates the Eucharist they use the same words as he does in proclaiming their faith; likewise when an Anglican celebrates they all use the same words as him; they all believe in the real presence of Christ in the sacrament of the altar. So, on the Lord's day, all of us, Anglicans and Catholics, come together in order to celebrate the Lord's victory over death and division; we repeat his words, praying that we all may be one as Father, Son and Holy Spirit are one; we all bow as one at the consecration in acknowledgment of his real presence. And then when the Lord commands us, 'Take, eat; this is my body', something strange happens. A number of us do what he tells us to do one week but others do not, whereas the next week those who last week did take and eat do not now do so. It will surprise no one, therefore, to be told that such a pattern of behaviour seems to become more and more incredible with every week that passes, until it is quite literally beyond belief. In fact I doubt whether even one single person standing there at that moment can believe in his or her heart of hearts that our behaviour is in accordance with the will of our Lord and Saviour Jesus Christ.

In the light of that heart-rending experience we may perhaps understand better the *cri de coeur* of our present Pope when he said: 'It seems to me that the question we must ask ourselves is not so much whether we can re-establish full communion but rather whether we still have the right to remain separated.' It is true that when he said those words he was speaking to Patriarch Diodorus; but was he not also voicing a wider longing of the whole people of God? Did the Pope not show himself to be one of those church members of whom Karl Rahner has written, 'the official doctrine of the church may sometimes have to adjust itself to what actually goes in the heads and hearts of church members'? Because what the people of God actually believe is always somewhat ahead of the official doctrine.

3rd May, 1982. Tantur

This evening Dorothy and I went to the reception being given at the Mayoralty by Teddy Kollek for a group of visiting American mayors. We had been in some doubt whether to go since we were also invited to a reception at the Russian Mission in Dabbagha Street. However, we were very glad in the end that we did go because scarcely any other head of a Christian institution in Jerusalem was present, and Teddy Kollek seemed rather put out at the absence of the Christians, even after I told him about the other reception. But by going to the Mayoralty we found ourselves obliged to listen to some pretty obnoxious speeches – especially from one of the American mayors who produced a naval hat which he placed with mock solemnity on Kollek's head, saying amid loud guffaws that he thereby made him an honorary commander of the nuclear submarine that had just been launched from their city. What kind of a city has that kind of a Major!

I wonder what these junketing American mayors would have said to the Lutheran pastor from the Redeemer Church who came in just at this point, looked round to try and spot a friendly face and then came over to us? He was literally shaking with anger as he whispered to me that he had been present this afternoon at the Holy Sepulchre when violent incidents had taken place. Some students from Christian school had been sitting in the courtyard of the Holy Sepulchre in a peaceful and orderly demonstration against the Israeli government's plans to impose 'autonomy' upon the West Bank. Then along came a swarm of Israeli soldiers, uniformed policemen and secret police who started beating the students up, the secret police being the most vicious. Matters might have got completely out of hand had not the Christian leaders in the Old City, Patriarchs, Custos, etc., been

110

summoned. They, in a rare act collaboration, formed a circle around the students to protect them and lead them to safety through the crowd of Israeli soldiers and police.

7th May, 1982. Tantur

The monks must get very weary of going through the same experiences time and again, responding each year to the bright new ideas put forward by scholars which turn out to be the same as the ones that did not work in previous years. There was just a trace of such weariness even in the twinkling face of Fr Adalbert today when I announced to him that for the last two weeks, and for the foresee-able future, there was no Anglican priest now wishing to take advantage of the provision we made for them to celebrate the Eucharist on a weekday. Very few people, apparently, had attended the two or three celebrations that had been held. So he and his little Benedictine family can now return to their customary order of celebrating Mass in the morning every weekday – a reward, presum-ably, for the graceful way that they agreed to forego their daily celebration in the first place.

17th May, 1982. Tantur

I cannot imagine, being on the verge of my sixtieth year, that I shall ever now get over my astonishment at the capacity of human beings to deceive themselves.

Ten days ago we discovered who the Institute thief was; and we dismissed him. There was a sigh of relief all round, as if to say, 'Well, that little drama is now over.' But, so it seemed to me, that was not good enough; the episode did not end with the thief's dismissal, because a lot of other people had incurred guilt through pointing an accusing finger at individuals whom events have revealed to be innocent of the crime.

I thought it might be heavy-handed on my part to remind the community of the Talmudic teaching that one who speaks evil of others loses his share in the world to come unless he repents, and that a part of such repentance is to inform the maligned person of what you said, even if he is unaware of it. Since we are living in a community with a highly Christian profile I thought it would be sufficient for me to put up a simple notice on our information board announcing that the thief had been dismissed, from which it was clear that innocent people had been falsely accused. I reminded everyone who had pointed the finger of suspicion at the innocent that we are each of us obliged to make reparation for such actions.

Though the notice was posted ten days ago Yaser assures me that no one has come to him and apologised for having wrongly suspected him. And he tells me that none of the other common suspects have received any apologies either. That does not altogether surprise me, but what absolutely astonishes me is the number of people whom I heard voicing their suspicions soon after the robbery, but who are now talking as though they never said a word against Yaser and others.

It is enough to make you wonder whether the words we speak in chapel, in the hymns, prayers and readings, mean anything at all, or whether they are not a form of religious muzak, analogous to the background noises in a supermarket.

4th September, 1982. Wells, England

Driving over to the West Country yesterday, after attending the memorial service for David Brown[3] in Guildford Cathedral I kept reflecting on how some people give a lift to your heart whenever they come into your mind, especially if there is the prospect of seeing them soon. David, so far as I was concerned, was such a person.

Apart from anything else he was the ideal Tantur scholar, an answer to the Rector's prayer. For David soon made an appointment to see me in order to spend an hour or so explaining exactly what he intended to do at our

112

Institute; how he was going to work at his studies, his writing and the field trips and how he proposed to play his part in the common worship and daily life of the community. 'Here is a man', I thought to myself, 'who really believes in redeeming the time. There is something unmistakably low church – even free church – in the earnestness with which he regards his obligations towards the diocese that has given him leave and towards the British Trust which is, supporting his Sabbatical financially.'

That talk was only the first of many with David which I enjoyed as did so many other members of the community. All of us used to brighten up when David would appear with that lovely warm smile of his. On a number of occasions David and I took longish walks through the olive groves west of the Institute and up beyond the Israeli settlement of Gilo. And on each occasion, though I did look forward to the walk, at the same time I knew that I was going to be put upon my mettle: David was going to tax me with some explanation of the gap between the teaching of our Lord and the miserable performance of the Church, especially the Roman Catholic Church (of which I am a member) but also of his own Church, which he feared was 'developing a Papal style'.

So much of our conversation during those walks was summed up in one sentence from a letter which David wrote to me soon after the Pope's visit to England and not long before his own death. 'We have enjoyed the Pope, but I personally find it difficult to reconcile the Church with the Gospel records – so that I feel ill at ease – never mind – perhaps the fault is in me.' That last sudden switch of direction is so typical of his mind, which was consistent but not unilinear. On one occasion, for instance, after he had been pushing me very hard about the inadequacy of the Church I said somewhat wrily, 'Well, after all, it's not me but you who are a bishop! Presumably you are in favour of disestablishing the Church of England?' In this response, much to my astonishment, he came out with a very strong defence of the established Church in England.

One of the planks upon which his defence of the established Church rested was the fact that it enabled him to put forward a socialist point of view in the House of Lords. This position, in its turn, took me by surprise; and on the basis of my own yet more radical political position I probed his manner of reconciling his gospel-based socialism with his episcopacy over England's rich stockbroker belt. David's response was philosophically unsatisfactory yet wonderfully satisfying at a deeper level, because it conveyed to me his unfeigned love for his unusually affluent flock, in spite of the difference between their lifestyle and ideology and his own. By 'conveyed' I mean to say that some of his warmth towards those under his charge penetrated my own bones.

Not that David's radical political vision was an easy option for him. It involved him in agony, which all of us at Tantur recognised during those evenings when we gathered together round a television set and watched the unleashing of war in the South Atlantic. David was beside himself with misery and incomprehension at the sending of the expeditionary force, and he raised with me the question of whether those British who were then living at Tantur might not make a common protest. In the end, however, he decided to take the responsibility upon himself and sent a personal letter of protest to the British Ambassador in Tel Aviv.

Because he himself was so sincerely engaged, everything David did was engaging. As, for example, when he spoke to us at one of our Thursday evening Rector's 'at homes'. He spoke so beautifully about 'the gentle side of Islam' that none who were present will ever be able to dismiss Islam as a wholly harsh religion. I myself was so moved by what he had said that I asked him some days afterwards how he had arrived at such a benevolent view of Islam when, as I knew, he had been brought up to view non-Christian religions most severely. That was true, he said – when he first went to the Sudan he had regarded Islam as the work of the Evil One.

114

'How, then,' I asked, 'did you come to change so profoundly?' 'Simply through reading the Gospels', was his reply. I found his reply most unconvincing because, as I pointed out to him, he had been reading the Gospels for over thirty years before he changed so drastically. And though David kept on insisting that it was just reading the Gospels that had changed him I would not accept that account and I pressed him somewhat relentlessly to think again.

Eventually his face lit up and he offered an explanation which I believe to be worth recording.

In those days David used regularly to ride northwards out of Khartoum, and day after day he would pass a large Muslim graveyard. There he would notice Muslim women praying beside the graves of their loved ones, husbands, fathers, mothers, sisters, brothers and children. Then one day he said to himself, 'I simply cannot believe that God rejects the prayers of these women. Our Heavenly Father is certainly hearing the heart-felt, sincere prayers of those Muslim women. To them Islam is surely a means of grace.' David's prejudices against Islam had gradually been worn down by the prayers of those simple Muslim women, unaware that they were affecting profoundly the life of a chance passer-by who was one day to become an Anglican bishop and an acknowledged advocate of closer relations with Islam.

A few days before he and Mary left Tantur, my wife and I were priviledged to share in a memorable moment of that Christian-Muslim warmth advocated by David.

It was a bright, lightsome day, a Friday. The previous evening David had delivered his Tantur Lecture on which he had worked very hard. Knowing how hard he was working I had promised David and Mary that the day after his lecture I would drive them down to the Mediterranean at Ashkelon with my wife, and we would all enjoy a carefree day.

And so it proved. On the beach at Ashkelon David sang and joked; with no more than his three or four words of

115

modern Hebrew he entranced an Israeli soldier sitting at a nearby tea-bar. We all frolicked around in the waves and sang a blessing over our picnic lunch. It was a heavenly day, a day also of deep peace as we drove back in the evening through the lovely hills rising towards the Bethlehem-Hebron ridge.

At one point, as we were coming over the crest of a hill we saw an Arab woman standing by the side of the road, a heavy-looking basket beside her feet. So I stopped the car and invited her to get in. She said she was going to Hebron and would like a ride as far as the bus stop on the Bethlehem-Hebron road.

For the next half hour we four English folk attempted – often with hilarious results – to sustain a conversation with our Muslim passenger. Obviously David, being our Arabist, achieved the greatest success, but sometimes his classical Arabic ran way off from the Hebron dialect of our new friend. At which point David would lament having had to spend so much time in the past over texts and so little time over spoken Arabic.

But in the end it did not matter because the Muslim woman needed no words to feel the warmth of her welcome – as she showed beyond doubt when I halted our car at her bus stop.

In order for our passenger to alight Mary herself had first to step out of the car. This Mary did and was then standing by the door ready to step back inside when our Muslim friend took her by the shoulders and kissed her most beautifully and lovingly. Then as we drove away she stood there calling down blessings upon us. She chanted '*Ma'a selame*', and again '*Ma'a selame*'. That is, 'Peace be to you'. *Ma'e selame,* David.

30th September, 1982. Letter to the Tablet

I am so grateful for having been trained as a historian. It really does help you to put into perspective events which could easily lead you to make rash judgements if you didn't have such a training.

Take the other day, for instance, when I was standing on the tarmac at Ben Gurion airport, having just alighted from the charter plane from Luton. Most of my fellow-passengers had departed in buses for the airport terminal and I was gazing rather dreamily at the Israeli Defence Force soldier stationed some fifteen yards away. Both his green beret and his uzi machine gun spoke of uncompromising power. My daydreams, however, were suddenly interrupted when someone from behind tapped my elbow and announced, 'Security'. It was a security officer who told me to go with him over to the security van for questioning. As I did so I saw my fellow passengers looking at me suspiciously.

For the next quarter of an hour the security officer and his aides questioned me in the politely menacing manner which is second nature to those in their trade. After a time they seemed to get bored with my answers to their questions and the officer said, 'OK. We'll take you to the terminal.'

Knowing how essential security precautions are for Israel I did not attach great importance to the incident. Rather I smiled to myself as I thought, 'Well, since I am six feet six inches tall and have blond hair, at least they could hardly have taken me for an Arab!' Nevertheless, I did begin to wonder whether I may not look sinister and subversive a few days later when I was walking along the road to Jerusalem and found myself brusquely accosted by two Israeli policemen on a motor bike who also interrogated me – though much less politely this time than the airport security officers had done.

These incidents would hardly be worth recording were it not for the fact that so many visitors to Israel, and even long-term foreign residents, are prepared to make sweeping judgements about this country merely on the basis of such small everyday incidents which have affected them personally. I am sure that we should, on the contrary, try to keep such small incidents in perspective by seeing them against the background of the long history of the Jewish people and their struggle to establish a state.

Israel will continue to be misunderstood unless one fundamental truth is recognised and never for a moment lost sight of. This fundamental truth is that the Jews of Israel are still in a state of traumatic shock as a result of one of the most terrible deeds in all human history, the so-called Holocaust. When one states that truth to Gentiles nowadays their reaction invariably shows that they feel they have heard the same story so may times already that they automatically switch off, having long ago dismissed the Holocaust to the distant realms of history. In so doing they make a terrible mistake. Because for Jews, especially for the Jews of Israel, the Holocaust is as present a reality as their daily bread.

As a Sephardic Jew from France has written:

Affliction dies away in time, but shame and humiliation ever renew themselves. A shock not psychologically dominated is called a trauma. People afflicted with a trauma are mentally diseased. Every psychiatrist knows that a person afflicted with a trauma unconsciously strives to recreate the situation that is at its source, in order to be given a 'second chance' to act differently. Ashkenazi leadership in Israel unconsciously tends to provoke a new holocaust – a holocaust when Jews will die not 'like vermin' but as heroes and in a way commanding admiration. I claim that this alone is capable of explaining Israeli behaviour (Gustav Kars, *New Outlook*, January/February, 1982).

Whether or not this insight alone can explain Israeli behaviour there can be little doubt that it does help somewhat. How otherwise can one understand Menachem Begin's letter to President Reagan on his sixty-ninth birth-day, when he wrote concerning the Israeli encirclement of

Beirut: 'I feel empowered as Prime Minister to instruct a valiant army facing "Berlin" where, amongst innocent civilians, Hitler and his henchmen hide in a bunker deep beneath the surface'?

Mr Begin's statement confirms what we know about him from his own writings and from the evidence of many of his contemporaries and colleagues: he is still struggling to live out, to outlive, that trauma, that nightmare into which he was plunged by the unbearable cruelty inflicted forty years ago upon his closest and dearest ones simply because they were Jews. In order to succeed, as Gustav Kars says, Begin needs to 'recreate' that dreadful situation in which every *goy* in the world, every single one of them, was against the Jews. But this time he, Menachem Begin, will not allow his people to be humiliated but, like a true hero, will lead them to victory against the whole world. He will establish 'for ever' *eretz Israel,* the land promised by God to the Jewish people for ever, where they can be safe from the cruelties and humiliations that the *goyim* have inflicted upon Jews since as long as the memory of man runs.

It hardly needs emphasising that the nightmare just described is not peculiar to Menachem Begin. In one measure or another every Jew is plunged into it – especially, as I have said already, the Jews of Israel. One needs also to bear in mind a further effect of being in a state of traumatic shock; that is, you simply do not hear what is being said to you by other people. Not that this failure to hear is due to ill will or obstinacy. It is simply that the noise produced in your head by the sound track of your nightmare drowns all other sounds.

Nor is it merely that Israel as a whole does not take in what the rest of the world is saying, but that even within Israeli society no one seems to listen to anyone else. That, presumably, is why most people here shout so loudly, in the vain hope of compelling some other one to listen to the story which they are ceaselessly telling themselves inside their own heads. This observation, I hasten to add, is by no means original and was expressed to me in almost identical terms on separate occasions by two professors at Hebrew University. In comparing notes with them about teaching in California each of them said to me what a pleasure it had been to have had students who actually listened to what you were saying, since 'in Hebrew University the students don't listen to you at all. They just wait until you finish, then they immediately explain to you why you are wrong and they are right.' After which one of my professor friends added very sadly, 'This is the root of our parlous condition: there is no communication here – not even between husbands and wives.'

20th October, 1982. Tantur

One of the handicaps which afflict colonialist peoples is blindness about their own behaviour. Even more than the generality of human beings they are unable to see themselves as others see them. Not until they cease to be colonialists, so it seems, does the dark cloud of ignorance lift from before their gaze. That, at least, was the opinion of a recent British Consul General in East Jerusalem who had spent many years previously in the British Colonial Service. He told me once that it was not until he saw the Israelis strutting around the West Bank so arrogantly and lording it over the Arabs that he realised how he must have appeared in the eyes of the native peoples over whom he had at one time exercised power. I was reminded of the Consul General's remarks today at lunch. The guests at our table included our friend, Judith Simon, as well as as Naomi and Ann, two American friends of hers who are very active in societies for the support of Israel. Usually in our dining hall we all collect our meals from a common table, but today, out of consideration for our guests, I asked Mohamed, our strong handsome cook, to serve those whom I had invited to our table.

To my astonishment and embarrassment all our three guests at one point during the course of the meal launched into a loud denunciation of the intransigence of Arabs –

and that at the very moment when Mohamed was leaning over them to remove their empty plates and offer them more food! 'You just read the Koran', Ann said, 'and you will understand why we find it impossible to make peace with the Arabs. They are told in the Koran to carry out *jihad*, holy warfare, against us Jews; and all they are waiting for is the opportunity to do so.'

Leaving aside the strange assumption that they are better acquainted with the Qur'an than the rest of us who were sitting beside them, I could scarcely believe the evidence of my own eyes and ears. Here were three well educated, intelligent and quite amiable middle-class women denouncing a man's people at the very moment he was serving them so pleasantly and courteously. Yet I could not be angry with them when I remembered how many British men and women in our colonies I had observed similarly discussing the 'natives' who were serving them: in each case the British and the Israelis respectively failed to take it in that the servant was a human being. They would not have behaved one whit differently had the 'servant' been a robot – such objects do not have feelings!

On the other hand I did become angry with all three of them when we were drinking coffee together afterwards in our apartment. Though I did not want to tax them directly with their thoughtless behaviour towards Mohamed I did try indirectly to awaken them to the fact that the man who had been serving them was a human being. I gave them an account of what had happened to him several weeks ago.

It was a Sunday, and Mohamed was driving a friend along a lonely stretch of road between Hebron and Beersheva. The friend was wanting to visit his sick mother in Beersheva and Mohamed has a battered old car which he uses for such journeys, at the same time charging a small fee to help support his large family. They were travelling along a hill road with no other traffic in sight when suddenly a group of 'Jewish' (i.e. Israeli soldiers) ordered them to stop. The 'Jewish' then ordered them out

121

of the car and told them to lie face down on the road in the dust. Once Mohamed and his friend had done as they were ordered the 'Jewish' nudged them with their boots and asked them why they were sleeping on this dirty road. Then Mohamed and his friend were made to sweep up the road in the area where they had been lying. After which they were allowed to carry on their way to Beersheva.

Part of my intention in recounting this incident on Mohamed's Sunday journey was to add that he had only told me about it after I had questioned him; and even then had not done so in blazing anger but resignedly and, as it were, sadly, as if puzzled that human beings should treat other human beings so brutally for no reason whatsoever. However, I hardly managed to add my gloss upon the story before all three guests were each bursting to be first to convince me that Mohamed was lying – 'it is part of the Arab mentality' – and then to quote instance upon instance of Arab brutality.

As regards any incidents of Arab brutality which they had witnessed personally, I replied, I believed them – because I trusted their personal truthfulness in exactly the same measure as I trusted Mohamed's truthfulness.

23rd October, 1982. Letter to the Tablet

I said last week that the Jews in Israel are still in a state of traumatic shock because of the holocaust, and as a result sometimes seem unable to listen to anyone else. Fortunately, however, the pessimistic judgement of my friend which I quoted – 'there is no communication here, not even between husbands and wives' – is not entirely accurate. Apart from anything else, he himself has a wonderful capacity both for listening to others and for communicating with them. He is one of those whom I had in mind when I remarked some months ago that 'these Jewish intellectuals are the salt of the earth.'

The occasion of my remark was the awarding of peace prizes in honour of Sylvia Shine which took place in

Jerusalem in the presence of the Mayor, Teddy Kollek, and other notables of the city. A whole series of speakers addressed themselves to the subject of peace with the Arabs; and they did so in a fashion which assured me that the Holocaust, though still an agony, was no longer a trauma for them. But there was one particularly striking speech that came from Rabbi Arthur Herzberg, the well-known American historian of the Jewish people. After rehearsing the injustices which were being perpetrated upon the Arabs of the West Bank by the Begin government he declared very emphatically: 'This government is poisoning the wells in this part of the world not just for one generation, not just for two generations but for generation upon generation.' Herzberg's speech was doubly courageous because not only did many many people in Jerusalem disagree with him but also, since he chooses to live in America, and not in Israel, he lays himself open to the taunt that he is not in the front line and consequently has no right to criticise the policies of the State of Israel.

In fact, of course, the existence of a free-speaking American Jewry may well prove a great blessing to Israel in the long run, since American Jews have a certain breathing space within which they can achieve a sense of proportion and perspective upon Israeli affairs. On the far side of the Atlantic they are not necessarily caught in that obsessional world which encompasses all who live in the Holy Land – even those of us who are temporary sojourners, even indeed remote reviewers of books about the Land to judge from a *Tablet* review which began: 'Pro-Jew or pro-Arab? The first question one asks of a book on modern Israel must always be this.' So far can the obsession with 'our problem' stretch.

Herzberg's speech, quoted above, was delivered some time before the invasion of Lebanon, though we were all aware even then that the invasion was imminent. But the time of his speech is worth recalling because the tide of protest against the policies of the Begin government had already begun to swell before that invasion; and the invasion itself has tended to blot out of our minds, and particularly out of foreigners' minds, the volume of protest that was being directed against Israeli policy in the West Bank during the first six months of this year. Some of the critical letters to the Israeli press, for instance, were of unforgettable nobility. I remember especially the one from Professor Abraham Wasserstein of Hebrew University. Precisely in the name of his sister and his parents who had been murdered by the Nazis, Professor Wasserstein denounced the repression being carried out against the Arabs; and his whole letter carried the repeated, compelling refrain, 'I am ashamed.'

Nevertheless, the Israeli invasion of Lebanon has genuinely changed not simply the mood but the very condition of the nation, at a profound level. Indeed one of my Israeli Jewish friends does not hesitate to say that the nation during these past months has been 'undergoing a sea-change'. The kind of self-questioning that one had thought to be confined to small groups of intellectuals has now spread to virtually every branch of the people on account of Lebanon. Which is not to say, of course, that all are agreed as to the answers. For an Israeli to agree with anyone else is like surrendering his independence – Israelis are the most argumentative people on earth.

But the debate within the nation during these last few months has demonstrated, first, how profoundly moral is the substance of the Jewish people and, secondly, how strong is the democratic instinct within the country.

When I speak of the Jewish people as profoundly moral I am not saying that I think their judgements are always right. How could I say that when they are forever contradicting one another? But I mean that the debate about Israeli policies within Israel has been raised to a moral level which is almost unique in the modern world. The contrast, for example, between the quality of Israel's self-questioning and both the American debacle in Vietnam and the British in Northern Ireland is striking beyond words. No one in the USA managed to lift the level of public self-examination about US policy in Vietnam to the moral level; whilst the British in Ireland have failed miserably over the centuries to do so and are now bogged down forever, it would seem, in the morass of pragmatism. Only the debate engendered in France by such towering personalities as Mauriac, Marrou and Massignon at the time of the Algerian war of independence seems to me comparable in depth with the present struggle for righteousness in Israel.

No secret was made of the fact that quite a number of the Israeli soldiers doing their duty in the Lebanon were against the war from the beginning, whilst even more of them protested against extending the campaign as far as Beirut. Indeed, some of them on leave from the front held public meetings to protest against what was happening; whilst all the world knows that a distinguished young soldier, Colonel Eli Geva, asked to be relieved of his command, rather than take part in an attack upon Beirut. Moreover, though relieved of his command, he was not punished for his stand. Neither, apparently, was the son of interior and religious affairs minister, Josef Burg, when he took an open stand against the policies of the government. That such events should take place whilst the country's soldiers are in action is surely quite extraordinary, and it is scarcely surprising that many people within Israel felt that such events should not be allowed to happen. But in fact they are a sign of a society that is longing to be healthy.

How strong that longing is may be gauged by one of the most moving aspects of the Lebanese campaign: a number of parents of soldiers who died in Lebanon have openly declared that their sons died in an unnecessary war. That is an incredibly courageous statement on the part of parents. What could be more agonising than to acknowledge to oneself and one's community that one's beloved son has died unnecessarily – not for a good cause, but for nothing? I find it hard to imagine how a parent could find the courage to make such a declaration. During the period of the Vietnam war was it not the seeming impossibility of such a declaration which served as one of the psychological obstacles to making peace? If the US were to make peace with the Viet Cong, it was said, it would be tantamount to telling the bereaved parents of thousands of soldiers that their sons had died in vain. How could you do that?

So in order to prove that the dead had not died in vain you had to send more young men to die after them.

The issue of whether the US action in Vietnam was wrong or the Israeli action in Lebanon or the British action in the Falklands is not one to which I am at the moment addressing myself. I am simply recognising that in virtually any military action, as any soldier knows, there will be occasions when you wonder whether what you are doing could not have been avoided and whether you may not be risking your life in vain. And I suggest that it is a sign of national maturity when such doubts can be openly raised.

But even those of us who live in Israel were amazed, I think, at the demonstration in Tel Aviv when it is calculated that one Israeli in ten gathered in the Municipal Square to register their concern about the Lebanon campaign. Naturally we anticipated that certain of our friends would be there – those, for instance, who belong to the *Oz ve Shalom* group, religious Zionists who 'are gravely concerned about the drift in Israeli politics, especially within the religious parties, which threatens to undermine Jewish values and Torah principles for the sake of a parochial ideology'. Nor could we doubt that the *New Outlook* team, whose inspirer, Simha Flapan, has for more than thirty years struggled without ceasing to promote Arab–Jewish friendship, would be in the square. But the crowds in Tel Aviv included many who had never previously participated or even thought to participate in such a demonstration. Amongst them were Yeshiva students usually regarded as ultra-nationalist. 'One discerns a certain fall from innocence among these religious soldiers, who suffered a large casualty rate in the war', is how one observer put it. But the shock waves that went throughout the country must not be attributed simply to a large casualty rate amongst the religious, since subsequent weeks have revealed more and more rabbis also declaring themselves – Rabbi Yehuda Amital, for instance, head of the well-known Har Etzion yeshiva, and many others. Also we have lately heard the observant education minister, Zevulun Hammer, recording a change of heart when he said: 'Our minds must remain open to many ways in which our living in Judea and Samaria can be assured, and we must make every effort to achieve a solution that would not be just military.'

12th November, 1982. Letter to the Tablet

Last week I described the moving attempt within Israel to ensure Jewish values. But in one respect especially this should not be misinterpreted. It should not be seen as providing *carte blanche* for every critic of Israel to indulge his prejudices or his desire to hit back at Jews for any unfair criticism which they may have heaped upon him at some time. In particular it seems to me inexcusable to characterise Israeli policy in language and idiom which gained currency through the dreadful events of the period from 1933 to 1945 in central Europe, using terms such as 'holocaust' and 'genocide' and 'Gestapo'. If Israeli critics themselves choose to employ such exaggerated language, that is their privilege; but it is not a privilege of which others should avail themselves. Admittedly it is the case that a section of the Jews in Israel are intent upon driving the Palestinians out of the West Bank on the specious plea, put into currency by Arik Sharon, that 'the Palestinians already have a state – it is east of the Jordan River.' And that same section of the public does not trouble to conceal its delight that 160,000 Palestinians have emigrated in the last fifteen years, or its intention of forcing the rest to follow them. But that is not 'genocide'. It is immoral, of course, and cruel, and it is unjust towards the Palestinian people who so love their land. But it is not 'genocide'.

Again, it is true that the Arabs on the West Bank are continually being harassed, regularly in minor ways and often in grievous ways; and sometimes Arabs have been killed without due cause. Nor is it any consolation for a bereaved Arab family to be told that virtually every army of occupation one can think of has behaved more ruthlessly than the Israeli army on the West Bank. But no one who knows anything whatsoever of the period from 1933 to 1945, especially of what happened to the Jews, could ever describe the Israeli army as a 'Gestapo'. At no period, for instance, would the Gestapo have anywhere permitted the publication of the English language weekly *Al Fajr,* a radical Arab newspaper which is essential reading for anyone who wishes to keep up with day to day events on the West Bank and Gaza.

Again, it is inconceivable that a 'Gestapo' would have allowed any of its officers to behave as certain Israeli officers have been allowed to: they held a press conference denouncing some of the practices of their own army on the West Bank; and their accusations have led to the arrest and sentencing of Israeli soldiers.

Moreover there are certain groups of people, especially, who should have the basic decency to refrain from such totally inappropriate idiom – the Germans, obviously, but also Western Christians.

British people always seem surprised when I tell them that I know of no single Israeli who does not think that the BBC is adamantly prejudiced against the State of Israel and that the BBC is in that respect representative of British public opinion. The British would be less surprised if only they could bring themselves to imagine the image of Britain that is the background which Israelis see when they are hearing the pronouncements of the BBC. That image, for most Israelis, is of British colonialists who executed

Jewish freedom fighters in the Mandate period and then, in the person of Ernest Bevin, closed the doors of the Promised Land in the faces of hapless refugees who had survived the Nazi concentration camps. Therefore, when any British person, and particularly a British minister, makes a statement critical of Israel's policies, the Israeli citizen automatically sees the statement as a function of an anti-Israeli, not to say anti-Semitic stance, which is all that he can expect from the British, granted the image he has of them.

Of course, the Israeli reaction is not balanced. But who should dare to demand balance of a people just emerging from an era of such oppression? Not at any rate the British, and even less the world Christian community, since so much of the persecution of Jews throughout the centuries has been carried out in the name of Christ, not simply by ignorant Christian peasants but even more by high-ranking Christian prelates. That unpalatable but undeniable fact surely demands of Western Christians, and especially of Christian prelates, that they afford Jews space in which to vent the anger that has been piling up inside them over the centuries. Christians have a calling to stand inside that space and absorb Jewish anger precisely in the name of Christ who said: 'If anyone presses you to go one mile, go two miles with him.' Western Christians are failing the call when they instantly react by rejecting Jewish anger and hitting back with self-exculpatory apologies.

That sentence might well strike the proper note on which to end this account of the mood in Israel, were it not for the fact that my account leaves out something which I have come to value as the most helpful feature of foreign correspondents' reports. That something is the smell, the feel of everyday life in the country being reported upon. Although, to give a different example, I had read a great deal about the Soviet Union before the year 1970, it was only in that year, when I went to Russia, that I acquired any feel, sense, or smell of everyday life in the country. And the volume of letters I received after broadcasting my impressions of Russia on Radio 4 showed me that many other people have the same need as I have, and that it is the retailing of ordinary incidents which satisfied that need. Hence I offer the two following incidents from my own recent experience.

The first took place beside the swimming pool of a kibbutz where Gentiles are welcomed to come and swim, and where I have even encountered a group of Arab boys disporting themselves (which says something).

A Jewish woman fell into conversation with one of the swimmers and discovered, to her surprise, that he was a Catholic priest. At the front of her mind was the knowledge that the genial Mayor of Jerusalem, Teddy Kollek, had just turned down an invitation from the apostolic delegate to attend a reception in honour of the fourth anniversary of Pope John Paul II's coronation – because the Pope had publicly received Yasser Arafat.

So the Jewish woman said: 'What do you think of the Pope receiving Yasser Arafat?' Priest: 'Well, Arafat is not my favourite person. But I expect the Pope was trying to act as a sort of bridge builder.' Woman: 'But how can a spiritual leader condone a terrorist?' Priest: 'Well he received Yitzhak Shamir, didn't he? And Shamir was one of the leaders of the Stern gang whose founder Avraham Stern tried to do a deal with the Nazis. Most people believe that the Stern gang assassinated Count Bernadotte. And who assassinated Lord Moyne? And we know that Begin blew up the King David Hotel and was responsible for the massacre at Deir Yassin. And we know that Arik Sharon was the leader of the 101 squad. It's a funny business trying to sort out when a terrorist ceases to be a terrorist – if ever.' Woman: 'Do you know, I never thought that way before.'

Anyone conditioned by endless reports of Israel–Arab conflict could be excused for surmising that after the above conversation priest and woman parted as cool enemies. On the contrary, when the woman discovered that the priest did not have a car she kindly drove him home.

The second incident occurred in a taxi travelling from Tel Aviv to Haifa carrying six Israelis, five of them Jewish and one of them an Arab, a Christian. The Christian was quietly reading the New Testament as the taxi radio was broadcasting a speech by Menachem Begin. (That also says something: we listen to the radio continuously as though we are expecting any minute to hear that the Messiah has come in judgement.) When Begin said something particularly harsh the Arab passenger in the taxi groaned and exclaimed in disgust, 'Begin!' Instantly the taxi driver told him to keep quiet because he did not belong in Israel. At which the Arab equally vehemently retorted that he and his family had lived in the land hundreds of years before the taxi driver and his family; moreover he himself was an Israeli citizen who always tried to live at peace with everyone. But the taxi driver was not to be appeased and told his Arab passenger that soon he and all other Arabs would have to get out of Israel.

One could, of course, leave the story at that point. And one would then have simply added one more anecdote to that endless list of stories illustrating Arab–Jewish hostility which many people delight in. But the rest of the incident is far more significant: the five Jewish passengers in the taxi, each and every one of them, sprang to the defence of their Arab fellow citizen and rebuked the taxi driver in no uncertain terms. Some of them (if percentages are anything to go by) must have been supporters of Mr Begin; nevertheless they recognised when a principle was at stake. They exhibited a real sense of what democracy means, and I am not at all confident that a parallel situation with a taxi full of comparable people would have produced the same scenario in Birmingham, England, or Birmingham, Alabama.

These are, perhaps, minor incidents but they reflect the hopes of ordinary people. May they not be betrayed by those for whom the destiny of the Holy Land is an 'international issue' or an interesting television documentary and not, as for the inhabitants of the Land, a matter of life and death.

24th November, 1982. Tantur

One more addition to the seemingly endless series of 'solutions to the eucharistic question' has gone off the rails.

I ought to have had more sense. And certainly I should have exercised more caution last Friday when our American Jesuit friend, Dan, came to me for permission to try his solution to the thorny question of our Sunday celebration. My instinct was to distrust the proposal immediately. After all, there is something very contrived in an arrangement whereby you have a Jesuit conducting the service at one end of the altar whilst a Lutheran minister stands by at the other end ready to pronounce the Lutheran words of consecration over the offering at his end after the Jesuit has first pronounced the Catholic words over the offering at the far end. The intent of this contrivance was that everyone, Catholic and Protestant, would feel at ease in coming to receive communion.

On seeing my initial hesitation about his scheme Fr Dan assured me that he had discussed it with Fr Adalbert and our Lutheran colleague, Professor Reinhardt, and they offered no objection. Disarmed by this assurance on the part of the three most senior, respected and competent members of the house of Tantur, I agreed to the scheme. I ought to have had the sense to see that an arrangement made by an American-speaking Jesuit, a German-speaking Lutheran and a Catalan-speaking Benedictine might well gloss over certain misunderstandings!

On the day itself, inevitably, the order of service made things worse rather than better. From the beginning, for instance, we had the uncomfortable feeling in chapel that we were taking part in an experiment rather than sharing in a liturgy. And then the position of the priests at different ends of the altar only deepened the sense of division. And, even worse, it split the congregation into Roman Catholics at one side and 'all the others' ('the odds and sods' in British Army parlance!) at the far end.

To crown it all, I discovered afterwards that Fr Adalbert had not understood the proposal fully in the first place, and that Reinhardt was not happy at the implication that he did not mind to whom he gives communion.

It is a great tribute to the community that no one afterwards made any fiercer comment than to murmur quizzically, 'It didn't quite come off.' Also, Fr Dan's fine homily reaffirmed the community's judgement that his mind and heart are far more Christian that the rubrics which he was trying to bend.

1st December, 1982. Christmas Letter to the Tablet

'It must be simply wonderful to be in Bethlehem at Christmas-time – so long as the Arabs don't play up.' That was the message inscribed last year by a Californian friend of ours on the Christmas card which she sent us. If only she could have foreseen the ever-deepening waves of irony that her message aroused in us she would have been astonished.

After all it *is* a cause for wonder as soon as one wakens each day to draw back the curtains and see from one's windows the town of Bethlehem on a hillside just opposite, its university buildings and the Church of the Nativity so clear in the light of early morning that one feels as though one could easily reach out and touch them. Similarly, were I to walk out on to our terrace and pick up a stone, then – if my cricketing arm has not entirely lost its vigour – I could throw that stone as far as that rocky path running below our west wall which Joseph trod, or so our Arab neighbours tell us, on the eve of the first Christmas as he led his donkey along bearing Mary and the child within her womb.

How is it, then, that I gave much less immediate assent to our Californian friend's message than I did to the words of *The Times* correspondent who last year headed his Christmas report with the words, 'O tragic town of Bethlehem'? And not much more immediate assent than I gave to a bitter article by another foreign journalist, entitled, 'O little town of guns and soldiers'?

The answer is simple. Our Californian friend sees Bethlehem and its Arab inhabitants in the light of misapplied fairy-tale and mischievous propaganda, whereas the two journalists in spite of their variously inadequate visions, have at least caught a glimpse of the reality of Christmas in Bethlehem.

Suppose, therefore, that I try to gaze upon this Bethlehem and the Holy Land at Christmas with the eye of faith – even my little faith – do I see anything further than a misplaced fairy-tale, mischievous propaganda and unredeemed bitterness?

What I see first of all, with the eye of faith, is Arabs – not 'playing up' as my Californian friend feared, but trying to find some way of putting bread into their mouths. That has been difficult for them this year because much of Bethlehem's prosperity in the past – minimal though it may have been – has been derived from the tourist trade, which is now in decline. And visitors who despise the tourist trade and speak of the souvenir shops and hawkers as spoiling the pristine atmosphere of the 'little town of Bethlehem' might well pause to remind themselves that it is the profits from those tawdry little shops that have often to feed as many as twenty or thirty mouths in the extended families to which they belong.

For in Bethlehem ('the house of bread', as the Hebrew name signifies) daily bread is not easy to come by, especially for those 15,000 or so Arabs, almost entirely Muslims, who make up the population of the three refugee camps situated on the outskirts of Bethlehem. Many of those in the camps who are able to find work go each day to help construct housing projects for the Israelis. And as one sees them trudging to their work in a morning one cannot help reflecting on the irony of their position

– building fortresses for their new rulers in order to be able to put bread into their own mouths and the mouths of their children. And yet these same Muslim workers never inspire pity. They are too proud, too much their own men to permit such a response. You feel the truth of that, especially in the afternoons, if you happen to be passing a group as they are waiting by the roadside for a bus to take them out of Israel and back into the West Bank. On such occasions you may observe a handful of them, weary-looking, cement all over their clothes, stone-dust clinging to their eyebrows and their hair; and then the next thing you will see is that each of them takes up a stand shoulder to shoulder with his neighbours, turns towards Mecca and in unison with them begins the rhythmical sequence of ritual gestures prescribed in the prayer of Islam. I myself am still moved by that clean, uncompromising confession of faith just as much now as when I first encountered it forty years ago in the desert of Sind.

In that uncompromising position our Muslim brethren are more fortunate, perhaps, than our Christian brethren in Bethlehem because the Christians have to tread a path that is fraught with ambiguity.

To begin with, they are Arabs. Arabic is their language; and the Arabic language is more than a computer-like means of information; it represents a whole world in which a person feels himself at home, at his ease, confirmed in his identity. Yet the image which is imposed on them as Arabs by the world outside their home, as by our Californian friend, is an image that alienates. 'Who are these people?' said an American visitor, speaking in the name of her whole tour party, after she had been received by some of our Arab staff. 'They are Arabs', I said. 'Arabs!' cried the tourists in alarm, as if to say: 'Then they are terrorists! And we are in danger of being murdered in our beds!'

There is something almost comic in such a reaction when one knows the real nature of the Arab Christians of Bethlehem and neighbouring Beit Sahur and Beit Jala. Amongst them one finds gentleness and kindness of a

135

quality that I have experienced nowhere else except in certain parts of Connemara. In fact, the gentlest eyes and voice I have ever known belong to my devout friend Issa. There was even no note of anger in his voice last winter when he explained at my request what had happened to him one day the previous week. He said quite simply that after he had come out of church on that particular day some Israeli soldiers had surrounded him and several other Arabs walking down the street and made them all stand facing a wall with their hands held high, palms against the wall. They had not been cudgelled, he said; and after they had stood in that position for three hours the soldiers had just let them go without any explanation. He had suffered no harm, he assured me; the only thing was that his shoulders still ached.

Issa has a most beautiful voice and sings in the choir of St Catherine's, the Catholic church within the Church of the Nativity. But he will not be singing there on Christmas Eve, because Midnight Mass in the church of the Nativity is really for the tourists. If you want to join in the Mass you have to obtain a ticket beforehand and then to run a gauntlet of road blocks thrown around the township. Eventually you come to the edge of Manger Square and meet several walls of soldiers who will quickly let you through into the church once you show your ticket. The efficiency of that operation will spare you the sight of Manger Square itself where raucous and often drunken young men and women from outside Bethlehem roam around within the walls of soldiery.

So it would not be at all surprising if Issa were to be angry. He has many grounds for being so. He could justifiably be angry against the foreigners who take over his parish church on Christmas Eve. He might very well rage against the Israelis who are occupying his native town, producing conditions which drive his children to emigrate from their own township. It would be understandable if he were to spit in the faces of those evangelical Christians who come from abroad to hail Menachem Begin on the

Feast of Tabernacles and who proclaim that resistance to his policies is 'anti-God'. Nor would it surprise me if Issa were to criticise his own church leaders who maintain such a close clerical control over the People of God that the people are almost asphyxiated.

But Issa does none of these things. When I met him in the bright sunlight of Manger Square on Christmas Day after Mass and asked him whether he was sad not to have been able to celebrate Midnight Mass in his own church, he smiled and said, 'No. Is better. Last night was good for the tourists. This morning is better for the Arabs – the children come.'

So I hope that this Christmas my Californian friend will worry less about the Arabs 'playing up'. And with the eye of faith I would like her to see through the 'tragic town of Bethlehem' and the bitterness of 'guns and soldiers' to the lovely, gentle smile of my friend Issa – because peace begins with a smile.

And just in case she did not realise it: Issa is the Arabic name of an earlier native of Bethlehem – Jesus.

20th January, 1983. Tantur

The thought of giving a lecture tomorrow at Nes Amim[4] is making me uncomfortable. I don't see why I should feel like this since what I intend to say was, so to speak, cleared by the members of the Ecumenical Fraternity last June when I spoke to them on the same topic: that is, 'The Christian Response to the Holocaust'. All members of the Fraternity are known throughout Jerusalem to be devoted to the Jewish people and one of them, a distinguished Hebraist, said to me after my talk last June that it was the only one he had heard on the subject given by a Christian with which he had no quarrel whatsoever. Moreover the Nes Amim pastor, Arend Boersma, was present on that occasion; and since it is he who prompted the invitation for me to go and speak there I presume he wants the people at Nes Amim to hear what I have to say.

Yet no matter what consoling considerations I may urge to myself inside my head the thought of Nes Amim makes my heart heavy – partly, no doubt, because that community has touched off weird vibrations within me ever since I went there six years ago. Before that first visit I was favourably inclined to them because I agree with their foundational belief that Christians have a duty to make some effort, no matter how inadequate, at reparation towards our Jewish brethren for the evils that Christians have inflicted upon Jews. But on arriving at Nes Amim I quickly sensed that in their effort many of the members there had fallen into a familiar trap. It is the same trap into which we are all likely to fall when we decide – usually on a generous impulse – to identify ourselves with some group other than our own. Before we know where we are we start using that repulsive word 'solidarity', and keep repeating that we must show our solidarity with the group that we have chosen to identify with. Since my own primal group is the working class of Northern England I can see the process at work most clearly in the case of those members of the middle class who seem to imagine that the working class needs them to prevaricate on many issues in the name of solidarity – even lying, if need be. Whereas what members of the working class need, above all, is the same as other classes need; that is, truth.

There are so many other examples of this corrupting process at work; in Ireland, for instance, whose history has been bedevilled by Englishmen and Americans taking up the Irish cause. In India and in Africa, amongst Arabs and amongst Russians, the same story is repeated.

For very understandable reasons a number of Dutch people, French people, Germans and others have recently chosen to declare their solidarity with the Jewish people. Many of them, however, it seems to me, have fallen into the trap I spoke about and now attach more importance to solidarity with the Jewish people than they do to truth. I felt this most strongly the last time I was there when every one of the Nes Amim members at my table unconditionally defended the Israeli invasion of Lebanon, as well as all the subsequent actions of the Israeli army in that land. One of them even praised the murderous Arik Sharon for being just the tough kind of person that you need for such a situation. So perhaps I should not have been surprised to discover that you cannot be accepted as a full member of the Nes Amim community unless you are prepared to bear arms in defence of Israel, a condition which obviously cuts out pacifists. Yet the State of Israel itself provides more scope for the individual's conscience than that. I can well understand how Nes Amim have come to their position; but should they not ask themselves whether they have taken a wrong turning somewhere along the way?

Amidst this confusion of my mind and my heart the main source of solace for me is that my host, Pastor Boersma, is a good and truthful man and presumably there are others at Nes Amim who do not demand that everyone toes the party line. Also, I take their invitation to go there as a sigh of friendship on their part.

22nd January, 1983. Nes Amim

'My worst fears were realised at Nes Amim' is the sentence with which I intended to begin today's entry in this journal but the sentence itself caused me to pause and ask myself whether it may not be truer at a deeper level than I would like to acknowledge. May it not be true that if one approaches an occasion in a fearful spirit then that very approach causes whatever one most feared to happen?

Be that as it may, the result of our visit was not happy!

Actually things seemed to be going very well for a time. My friend, Colin, a medieval historian, and myself were met by young Victor, an ex-student of mine who is working for a year at Nes Amim. We spent a couple of happy hours chatting with him and then with others over dinner. And there were about fifty or more members who later came to the lecture and followed it most attentively, so that I was feeling rather relaxed by the time I finished speaking. What happened at question time, therefore, took me off my guard.

A woman asked in strident tones why I had not dealt with the historical responsibility of the Christian Church for creating a mentality which made the Holocaust inevitable. Since such a crucial question (not to say begging of the question!) demands the utmost competence in historical research as well as deep integrity, I turned to Colin and asked him if he would care to make a comment, because his concern for the Jewish people has led him in recent years to study the matter in some depth. Colin kindly agreed, and provided a most careful, nuanced statement, characteristic of the gifted historian that he is.

But evidently such a careful statement was the last thing the woman wanted. What she was demanding of us was a denunciation, particularly of Martin Luther; and in pursuit of her demand she bombarded Colin with a series of quotes from Luther's coarse writings about Jews, quotes which she reeled off by heart in the manner of someone reciting a catechism. Being a conscientious historian, Colin tried to put Luther's statements into their context without in the least minimising their shamefulness. He then went on to say, quite firmly, that you cannot draw a straight line of causation from Luther's excesses to the annihilation programme of the Jews. 'Hitler's use of Luther', he said, 'was not derived from Luther but from his own psychological condition.'

At that point the woman exploded, and an atmosphere was generated which made it quite impossible for anything sensible to be said. So the meeting was brought to an end.

This morning Colin was clearly still distressed that his well-intentioned comments had not only provoked such a violent reaction but had even raised the suspicion that he, and possibly myself, were trying to 'absolve the Christian Church' from any responsibility for the Holocaust and that maybe we are surreptitiously anti-Semitic.

However, we both felt cheered when young Victor told us that our visit had acted as an occasion of liberation for him. After the meeting he had walked round on his own under the night sky laughing and laughing out of relief that the *moshav*'s suffocating party line had unwittingly been exposed: 'It was just the breath of fresh air that I needed.'

24th January, 1983. Tantur

It is inevitable, I suppose, that I should be continually using up much energy and time worrying about whether this community of which I am head is in good heart. On the days when I am exhausted and depressed the word that comes into my mind to describe some of the scholars is 'merciless'. They want what *they* want; they intend to get it and have no mercy on anyone who gets in their way. Always, on reflection, however, I recognise that the number of them who behave in that fashion is really quite small. On the other hand, in this community as in many others, they are the sort who often make the running, set the tone or fix the agenda – whatever metaphor you wish to use. It is also disturbing that frequently the merciless ones are precisely those who arrive announcing to one and all that their overriding concern is 'community-building' or 'peace-making' – or both!

To some extent I was forewarned about people who go around telling everyone that we must concentrate on 'building community'. I had already come across Bonhoeffer's remark that if someone arrives upon the scene talking perpetually about community then you can be more or less certain that they will turn out to be a pain in the neck of the existing community on to which they have descended. What such characters usually mean is that they have devised a scenario for a community in which the rest of us play supporting roles to themselves, who are to star as the central characters in the drama. A community can carry one or two people like that, but if you get more than a certain percentage of such prima donnas the tension of the drama becomes intolerable for the other members.

Lately, in the course of a seminar, I told a story bearing on these matters which I hoped might be heard and taken to heart by our small set of 'community-builders'. It was about my friend Fr Aidan when he was asked to help in a mission to an English university. The task given to him was neither to preach nor to lead study groups nor even celebrate the liturgy but simply to be around, wandering into coffee bars and common rooms or chatting with students and staff in corridors or at sporting fixtures – in a word, to pick up a sense of what the members of the University were thinking concerning the mission.

In the course of performing his task, however, as he told me later, he stumbled across a puzzle of his own. Never having been a university student himself he was puzzled to work out 'what made this institution tick'. So he paid particular attention to the members of the University as they circulated, taking notice of how they related to one another. 'And eventually', Aidan said, 'one day the penny dropped. What did those people exchange with one another when they met? You'd be surprised – they exchanged grievances. So the currency of that University is grievance.'

Never previously had I come across that particular insight into the way human societies work: any body of human beings, like any physical body, depends upon its circulation; it depends upon what the members put into the blood stream of the whole body, because what you will get back when the blood circulates will be what you put in. If you put in grievance, you will get back grievance. If you put in kindness you will eventually get back kindness. So all of us should examine ourselves honestly and ask ourselves, 'What do I put into circulation within this community?'

Fr Aidan's observation about the kind of currency that circulates throughout any body of human beings helped me to understand something that had puzzled me about

142

many monasteries and convents that I have known. It is that in spite of their high ideals and the striving after goodness of the individual monks or nuns some fail to form a good community, whereas others seem to manage it naturally. Take, for example, that religious house in Batley. On the face of it you would not expect it to be outstandingly successful as a community because almost all the individual members go out every day to pursue their own specialities and they appear to do very little in common, and yet you always feel warm and at home there. After racking my brain for long enough I finally hit upon the explanation. It is Brother Albert. What could be more surprising! For Albert is now very broken down; he shuffles around the house in his slippers, devotes ages to reading the morning paper, smokes a good deal and spends much of the evening sipping his whiskey and watching television – hardly what they call 'a model religious', and yet I am convinced that it is mainly Albert who sets the currency of goodness and kindness circulating through that community.

When you ring the monastery door bell, for instance, it is Albert who come shuffling along and opens the door, always with a kind smile on his face. 'Hello, Donald', he will say, 'how are you? Do come in. When did you eat last? Well, in any case, come and have a cup of tea . . .' Or, if it happens to be a tramp who calls, Albert will afford the same welcome, but to the tramp he probably says instead, 'Would you like a cigarette?' And so it goes on all the day, with Brother Albert circulating kindness and consideration throughout the whole building, so that when the 'model religious' return in the evening they find themselves in a current of kindness and consideration.

It was the thought of Brother Albert which two weeks ago left me putting one question mark after the brilliant lectures given to us by Fr Jerry Murphy O'Connor. Taking as his point of departure the Christian Church at Corinth in the first century Fr Jerry drew out of St Paul's letters to the Corinthians certain principles that have to be fulfilled

143

in order to have an authentic community. The principles he stated were so demanding as to scare the living daylights out of us.

So it was partly out of fright and partly out of exasperation that one of our number defiantly asked Fr Jerry whether he had ever come across a community that was authentic by his criteria. 'No!' he replied, 'at least, not in the Western world.' 'Well, where then?' came the retort. 'In the base communities of Latin America', said Fr Jerry. 'Well, why there?' was the next exasperated rejoinder. 'Because they have no choice', said Jerry. 'For them community is a matter of life and death. And their commitment to one another is, therefore, for life – for good, until death. I know of no communities in the Western world of which you could say the same.'

In those staccato sentences Fr Jerry seemed to me to be presenting us with tremendous insights into the meaning of community but his use of them was flawed through their being given such an all-or-nothing application: either perfect, authentic community or no community worth speaking about. Against that application, however, the figure of Brother Albert shuffling around the Batley house rose in protest. Albert is not perfect; nor are we at Tantur, yet we do achieve some measure of genuine community if I am to believe what one of our scholars said the other day. Since he is someone whom I had had to rebuke severely in the past for kicking over the traces it was all the more impressive to hear him saying, 'It is a real miracle that community is achieved here at Tantur considering that the scholars come for such a short period, and each with their own agenda.'

There was a further implication of what Fr Jerry had said which only became clear to me as I thought of one scholar's indignant explosion, 'Well, you can't expect us in the USA to devise an artificial situation of life and death just so that we can have what you call "authentic community".' The more I thought about that remark the more I wanted to answer the man, 'You don't need to devise a situation of life and death in the USA – or anywhere else on earth, for that matter. I don't simply mean that every human being is always in a life and death situation if only he realises his situation; I mean, even more, that the entire human family, as a family, is now facing death from nuclear weapons and pollution. You don't need to devise any artificial situation; all you need do is to see what is in front of your very eyes. So perhaps the greatest contribution any of us can make to community-building is to awaken one another to our life and death situation, but to do so in such a manner that we don't scare people to death.

27th January, 1983. Tantur

Having been asked to speak this afternoon in the Cenacle on Mount Zion, during the service which is part of the Week of Prayer for Christian Unity, I spoke as follows:

We are soon to eat *matza,* i.e. unleavened bread, the bread of affliction as it is termed in the Scripture, *lehem oni* as opposed to what the Talmud calls *matza ashirah,* the bread of opulence.

Now very few of us here, I imagine, eat the bread of affliction in the original sense of the term – most of us do not belong to the oppressed people, nor are we hungry, or homeless, or ill-clothed or in prison – all those characteristics which qualify people to eat the bread of affliction.

How then do we here dare to carry on with this ceremony of eating *matzot?* What can we do to avoid making this ceremony into just a piece of play-acting which is simply a part of the annual Jerusalem January round?

May I suggest to you that we should think of what we are about to do as a token of our determination, each in our own calling, truly to eat the bread of affliction by sharing our energies, our very lives, with those who alone give meaning to our ceremony? Those who in the literal sense of the word eat *matza,* the bread of affliction. Those in prison whether in Teheran or Vladimir or Ramallah;

the homeless, whether in Lebanon or Afghanistan or El Salvador; the hungry, the sick and the lonely who are all about us, whether in Kfar Salem, the Musrara, or in Gaza.

Whenever we eat bread that is provided for us we consume part of the life of those persons who have put their energies, which are their life, into that bread. Their lives have been transformed into bread for us. Let us in our turn transform that bread into life for them. Or, as Mother Teresa never tires of saying to her sisters: 'Let the people eat you up.' [At this point in the service each member of the congregation ate a piece of *matza*.]

By eating the bread of affliction together we have signified in God's presence our determination to work for the day when no one whosoever will be hungry or in prison or homeless or lonely or sick. Perhaps that is precisely the manner in which we are called to work in the present age so that under God's providence even Christian unity will be achieved. First the bread of affliction; and only then the bread of the Eucharist.

Until that day dawns let us take courage from the words of the Korean poet, Kim Chi Ha, who has suffered many years of imprisonment, hunger, loneliness and sickness at the hands of a tyrannical government, and who knows what it means to eat the bread of affliction.

The poet says:

> Bread is heaven
> You can't make it on your own
> Bread should be shared
> Bread is heaven
>
> We all see
> The same stars in heaven
> How natural that we
> All share the same bread

Bread is heaven
As we eat
God enters us
Bread is heaven

Oh, bread
Should be shared and eaten by all

In Jesus' name. Amen.

Not everyone was pleased with my attempt to relate the theme of affliction to the affliction going on under our noses, in this Holy Land.

12th February, 1983. Tantur

I expect it had to happen sometime! Since Christmas I have seen a group of Catholics in the house slowly wind themselves into a tight little knot, each drawn towards the other by those aspects of their individual personalities which are narrow and fearful. There seemed to be a good chance of halting and reversing the process at one stage because they all have generous qualities. And I am at fault for not taking time to speak with each of them earlier and win their trust. Now I imagine it is too late. The individual fears of each one of them have become so closely interwoven with the fears of the others that they are caught in a knot which probably cannot be loosed by words. Only experience can now either unravel or, more likely, cut that knot.

It was also a mistake on my part today to call them together as a group in order to get them to see why their behaviour has prompted some of our non-Catholic members – as well as two Catholics, for that matter – to complain to me about Catholics forming a sect within the community. These Catholics sectaries indignantly denied that there were any grounds for the complaints, and I really do believe that they genuinely do not see how their behaviour has given rise to the complaints. Individually they might have been brought to see it, but by calling them together as a group I had already, so to speak, put them all in the same bag. In response to which even their individual body movements coalesced into one undifferentiated pattern, heads down, lips pursed, heels dug in.

Watching it all happen these last six weeks or so has been rather like watching the rerun of a film to illustrate patterns of Catholic behaviour from the period before the Second Vatican Council. One has seen the same flocking together, backs turned against the world, the mutual comforting in half-truths, the same sound of exclusive laughter at some in-group joke and the same inability to see themselves as 'outsiders' see them – every feature summed up so succintly by the French phrase '*esprit de chapelle.*'

The end-term of this sectarian behaviour is that the priests in the group have told me this evening that they are not prepared to take their turn at presiding over our Sunday Eucharist. Since the only other ordained person who has not so far celebrated also refuses (career ecumenist though he is!) I am now left without a celebrant for this coming Sunday. Because I cannot decently lay the burden upon the Anglicans, who have already borne more than their fair share.

15th February, 1983. Tantur

I am at my wits' end about what sort of service to arrange for Sunday. Of course the easy way out would be simply to hold a service of the Word, in which case no one need be upset, especially if the service were to include an anodyne sermon such as makes no demands on anyone, including the preacher. To follow that course every week, as many people recommend, would obviously make my own life incomparably more comfortable. On the other hand it would destroy the whole *raison d'être* of the Institute as a centre of ecumenism. It would allow us to walk round

148

the central issue of Christian division. Then we should simply become what some people here seem to desire, an outstandingly comfortable base where scholars can stay whilst taking part in a subsidised reading party in the Holy Land.

So, if our liturgy is to be something more than an empty ritual, our service this coming Sunday must in the first instance reflect our bankruptcy as a community whose ordained ministers are not prepared to celebrate the Eucharist.

What we must do, then, is to come together as usual but, in honest acknowledgment of our bankruptcy, to eat *matza* together, that is, unleavened bread, the bread of affliction as it is termed in the Scripture – *lehem oni,* as opposed to what the Talmud calls *matza ashirah,* the bread of opulence.

But for Christians to be content with *lehem oni* alone would be a sign of faithlessness. First the bread of affliction, certainly; but also then, surely, we must ask in faith for the bread of the Eucharist. Without the words of consecration pronounced by an ordained minister? The answer to that question, surely again, has to be that in extreme circumstances such as a threat to life itself, or a bankruptcy, then the ordinary rules for everyday situations are inadequate and so cannot be binding.

In extreme situations we are stripped of our customary supports, such as an ordained minister, and we have to act, therefore, in naked faith. We must, in this case, take the bread for the Eucharist and recite together the words spoken by Jesus at the Last Supper, trusting that if we do so in good faith then he will be as truly present in the food we partake as he ever is when the words of consecration are pronounced by an ordained minister.

In order to avoid disconcerting the Catholics any more than is necessary we will not assemble round the altar as if we were usurping the role of the absent priests but instead we shall form a circle behind the altar.

149

20th February, 1983. Tantur

I am in two minds – even three or four minds – about whether what took place in our chapel today was truly 'right and proper'. Did my initial emphasis upon our bankruptcy and our need to eat the bread of affliction have the effect of putting the recalcitrant priests in the dock? On the other hand, two of the Anglican priests present said to me afterwards that it was a very salutary liturgy and a necessary reminder to us all that celebration of the Eucharist is not a possession of the ordained minister but is a gift of the Lord to the Christian community.

Still, though my heart feels clean from the day, my mind is still not clear about it. I take some comfort in recalling that the Last Supper itself, celebrated by Jesus, was by no means a smooth ritual performance which disturbed no one. In fact I have just read through the accounts given by Matthew, Mark and Luke and can but conclude that the occasion in the upper room was very turbulent indeed.

5th March, 1983. Kifr Harris

Around sunrise this morning John and I were taken by Khalil, our friend from Bethlehem University, to visit his native village of Kifr Harris, which is situated in the hills to the west of Nablus.

Our day began typically; that is, inauspiciously. The *sheerut* which we were sharing with five Arabs had only travelled a few miles along the road from Jerusalem to Nablus when we were halted at a road block. The Israeli soldiers, flourishing their machine guns, ordered us all out of the *sheerut* so as to examine our identity documents. Fortunately the Arabs' documents were beyond suspicion and the soldiers allowed us all back into the *sheerut,* though not without giving John and myself some hard stares, as if to say what were we up to with these potential terrorists.

Once past the road block, however, the whole atmosphere inside the *sheerut* quickly began to change. Our companions visibly relaxed; their bodies became less tense the further we drove from Jerusalem, and they started speaking and breathing more easily.

The change was particularly noticeable in Khalil. As soon as we stopped in Nablus his face took on a smiling appearance such as I had never seen on him previously. The sounds of children calling to one another and the greetings of stall-holders as we walked along the streets, every aspect of the city, seemed to assure him that here he was safe amongst his own people. Almost like a wealthy landowner displaying the riches of his estate to distinguished visitors he led us into a café which is owned by one of his relatives, but which, in all conscience, is extremely seedy. The relative was trained as a lawyer in Beirut but does not work as an advocate in the civil courts here because in common with a score of other lawyers in Nablus he is 'on strike against the Israeli occupation courts'. For this strike action each of them is paid 100 Jordanian pounds a month by the government in Amman. Those amongst the Nablus lawyers who do work in the Israeli courts are not ostracised by the people, as one might have expected, because everyone recognises that the Arab community needs to have *some* representatives speaking for them in the Israeli courts.

I asked this striking lawyer what would happen to anyone who tried to protest against the recent imprisonment of the four youths from nearby Jenin. They had been arrested for not informing the police when an alleged terrorist was supposed to have attempted to persuade them to join his organisation. The man laughed incredulously, as if to say, how could anyone ask such a naive question? He said, if you did so then you also would be put inside. One of his brothers has been two years in prison already for making such a protest. And since another brother is in Kuwait studying, he himself has to keep the family going by running this decidedly ungrand café.

In mid-morning we left Nablus and drove westwards through hill country dotted with Arab villages. Where the land has been cleared of rocks the soil is very rich, which is one reason why the Gush Emunim are determined to establish settlements in this area and gradually force out the Arabs. Khalil's own village of Kifr Harris is under particular threat from the Gush Emunim because it is the site of the tomb of Caleb, an Old Testament hero; and the Jewish fanatics regard it as their sacred duty to take over and occupy every such holy place and its vicinity.

However, none of those threats seemed this morning to becloud the mind of Khalil whose inner joy mounted at every turn of the road that brought us nearer to his beloved village. And his joy was complete when eventually he led us up the rocky path to the door of his home where his old father came to greet him. Father and son embraced each other long and lovingly.

There was an element of relief in the father's greeting to his son, as we soon learnt from Khalil, because during the previous night a company of Israeli soldiers had descended upon the village, arrested four of the menfolk and taken them away to who knows where. General opinion throughout the village seemed to be that there is an informer amongst the three thousand inhabitants who must have reported to the authorities some scathing conversations about the Israeli occupation made by the four men arrested.

These sudden swoops in the night upon Arab villages, resulting in arrests, particularly of young men, are a source of constant terror to the people and Khalil's father had feared that maybe what happened in Kifr Harris had simply been part of a general sweep throughout the whole West Bank. He was frightened that Khalil also, in Bethlehem, had been thrown into jail. However, he soon recovered himself; and his wife began a ritual fussing over John and myself, apologising for the fact that we certainly came from more lavish homes than theirs and that they could not receive us at the level of honour to which we are accustomed. Still that ritual was not over-prolonged, and in no time she had an enormous mat spread on the floor with pillows and coverings for each one of us. Sitting between Khalil and ourselves the old father, now seventy-four but still very strong and fit, made sure that our cups of coffee were constantly replenished from the handsome pot which was being kept hot upon a brazier.

They burn wood from their extensive olive plantations in order to keep themselves warm but at the same time they leave their doors open to prevent the rooms becoming filled with smoke, an arrangements which probably explains why they are such hardy people – their bodies have to develop a great capacity for the inner regulation of heat and cold. Since I am not endowed with that capacity I was very glad to be wearing my duffle coat.

Also, these village Arabs, as I have noticed before, have an equally astonishing capacity for eating, which they assume is shared by all people. This they showed by bringing us great handfuls of nuts, and spoonfuls of the most heavenly honey I have ever tasted – so heavenly, in fact, as to leave me feeling that all the honey I had hitherto tasted cannot have been real honey. Only this honey was real which Khalil's father takes from his hundred and fifty hives and whose absolute purity he attributes to the fact that he never gives his bees sugar; hence they feed only on the wild flowers in these unpolluted hills. The old man glowed with delight when we told him that after tasting his honey we would always remember his home as *Beit-al-nahil* (House of the bee).

In the meantime the room had been unceremoniously filling up with children and adults. One of the adults introduced himself as Khalil's uncle, a construction worker, whose work place is near Tel Aviv. This means that he has to leave the village at four o'clock in the morning and does not arrive back home until six in the evening. As a reward for doing that six days a week he receives only a pittance on which to support his family. He and his wife have nine children, a boy and eight girls, one of whom is now married. Interestingly, he also acts at certain times as *mu'addhin*, the one who calls the faithful to prayer. When I learnt this I began to reflect on the truly popular nature of Islam. You could never have imagined such a character serving as a Christian priest, roughly dressed as he was and with calloused hands. My mind also went back to the day in Cairo when we visited the ancient Islamic University, the al-Azhar, where we were struck by the very simple, not to say primitive conditions in which the Muslim students from all over the world live and pursue their studies. No wonder, we reflected, that Islam is spreading so rapidly throughout the world when its ministers are prepared to live so simply. We had in mind, by contrast, the numerous young men of Christian families who are taken from peasant homes in Palestine or Africa or India and transported to luxurious seminaries in Rome, London or Chicago and there transformed into ecclesiastical careerists who are intent on never again returning to the rough life of their tribal ancestors.

After a couple of hours of warm conversation, talking about life in Palestine, England and California, both now and in earlier generations, a great meal was brought in by Khalil's mother and sister, who, along with other unnamed women, served us. We five men all ate from the same enormous platter which was entirely covered with recently made bread, two chickens and beans. This was followed by bowls of the tastiest roasted or cracked wheat gruel accompanied by salads and olives. The meal was made heart-warming, to the point of sacramentality, by the way in which Khalil's father and uncle would regularly pick up some choice piece of meat and place it with evident pleasure on our round of flat bread. This atmosphere of holy hospitality was further heightened by their habit, frequent amongst Arab hosts, of looking at you now and again during the meal and murmuring 'Ahlehn' (meaning 'You are truly welcome').

During the course of our meal one or two children and men quietly sidled into the room and either stood around or sat on the floor watching us eat. Mostly they remained silent but occasionally they whispered to one another, smiling a lot with their eyes. But once we had finished off our meal with delicious goat cheese and Arab coffee these spectators began to talk more freely and the whole room became lively as more visitors crowded in.

This enlarged group included someone who was obviously being presented to us as the pride of the village, the teacher of English. She was quite extraordinarily beautiful – and shy at first. She was nervous, I suspected, that the presence of these English speakers might reveal her legendary knowledge of English to be faulty. She need not have feared, for she was very intelligent and she corrected almost instantly any slight mispronunciation or syntactical error which she had made when I pointed it out to her.

For over an hour she read aloud some of the very complicated poems which these village children have to study for their examinations and we discussed the levels of meaning of different phrases, all the time watched intently by the crowd which had now gathered in the room. Eventually I saw that she was beginning to tire and so I spared her by singing for them some of the lovely songs that one meets in Shakespeare's plays. Then, for some reason which I cannot remember, I was persuaded to sing folk songs in Gaelic, which seemed to intrigue them.

But what brought the whole company to the pitch of excitement was theology. Khalil's uncle, the *mu'addhin*, having waited for the moment when his question to us would have its most dramatic effect, suddenly said to John and myself without any preliminaries, 'Why did Jesus never marry?' This question led to many others such as the relationship of the Qur'an to the Gospels; and, inevitably, since we were in an Islamic community, our hosts latched on to the issue of the Crucifixion. Afterwards, John and I both said to one another how unlikely it would have been to have had any similar theological discussion in a comparable American or English community.

Fortunately, perhaps, our taxi was by this time waiting to drive us the twenty miles or so down to the Jerusalem road and so we declined the pressing invitations to stay overnight in the village. We set off eastwards along a road that was now soggy with the late afternoon rain.

We had only been travelling four or five miles when a sight met us which immediately erased from our minds that image of Arabs impressed upon them during the last few hours. The image of Arabs as hospitable and friendly was replaced by the one which Israeli propaganda induces in nervous tourists: Arabs as the supreme terrorists. For about a hundred yards in front of us, strung across the road, barring our way, there stood a score of evil-looking Arab men, their keffiyehs drawn tight around their mouths and their shoulders hunched against the pouring rain. They put their hands out, palms towards us, indicating that we were to stop. As they did so I heard John, sitting next to me, catch his breath and I likewise felt my own heart begin to beat more quickly.

Our driver did stop and wound down the car-window. Two heavily moustached men leaned into the car and began to address him in staccato Arabic sentences. The sky seemed to grow suddenly even darker as they spoke.

Then, as firmly and calmly as I could manage, I said to our driver, 'What do they want?', wondering whether they wanted money or hostages or Lord knows what. 'They say, sir', replied the driver, 'that there has just been a wedding in the village hall and it is the custom for the woman to walk in her fine dress back to her husband's home. But the weather is so bad and the road so muddy that she needs to go in a car. But nobody has a car so, please, could they borrow the taxi for half an hour to take the woman to the husband's home?'

When we instantly agreed to this request the 'evil-looking terrorists,' were transformed in a twinkling into the same warm-hearted Arabs as we had come to know in Kifr Harris. They led us into the village hall as though we were some sort of heroes and there showered hospitality upon us, endless sweetmeats, unending cups of coffee and, to our dismay, one cigarette after another. And although neither John nor I smoke cigarettes, we both felt it would be churlish to refuse them on this occasion; and so each of us struggled thought the task of half-smoking one or two.

For three quarters of an hour we thoroughly enjoyed ourselves, sharing in the celebration of the wedding, so that when our taxi returned and we waved good-bye to our 'captors' I kept thinking to myself that perhaps peace would be achieved if only enemies could be invited to weddings.

Our driver had also received a generous welcome in the village hall, and he said to us how much he had enjoyed the day when he finally set us down at a bus stop on the Jerusalem road.

It was a desolate spot. The grey, rain-filled sky was closing in with darkness falling and we were actually beginning to feel nervous again – after all, this was 'Injun country' – when someone called to us from a barn-like structure behind us. We were being invited to shelter against the rain, and we were informed that the last bus had gone so we would have to hope for a *sheerut*.

In the half-darkness of the barn we discerned three men all engaged in making brooms. The dominant character amongst them was a strong-jawed, clear-eyed young fellow, enormously skilful with his hands; he could twist and tighten wire around the broom handle as easily as though it were cotton. A merry, self-confident fellow, he turned out to be the brother of a well-known Arabic author. He himself is a writer and a great reader, mainly of books translated into Arabic. His favourite work is Tolstoy's *War and Peace* but he also admires Hemingway and Sartre. For Marx and Lenin he has no time at all – too arid and intellectual. His brother is in an Israeli prison, and when I asked him whether he himself had ever been in prison he grinned, threw back his head and exclaimed, 'Not yet!' When I questioned him further as to to whether the Palestinian people had created any poems

157

or songs of resistance to Israeli occupation he answered very affirmatively. To prove his point he sang us one, a haunting one, with the refrain, 'Will you come and visit me in prison, my beloved?' When John then asked him if he knew the name of the poet and composer he again let out a loud laugh of amusement, put his finger to his breast and said, 'I am the one.'

This fascinating encounter with a genuinely popular culture only came to an end when a *sheerut* drew up, but not before we had discovered that there was a fourth man sitting on straw bales at the far end of the barn. Dressed in a worn *ghalabiyeh* and wearing heavy, broken-down boots, this mild-looking man came outside at the same time as ourselves. He was on his way to the mosque in order to call the faithful to prayer, because he is the local *mu'addhin*, another witness to popular Islam.

On the way back to Jerusalem in the darkness our Arab companions in the *sheerut* grew more and more silent and withdrawn the nearer we drew to the Holy City. They were tensely anticipating the inevitable road-block, which duly confronted us just outside Jerusalem. This time the Israeli soldiers did not make us get out of the *sheerut;* but they flourished their machine guns all the more vigorously. By the time they waved us on the atmosphere inside the *sheerut* was electric and the thought suddenly struck me that any young Arab who puts up with this sort of treatment day after day without engaging in some form of resistance must eventually come to feel that he has no balls, that he has been castrated.

3rd April, 1983. Ein Karem

This has been such a beautiful, relaxing day. To begin with I was able at dawn to take a long time over my yoga asanas and my breathing exercises. As a result I have found myself breathing really deeply all day, inhaling peace from the incredibly rich scents which fill this enclosed garden of the Sisters of Sion, who with the aid of a warming sun have nurtured such a dense growth of bushes and flowers of every variety. And the variety of bushes and flowers further ensures the presence of a rich variety of birds and insects and bees. I love these sun-blessed places on the earth's surface where the warmth bathes you in waves coming not only from the sky above but also from the ground below and from every side. How could you not grow relaxed in this peace-filled, scent-laden spot?

For most of the day I walked at my leisure around this womb-like valley of Ein Karem in the middle of which, and on its slopes, the houses of the village nestle, much as Jesus was folded in the womb of Mary when she came from Nazareth to this hill-country of Judea to visit her cousin Elizabeth, in whose own womb was nestling John, later known as the Baptiser. The route I followed today took me along the hilltops from the Hadassah Hospital to Kiryat Ha Yovel, where so many Moroccan and Yemeni Jews have settled, and then to the Holocaust memorial at Yad Vashem and on to Mount Hertzl from where there is so fine a view over the city of Jerusalem.

As you walk around the heights above Ein Karem there is no way you can prevent yourself reflecting that Ein Karem declares itself to be an Arab village which is now occupied by strangers. Even though the ancient terraces are now overgrown on which the Arab villagers once husbanded their olives, nevertheless they speak silently of those who had owned them for centuries. Similarly the shape of the houses, the straggle of the streets, the steeples of churches over-topping the trees and the tall minaret set above the Spring of the Virgin all harmonise with the hallowed Arabic name, *Ein Karem,* 'the spring of the vineyard'.

By contrast one sees ugly buildings here and there, often bearing signs in Hebrew, whose very shape and location appear to have been stamped upon the landscape by an alien mind. They squat uneasily by the roadsides as if conscious that they do not belong. They are the work of Israelis.

I almost began to hate myself for noticing the contrast between Arab buildings and villages and fields on the one hand, which always seem to have an organic relationship with the landscape, as though they have emerged in harmony with it, and on the other hand Jewish buildings, roads and settlements. Almost all the latter, with the notable exception of those inspired by Teddy Kollek, look as though they have been imported wholesale from some place far across the Atlantic such as New York or Pittsburg. I do not see how any honest person can fail to be struck by the contrast. Even some of my most patriotic Israeli friends agree with one of their number, Naomi, who lately sighed to me, 'Why are our buildings and settlements so ugly compared with the Arab villages?'

So I took comfort later in the day, as I was strolling through Kiryat Ha Yovel at being able to watch Jewish families relaxing in the evening sun for the start of Sabbath whilst their younger members were playing soccer and basket ball with great enthusiasm, and whilst the fathers of young families were earnestly cleaning their cars or carrying out improvements to their houses. The atmosphere in Kiryat Ha Yovel was pleasant indeed and I was pleased for these people who must be happier here than ever they were in Morocco or Yemen. Here they obviously feel to be at home.

12th April, 1983. Tantur

Once again the Eucharist has become an occasion of acute tension within the community. The tension has been heightened this time through Professor Girard, of the French Reformed tradition, who has a capacity for stating issues very clearly, and so making the rest of us strain our intellects to render our own positions as clear as his. In face of his persistence I sometimes think communities only survive because most of us amble along

160

from day to day in a bovine fashion and don't turn every step of the road into an intellectual or spiritual crisis.

His proposal is that since Tantur is an ecumenical institute then every person who is chosen to celebrate the one Eucharist here on Sundays must be prepared to give communion to everyone in the community. Anyone not prepared to do so should not be invited to celebrate.

Listening to Girard and admiring the elegance of his exposition I was nevertheless reminded of the dry comment made by a critic of Voltaire: 'His mind was a chaos of clear ideas.' Because if we were to put his scheme into practice we would, amongst other disasters, fall into chaos! It is obvious before we start, for instance, that Catholics and Orthodox would be excluded; and so would many Anglicans and Lutherans who all set boundaries to mark that faith in the Eucharist which they regard as necessary for its celebration. In fact I am not at all sure that Girard himself would be allowed to celebrate under his own rule! I know, for example, that he does not regard Moonies as Christians, yet they claim to be followers of Jesus. Would he give communion to a Moonie? I also know that he attaches great importance to ordination. So would he himself feel free to go to communion if the celebrant belonged to a Christian group for whom ordination is not a prerequisite for presiding over the Lord's Supper?

None of these considerations seem to have occurred to the rather vociferous minority who welcomed Girard's remarks with enthusiasm. And it is understandable that their minds should not immediately start running towards the consequences of his statement as my mind did: short-term members of a community do not instinctively see the long-term implications of attractive proposals. One headache which I saw looming ahead was the complication that is bound to arise next year if we have as members of the community not only the usual Christians but also, possibly, Buddhists, Hindus, Muslims and Jews in their capacity as scholars at our Academy of Peace. I have known occasions when Hindus, Buddhists and even Muslims have received communion from a Catholic priest on the grounds that they were also followers of Jesus. So under Girard's rule, no Girard!

The most fundamental objection to his proposal, however, is that the Institute here does not claim to have *achieved* ecumenism; we are working towards ecumenism. And I find it somewhat presumptuous for anyone to go around with an 'ecumenism barometer' measuring the degree of ecumenism that others have achieved and then granting them 'pass' or 'fail' marks on the basis of the barometer readings.

5th May, 1983. Tantur

How extraordinarily difficult it is for us, Jews and Christians, to really meet and discuss our beliefs without getting carried away by currents of underground feeling within us that arose thousands of years ago, before any of us were born. The effect is that such currents are continually creating eruptions of anger, resentment and hatred between us that surprise us by their suddenness and violence. Such eruptions can spring up even between Jews and Christians who are personally good friends.

One such incident happened last year when I was just beginning to familiarise myself once more with the many groups around Jerusalem devoted to Christian–Jewish dialogue. In the course of doing so I kept noticing how often people characterised Christian–Jewish dialogue as 'asymmetrical'. Puzzled as to how this term applied to the dialogue and what were its implications I turned to Professor Shamir, a very open-minded friend of some years standing. I asked him what the term meant and he replied, 'It means you need us, but we don't need you'. Coming from him the words themselves startled me; but what took me aback still more was the arrogant tone of this usually genial Jewish friend.

Though even Shamir's attitude was as nothing compared with that of a Rabbi who was lecturing not long ago to a large audience composed of both Christians and Jews. He was quite properly praising the heroism of Rabbi Akiba in the year 135, reminding us how under torture from the Romans Akiba's last words were the defiant, 'Hear, O Israel, the Lord your God is One.' And then our lecturer added, in a quite venomous voice, 'unlike the cry of despair from a crucified Jew a few years earlier'.

Nor was it only the Christians in the audience who were stunned by this sudden eruption in the middle of an academic discourse.

Yet I realised last night that Christians should try not to take offence at such fierce remarks, because similar underground currents often produce conflict amongst Jews themselves.

What happened last night was that Professor Horowitz delivered to our group a very well thought out lecture on the subject of changes since the Second Vatican Council in the attitude of Catholics towards questions of human rights. As his lecture proceeded I imperceptibly began, as one does around these parts, to sense a wave of resistance to what he was saying running through the group. The reason for this escaped me at first but then became crystal clear, as I explained to my guest, Fr Michael, during the break for refreshments that always precedes discussion of the lecture.

Fr Michael said to me, 'What happens now?' 'I'll tell you what I think is going to happen', was my reply, 'I am pretty sure that some of our Jewish friends here realise, within the penumbra of their minds, that if they accept as true what Horowitz has been saying then they will also have to accept that present Israeli policies on the West Bank are morally indefensible. But that is what they certainly have no intention of recognising. Their anger over the dilemma into which Horowitz has placed them goes so deep that they cannot face it. And so they will displace their anger on to Horowitz and attack him personally.'

In what followed it was as though the participants were faithfully acting out the script that I had given them, except that the attacks upon Horowitz were even more vicious than I had envisaged.

None of the Christians present said a single word; they seemed paralysed at the animus that was being displayed. And I certainly had no intention of heightening the swirling passions by injecting my diagnosis of what was going on.

6th June, 1983. Tantur

'Well done, Yorkshire!' I say that because of the lightning response of the TV producer, who was phoning from Leeds this afternoon.

He had telephoned me several days ago asking if I could put him into contact with any Arab Christians who might be willing to give their views of the accord for Lebanon recently drawn up by the Israelis, the Gemayels and the Americans. At first I hesitated to do so, knowing that whenever an Arab raises his head he is liable to get it kicked in. But eventually I gave him the names and phone numbers of three Arab Christians who are strong-minded enough to say 'No' if they don't want to have anything to do with the proposal.

When the man called me up today he did so in order to thank me for the help I had given but also to convey his disappointment that none of my Arab friends had proved willing to accede to his request. 'They seemed very reluctant', he said, 'to go into the Israeli television studio in Jerusalem.' 'Does that surprise you?' I commented with astonishment. 'Yes, it does', came the reply. After a short pause during which I reflected on how little sense even educated people have for the realities of life in this land, I said slowly and deliberately, 'Do you realise that there is almost certainly someone listening to our present conversation?' 'No, I didn't', said the startled voice at the other end of the phone in distant Leeds. But then, quick as a flash, the Yorkshire voice said, 'Well, to whoever is listening . . . *shalom!'*

164

I hope the listener appreciated the quick wit as much as I did.

21st August, 1983. Tantur

Never again, I vow, shall I call another human being 'a nut', not after today. At the same time I can scarcely be blamed for calling her 'a nut' in the first place, when she phoned one evening two weeks ago.

Our dinner party was in full swing when the phone rang and our confused receptionist up at the desk announced that a woman wished to speak to me; but he couldn't make out what her name was. So I said, 'Put her through.' Then when I announced myself over the phone I was greeted by a staccato voice saying, 'This is . . .', followed by a strange name that I could not catch. But I caught only too well the next sentence: 'I am Jewish and have been in Assisi and there St Francis told me to talk with you.'

Inwardly I emitted a long drawn out groan. 'Here we go again!' I said to myself. Because at least once every week, sometimes twice, and even occasionally more often, some character or other either phones or writes or just appears at our reception desk with a plan for saving the world or announcing the end of the world. And for some unaccountable reason they have cast me for some role in this impending scenario. Every time it happens I am reminded of the statement by Danby, the great Anglican scholar, that whenever he was lecturing in Jerusalem he could always be confident that at least six members of the audience facing him considered themselves to be the Messiah. Nor do our beloved Arab receptionists seem capable of screening me from these and other unexpected visitors – probably in virtue of the Arabs' admirable inability to understand why anyone would not be glad to welcome any visitor at any time. That inability left me one afternoon entertaining in our apartment at one and the same time an Arab shepherd, a German professor and a French Cardinal Archbishop. The latter had called because of his concern for Christian–Jewish relations; the German professor wanted to discuss the New Testament and the Arab shepherd wanted me to expel other shepherds who were grazing their flocks in our grounds over which he claimed a monopoly for his sheep and goats.

But to return to our messenger from Assisi. I said to her, 'Where are you?', dreading that she would say she was at our reception desk, in which case I would be trapped. To my great relief, however, she said she was phoning from Haifa. That at least gave me a breathing space, and we arranged that she should come to lunch with her husband (who, I gathered, was a famous author) at twelve thirty today.

But in view of our initial conversation I knew it would not prove so simple as that! Nor did it. In subsequent phone calls I was asked to arrange for someone to take her husband and herself along the Stations of the Cross in the Old City of Jerusalem, because her husband knows nothing whatsoever about Christianity. That experience was tentatively arranged for them but then it somehow slipped off her programme without a word – and so off mine! Moreover she several times changed the time at which the two of them would arrive for lunch.

Finally it was agreed that lunch would be at twelve thirty. So, not for the first time, I asked the community if they would be so good as to switch the time for lunch again, from the usual hour of one o'clock, to which they generously acceded.

But at twelve thirty there was no visitor in sight, nor at twelve forty-five, by which time I was wondering if it was my duty to remonstrate rather sternly with our visitor when and if she were to arrive.

Then, at one o'clock, just as I was about to tap a glass to signal the grace and begin the meal notwithstanding, we heard a noisy clatter along the corridor outside the dining room. The door was flung open and there strode in a big, fat, smiling woman followed by a small, pensive-looking man. And instantly I liked her. Why I should have liked her immediately I cannot explain. Of course I can think up reasons, such as that she behaved so warmly towards our Arab cooks, to whom she spoke in voluble Arabic, both accomplishments unusual in our Jewish visitors. But perhaps the real reason, despite my ingrained scepticism, has something to do with St Francis.

I say that because of what happened after lunch. She asked me to provide her with brochures about the work of the Institute and for that purpose we had to go across our garden to my office. There I opened the door and walked straight across to my desk in order to find the required brochures; but scarcely had I begun searching for them than I heard my visitor's powerful voice behind me proclaiming, 'There! I told you I would come to see him.' Astonished, and wondering whom she might be addressing, since there was no one else in our end of the building, I suddenly realised that she was standing reverently in front of a slender board hanging upon the wall upon which I had fixed the full length portrait by Cimambue of St Francis displaying the stigmata.

Preoccupied as I had been over lunch I had completely forgotten that I had placed that powerful depiction of St Francis upon the wall of my office. St Francis' eyes are so piercing and unrelenting; and they were saying to me, 'Unbeliever! Never again call anyone "a nut", not even in your mind. If you had been a citizen of Assisi during my lifetime you would probably have called me "a nut".'

(For the sequel to the events of this day, see p.224)

22nd August, 1983. Letter to the Tablet

I don't know why I should have been surprised – after all, every precedent going back thousands of years assures you that trying to act justly in the Holy Land constitutes an invitation for someone to stone you. Still, I was taken aback when I opened the letter. It was from Los Angeles, and had been prompted by an article of mine entitled 'Peace in the Holy Land?' As I read the letter, I had the feeling that the words were jumping out of the pages to bite me: the man was accusing me of having been duped by the Jews into believing their version of recent history, which was all lies. They deserved what had happened to them, he said – and there was more to come.

I felt sorry for the man who had written it – evidently an American Catholic – when I imagined the misery of living within such a skin. At the same time I was truly grateful to have been the recipient of such a letter, to have myself been the object of an anti-Semitic outpouring. For although I have read much anti-Semitic writing over the years, never before had I experienced the sensation of the filth being heaped on my own head. What it must be like to receive such venom constantly is beyond imagining.

And then there came a second letter, this time from the east coast of the United States, on account of the same article (on peace: God help us!). I was now charged with supporting 'the murderous Arafat'.

By good fortune, however, I had lately been reading a book by Ronald Storrs, *Orientations*, in which Storrs, who was at the time military governor of Jerusalem, describes being summoned to Downing Street by Lloyd George. Storrs feared the worst when the Prime Minister pointed to a pile of letters of complaint against Storrs and said they were from Arabs. Then he pointed to another pile of accusing letters from Jews. After which Lloyd George assured Storrs that he would be sacked if there were ever to be only one pile.

Storrs comments later: 'Two hours of Arab grievances drive me into the Synagogue, while after an intensive course of Zionist propaganda, I am prepared to embrace Islam'; he complains also that 'criticism of any Zionist method or proposal' is considered to be 'equivalent to anti-Zionism, even to anti-Semitism'.

I sometimes think that nobody whatsoever actually listens to the Palestinians of the West Bank – neither those who speak in support of them, or even in their name, nor those who speak against them. Some people at least listen to our Jewish brethren, many of whom speak the same language as ourselves and, in many cases, went to the same universities as we did.

So I am all the more eager, when opportunity offers, to hear the comments of thoughtful Palestinians such as Ahmed whom I met again two days ago. And, as often happens, he made me really think.

I was attempting, as always, to 'put the other side' in the hope of increasing mutual understanding. Frequently there is a touch of arrogance about such an undertaking, because it assumes that one has reached a deeper understanding than that of either side. In the event the conversation revealed my own imperceptiveness.

In response to Ahmed's complaints about the Israeli occupation of the West Bank, I was trying to argue that it is less harsh than most occupations one knows about. He looked at me sadly, as though called upon to enlighten a moron, and then said: 'We have been occupied by the Turks, by the British, by Jordan. None of them were good. There was much cruelty from all of them. *But none of them stole our land.* What is happening at the moment is not occupation; it is conquest and stealing. And you watch it as though it was a play on television.'

Failing so frequently to serve as a bridge can be discouraging, so for encouragement I looked again at my journal for one day in March of this year.

'This morning I walked southwards out of Tiberias alongside the Jewish cemetery on my right, with the Sea of Galilee to the east, on my left. The cemetery is beautifully kept. Whenever I pass it, there are usually groups of religious Jews present, tending the graves of their beloved dead. There is always something very moving about seeing one's fellow human beings making their fragile protest against the seeming finality of death.

'But when I came to the end of the Jewish cemetery, I walked immediately into a different world, a wilderness through which there ran an overgrown path leading up the hill. For about a quarter of a mile I walked along the unused path, past ancient rubbish dumps and rusty abandoned bodies of cars. Gradually, I became invisible to the rest of the world, buried from sight by the tall, luxuriant yellow bushes on both sides. By now, however, through the bushes to one side, I could just make out some more graves – Muslim graves this time. They were totally abandoned except by the brilliant anemones and marigolds in which they nestled. And then, the path having turned, I again observed the high graves of the Jewish cemetery some ten yards away to my right.

'Standing there in the warm sunlight, all I could see eastwards over the yellow bushes were the Golan Heights, whilst westwards the land rose towards Mount Tabor. Scores of martins were skimming over and around me and myriads of insects were humming as they passed from flower to flower; so that all of nature seemed to be crying, "Life! Life!" And in a strangely compelling way the Muslims and the Jews, on either side of me, though dead, were also present in their such different cemeteries, the one so bereft of human care and the other so graced with it.

'In the presence of the living dead, I was sure that neither Muslims nor Jews would now mind if a lone Christian, standing between them, offered a prayer for all the commonalty of the dead, a prayer that all of us, Christians, Muslims and Jews, might even one day become human enough to tend one another's graves.

'Walking slowly back, afterwards, the Lord put a happy thought into my mind. When the winter rains sweep across that hillside they inevitably carry certain particles of the Muslim dead down into the Jewish cemetery: at the Resurrection we shall rise as one Body.'

10th September, 1983. Tantur

Sometimes you really do feel that there is an Evil One, a Satan, at work in the world, and especially here in the

Holy Land. Late on Thursday afternoon I even seemed to smell the traces of his passage amongst us, much as one can sometimes scent the recent presence of a leopard in the wadis above Ein Gedi.

I was pacing around the Institute, which is almost empty at the moment, in a certain anxiety about how things were going to work out the next day, Friday, because that was when we were to host the first Christian–Muslim Dialogue Conference ever to be held in this land. My anxiety was due not only to the fact that we were just about to step into unknown territory which might well prove to be a minefield but also because it has taken Geries and myself about eighteen months to prepare the ground for the Conference. At times it has seemed as though the mistrust and suspicion between Muslims and Christians hereabouts is so ingrained that we would never manage to bring them together. And I don't think, in fact, that we would have managed to do so had it not been for the good will of Sheikh Muhammad Al Imam Al Husseini. He it was who, so to speak, came to stand as guarantor of the good faith of Geries and myself in face of the local Muslim community – he is our protector, as it were. And his readiness to do so sprang entirely, I am sure, from a source which is so little recognised in modern society; that is, the heart. The moment that the Sheikh and I met about a year ago our hearts told us that we were brothers, and we each of us trusted our hearts. There have been difficulties since that moment, inevitably, but our mutual trust has each time smoothed them out.

All the same, the Evil One nearly outwitted us on Thursday afternoon! I was walking along the corridor leading towards our reception desk when I happened to glance up at the notice board. To my horror I saw pinned upon it a leaflet announcing a series of meetings to be held this very weekend in Bethlehem at which Abdul al Haqq, a convert from Islam to Christianity, would be speaking! For an instant a shiver ran down my spine as I envisaged what would happen the next day if our Muslim brethren were to arrive and see such leaflets fixed upon our notice boards. They would all have left instantly.

I had the leaflet off the board before anyone could utter the proverbial 'Jack Robinson' and went straightaway to Issa, the receptionist on duty, to find out if he had seen who had pinned the leaflet there. But he had not himself noticed it nor seen any stranger come in who might have done the deed. Nor did my subsequent enquiries of others shed any light upon the identity of the mischief-maker. However, I was less concerned about that than I was to go round the whole institute with my eyes skinned, looking to see whether there were any more of the offending leaflets about the place. I discovered two more before supper time. However, although I set Geries and the others to scour the place, thankfully no more were found. All the same I did not sleep as well as usual on Thursday evening – troubled, I expect, by a deep fear that I might have failed to detect one of the leaflets. And I was even more troubled, perhaps, by an awareness of how near we had come to seeing all our work of the past eighteen months brought to nought. Also I was disturbed by the depressing realisation that there are forces at work in the world so malicious as to want to destroy brotherhood.

However, in the event, the forces of good and not the forces of evil prevailed, thank God. Indeed on Friday afternoon I was even able to have a good relaxed laugh at something which happened, even though it was at my own expense.

As Rector of the Institute I clearly had to welcome our guests on Friday afternoon, all two hundred of them, virtually all Arabs. Equally clearly I had to ask for an interpreter to translate my words into Arabic. As far as I could make out the man appointed to do so made quite a reasonable job of the translation. But no sooner had the first session ended than a number of the delegates crowded around me to complain about the terrible mess the interpreter had made of translating my speech. From the haughty manner in which they criticised the wretched

172

fellow I realised that in part, at least, their indignation was a way of indicating to me how much better they themselves understood both English and Arabic than he does. However, Brother Bartomeu, who was standing nearby and listening to all this, provided me with a more charitable explanation: 'The interpreter was so hesistant', said Bartomeu, 'because he was waiting for you to say something. You simply stood there with your hands folded and spoke in your normal quiet, soft voice. On such an occasion as this Arabs expect a speaker to shout and gesture and generally behave dramatically. So your interpreter was waiting for you to do that; only then would he have known that you were saying something worth translating.'

Subsequently the truth of Bartomeu's reading of Arab modes dawned upon me. I recalled how startled I had been at the speech following my own when the dear Sheikh, the gentlest of men, kept punching the air and shaking his head, bellowing away, his eyes gleaming with excitement at what he was himself saying. In fact I became alarmed at the level of passion he was both displaying and evoking in his audience. 'Goodness', I thought, 'he sounds as though he is calling for *jihad*!' So I turned to the man sitting next to me and whispered, 'What is the Sheikh saying?' The man gave a gleaming, happy smile and whispered back, 'He is thanking you for your loving generosity in inviting us all to this historic conference.'

13th September, 1983

My apprehension about the repercussions of our Muslim–Christian conference have proved to be well grounded. From one section after another of the Israeli establishment I have already been receiving signals – in the unattributable fashion customary around here – that the Jews are displeased about our initiative and suspicious of what we are cooking up. How can there ever be peace in the Middle East so long as gestures of friendship between

173

any two groups are automatically regarded as gestures of hostility against a third group?

Also the sending of these signals makes me very cross with the media workers stationed in Jerusalem. Having recognised beforehand that our conference was likely to be misunderstood and misrepresented I had invited seventeen journalists, TV and radio reporters to come to dinner at the Institute when I would have explained to them what we were about so that there could be no misunderstanding. There is one question in particular that was bound to be raised yet again and to which I have replied until I am blue in the face. But I must continue to answer it. The question is, 'Why do you hold a Muslim–Christian conference and not a Christian–Jewish conference?' The answer which I seem to have to keep repeating over and over again is that, in the first place, there are numerous Christian institutions and centres in Jerusalem devoted to dialogue between Jews and Christians but not a single one devoted to Muslim–Christian dialogue. Moreover, here at Tantur Jewish scholars come in and out the whole time whereas we can hardly ever draw a Muslim into our circle. Again, a number of Jewish scholars have given Tantur lectures but not a single Muslim has done so . . .

If the media people had transmitted my answer to the public the suspicions to which we are now subject might have been dampened. Whereas not a single one of those invited turned up to dinner; and only two of them had the grace to reply – Jennie Goldman, the warm-hearted producer from *Kol Israel,* who was already engaged, and David Richardson of the *Jerusalem Post*, who had been called to military duty in Lebanon.

The behaviour of journalists frequently makes me seriously doubt whether journalism as it is practised can be regarded as what the Buddhists call 'right means of livelihood'.

174

8th October, 1983. Tantur

When those Jerusalem divines two years ago declared themselves so shocked at my proposal to place the question of nuclear weapons on the agenda for the Jewish, Christian and Muslim divines who had assembled in the holy city of Jerusalem I was at first astonished. Had they dug themselves so deeply into their various pits precisely in order not to be able to see anything outside their own particular pit?

Now, with the benefit of two years' living in the Jerusalem community I find their behaviour not so much astonishing as weird – eerie!

During these two years I have heard the following statements. I have heard a highly respected rabbi say that if Israel is ever in danger then he would be prepared for Israel to use nuclear weapons. When someone pointed out to him that such action might result in the destruction of all life on earth, he replied, 'Then so be it.' I have heard a Christian Palestinian priest say that if the only way for the Palestinians to secure justice is by way of a third world war with nuclear weapons and all their consequences, then 'OK'. And I have heard a Muslim Sheikh declare that if Islam is threatened then Muslims would be justified in using nuclear weapons.

When I look upon Jerusalem, aware of all these necrophilous passions swirling over and within the city with such intensity and then call to mind these priests of various faiths all mumbling away at the bottom of their separate pits, convinced that their particular mumblings are the only way the world can be saved; and when I further remind myself that they are all highly educated, and even in a sense intelligent within the limits of their own worlds, then an eerie feeling comes over me of the unreality of it all.

175

18th October, 1983. Letter to the Tablet

I never get used to the drive to Lod, no matter how many times I travel down that twisting road from the Judean heights to the plain where Ben-Gurion airport fronts the Mediterranean. It is as though that thin line through the hills brings out the very worst characteristics of Israeli motorists – boiling aggression and scowling faces which go far to explain why Israel has such an appalling record of death and injury on its highways.

And yet, though the journey generally scares me to death, I am always delighted eventually, when I get there, to be able to watch arriving passengers coming through the airport barriers. Waiting and watching becomes a kind of sacrament. From the very way that the individual men and women walk, you can almost read off in what manner each walks with God. And from their faces, especially from the glance of their eyes, you are drawn into one aspect after another of the human drama – the farce, the comedy and the tragedy.

But in every body and every face and every eye, there is one invariable, one constant: that is, the desire for recognition. It is true, of course, that certain of the arrivals try to hide their desire. Many of the English do so, as do priests and religious in general; but the effort is no good – it only underlines the desire.

However, there are some people who never seem to hide their desire for recognition, and that is the Israelis. As soon as those who are waiting and those arriving catch one another's eyes there is a veritable explosion of joy. Their faces light up; they laugh uninhibitedly; they wave fit to shake their arms off and then rush to the end of the barriers to embrace one another time and time again. In a sense all this has nothing to do with me, as I stand there patiently waiting for the plane that will bring my sober English friends; but nonetheless it always happens that

I once more find myself pulled into the drama – smiling slightly to myself at first, until finally I am laughing along with the chief characters and tingling with delight as I observe their happiness.

The only shadow that clouds my delight arises when I remember that I have still to drive up that dreadful road under threat from all those ill-tempered Israelis. At which point I have to ask myself whether those on the road and those in the airport can possibly belong to the same people. The answer is undoubtedly, yes, they do. But how can that be?

The explanation, I believe, lies in that matter of recognition. Watching those habitually closed, fearful faces and then seeing them suddenly open up into joy and happiness in the moment of recognition, I cannot help feeling that what this people needs is to be truly recognised. Then they would change – beyond recognition.

It was eerie watching the parade of Arab Scouts in East Jerusalem as they marched to commemorate the massacre in the Palestinian refugee camps of Sabra and Chatila. They marched in a wonderfully disciplined and dignified fashion to the solemn beat of their drums. They commanded the warmest admiration from all those watching the march – from all, that is to say, except the Jewish soldiers in their bottle-green battledress with their sub-machine guns grimly at the ready. The eyes of the soldiers were here, there and everywhere, scanning the crowds for the least sign of trouble. They seemed isolated and cold, alien beings from another world.

Yet it was not their isolation nor the menacing beat of the drums in the hot sunshine which provided an explanation for my sense of eeriness. It was rather the calm, untroubled, totally controlled manner in which the Arabs – both in the crowds and more especially in the parade – completely ignored the presence, the existence of the Jewish soldiers.

I had noticed on previous occasions the skilful way

in which Arabs manage to conduct themselves in the presence of Jews as thought those Jews simply did not exist. The first time was a year or two ago, in the staunchly Arab town of Hebron. I was standing only a few yards away from a Jewish soldier when an Arab whom I knew slightly saw me from a distance and came towards me to greet me. He set off to do so on a line that threatened to take him straight through the body of the Jewish soldier standing near me; so much so that I involuntarily lifted my hand to alert him to the danger, as if he had somehow failed to notice the soldier. In the event, however, my Arab friend passed within a hair's breadth of the Jewish soldier without even the slightest glance. Somehow or other he managed to reduce the soldier to a status even below that of a ghost. And that was what made me feel eerie, both in Hebron and in East Jerusalem.

After the parade, as I walked homewards along the Bethlehem road, which was quiet and almost deserted because of the holy day, I was pondering upon a story concerning the triumph of Nazism that has haunted me for many years. It is told by Karl Stern in his marvellously illuminating autobiography *Pillar of Fire*. There Stern describes how he travelled by train back to his cosy little home town in Bavaria just as the Nazi infection was beginning to take hold on the minds of Germans. His father met him at the station. And whilst the two of them were walking back home together as night was falling they kept encountering fellow-citizens of their acquaintance on the way. Some of these would no longer greet Karl and his father because of the Sterns being Jewish. It is precisely with such little acts of cowardice and hostility that all the terrible events of our terrible world begin – the lying, the tortures and the killings. Likewise the work of reconciliation begins with the act of greeting. Simply to greet another person, to recognise that person, is to partake in the sacrament of peace.

'Lost in wonder' is doubtless a cliché, but I have to say that no other phrase so well expresses the admiration I hold for Da'oud, my Arab Christian friend. He has lost his family lands to Jews and has had to endure almost daily harassment from them, yet I have never heard him speak even one word of hatred for them. When I call to mind the simmering hatred for Germans and Japanese which so many of us Britishers still harbour, the contrast helps me to understand how he manages to say: 'If we do not love our enemies, then we cannot call ourselves Christians.'

Nevertheless, he was very downcast indeed the other day. A close friend of his had suddenly been arrested and Da'oud had lain awake all night recalling all the fearful stories he had heard about the treatment of Arabs in prison and imagining what might be happening to his friend. But above all he was shattered by the killing of Palestinian refugees by their fellow-Arabs in Baddawi camp north of Tripoli. For him, the forces closing in on the Palestinians seemed to signify the extinction of the Palestinian people – his people – and their centuries-old culture. And the nations of the world were standing by, watching this final act, not concerned for the men, women and children being destroyed but hovering over them like vultures, waiting to see what pickings of power and wealth they might secure for themselves.

Within an hour of listening to my Arab friend, in despair at his abandonment by all the world, I found myself in a totally different atmosphere – the atmosphere of what St John precisely calls 'the world', where ambitious men and *soignée* women together generate that peculiar smell mingled of power, wealth and sexuality.

Since my friend Menachem truly does not belong to that world, in spite of his high office, he quickly drew me aside and began to speak of the events in Tripoli. After a time he said to me: 'Of course, I am deeply sorry for what has happened – especially to the women and children. But surely everyone in the world must now understand the fears of us Israelis, and why we need to be strong:

if the Palestinians do such terrible things to one another it cannot be imagined what they would do to us Jews if they were given half a chance.'

As we were driving home afterwards I began to daydream about the peace that might come about if only Da'oud and Menachem were to get to know one another. Unfortunately, there is a seemingly endless abyss between them over which no greetings can be heard.

27th October, 1983. Tantur

Last night could have proved to be disastrous to this community for the rest of the year. It may do so yet, of course, but I am not so fearful of that happening as I was last night. Still, if it does cause harm, most of the blame will be mine for issuing at the community meeting a rebuke which came from the wrong place inside me. As soon as I had spoken I knew it had come from the wrong place. So I immediately apologised. But that was already too late; the damage had been done. Other members of a community may be able to get away with such transgressions but when the head of a community commits the same transgression the consequences both for the whole community and for himself are inevitably more serious.

I, of all people, should have known better in view of all the times during the past forty years that I have given thanks for what I always think of, in traditional Celtic fashion, as *The Three Great Rebukes That Stopped Donald In His Tracks*. The first occurred in 1943 after I had entertained a barrack room of my fellow soldiers by running dialectical rings around a raw-boned Scot and his conservative political opinions. In the end, confused and totally exasperated, the good man bawled along the length of the barrack room, 'The trouble with you is that you're too bloody clever to live long!' With those words of an unquestionably good man all my cleverness was reduced to dust and blown out of the room.

My second rebuke took place in the French Carmelite monastery of Avon. There I made a sly remark one afternoon about the number of devout old ladies who used to come swarming around the friars – at which one of the friars, Fr Philippe, looked at me with steely eyes and asked, 'And who else do they have, except us?' My third Great Rebuke was administered by that most endearing of men, Professor of Old Irish at Dublin University, Gerard Murphy. In the excitement of a high-spirited conversation amongst a group of us I made a snide observation about Arnold Toynbee, tracing his ideological changes to his marital changes, only to be met with the deep-voiced admonition, 'Let us be very careful before we start taking away a man's good name.'

I have received other rebukes in the years between, of course, but those just cited are the ones that stand out in my memory as issuing from a clean heart. And because they were directed from a clean heart each of the rebukes found its mark in a rotten point in my own heart and thereby touched off a process of healing within me. The healing process, I have always realised, is still far from complete; but that in no way diminishes my gratitude towards my three rebukers. And it was in the light of my very gratitude towards them that I was now able not only to see how the rebuke I had issued had boomeranged back into my own heart but, even further, to find the determination not to sleep until I had uncovered that area of decay within me that had flared up into my angry words.

So it was that I went up on to the spacious flat roof of the Institute after the meeting and began to pace the length of it, forwards and backwards, time and again, for hour upon hour, trying to examine honestly not just the events of the evening but all the events throughout the whole of yesterday which had led to my flare-up. Nor was it long before I realised that my search had to go further back still, over months and years, in order to uncover the sources of my feeling of resentment against Alan and his circle. Because the more resolutely I tried to examine all aspects of the incident the clearer it became that by yesterday evening I was on the point of exploding with suppressed resentment, some of which had been boiling up within me for much of my life.

I felt that I had been working harder for half a century than most other people around me, partly through the need to earn my keep in this world and partly through a twisted sense of duty. And now I had run into a group of scholars who do not work half so hard yet are wealthier, who have been given the privilege of studying but who choose instead to sit for hours around the coffee room gossiping and idly scheming. I also resented the way I had been isolated during the course of the meeting. Such were only a few of the reflections that kept running through my head as I paced up and down in the darkness. And they could easily have been turned into a long bill of accusation against the community in general had I not seen my own resentment so clearly in the light of my Three Great Rebukes.

Was there something in myself, for instance, which, despite all of my pretentions to duty, would have preferred to live a leisurely life with plenty of money? with time to sit around, drinking coffee and gossiping? If not, then why do I object to others who live like that? Out of unacknowledged envy?

Objectively, of course, it is right that people who are not working hard enough to justify their wealth and who are forever mouthing high-flown sentiments over their coffee cups should be shown the error of their ways. But who has the right to show them? The only answer I could give to that question was that even though I was not the one to have administered the rebuke, nevertheless I was glad it had been administered, because it was needed.

And how fortunate I was in the opportunity to deal with all my turmoil on the high roof of the Institute, against the background of the silence of the Judean hills, and to be walking in the darkness of a moonless night, comforted by the glistening joy of myriads of stars. Under the influence of the night sky, the silence, the soft breeze from off the Judean desert and the sweet smell of the pine trees that reach up over the roof's edge, I found myself beginning to breathe more deeply and slowly. My whole body became more and more relaxed until eventually my heart melted and a deep peace came welling up within me, permeating my whole being.

I went down to our apartment a different person than the one who had climbed the stairs some hours previously. And I was doubly thankful that I had so firmly turned down Dorothy's suggestion that I should discuss with her the events of the evening. I refused because I needed all my resources to handle my own inner conflicts without taking on board the conflicts that anyone else might have brought to the situation. It is such a profound illusion to imagine that 'talking it over' is always a help – doing so often has precisely the effect of 'talking over' the real issues and sealing them under a wax of words.

But something very remarkable then happened. Although I felt at peace when I lay down to sleep, for some reason I did not sleep. Instead I continued to work away all night through those areas of myself that had been revealed as rotten. But I did so peacefully, no longer in turmoil. Certainly I cannot have slept for more than an hour, because I clearly heard the muezzins calling the pre-dawn prayer from several of our neighbouring mosques, and the distant stirring of the traffic while it was still dark as the Arab day labourers began their journey from the West Bank into Jerusalem. But what amazed me was that far from feeling worn out from all my mental struggle my heart was light, my mind clear, and I was ready to greet the new day with a smile and to regard my fellow human beings in the most benevolent light.

The whole episode has been a great lesson to me: if only you work away at the rotten areas of yourself on which the light of Christ has been shed, then the burden of Christ will prove so light as to be no burden at all.

31st October 1983. Visit to Ma'hadda.

I still don't know whether we made the right decision when we agreed that a small group of us should spend the day in the Arab village of Ma'hadda, which sits in a fold of the mountains eastwards of the city of Hebron. Two weeks ago we had witnessed for ourselves the damage done to a different Arab village by Jewish settlers in order to punish the Arabs for receiving foreigners and for revealing to them the injustices committed by the settlers and the Israeli army. As a result we resolved to be more careful than ever not to put Arabs into danger by contacting them unnecessarily. On the other hand, the message we received from Ma'hadda was that they were prepared to take the risk of reprisals at the hands of the Israelis if, as a result of our visit, their miserable situation were to become better known in the West.

This unheralded exchange of messages with the villagers also placed me in a rather delicate situation. In order not to attract attention our party had not to number more than nine plus our driver; and I knew that more than that number of scholars wished to go. I also knew which ones I wanted to see visiting Ma'hadda – responsible people who would behave discreetly and afterwards quietly do whatever they can to help the villagers. But there are two or three scholars, decent enough in their own milieu, who nevertheless are always wanting to get in on every act and who will always blather about it afterwards. They are precisely the ones, moreover, who kick up a fuss if they do not get what they want. I have already heard rumblings from them about what criteria I adopted for the make-up of the party – and I can hardly explain my criteria to them!

In the event the day went smoothly enough. We were taken to the middle of Ma'hadda where there stands a rather pathetic shrine, still not finished, in memory of the two young schoolboys of Ma'hadda who were shot dead by Israeli soldiers. We drank coffee with the boys' fathers in the village Centre and learned how the fascist rabbi Kahane had sent messages to them, after the boys' death, telling the villagers how many shekels Arab blood was worth – not many. The elders of the village also showed us where the Jews were steadily encroaching upon their ancestral lands in an attempt to drive them out – an attempt, the elders said, which would never succeed because now they would rather die than leave: the deaths of the two boys had in a way sanctified their *sumud,* their steadfastness to the land.

But the most striking and chilling incident occurred as I was walking alone with the most imposing of the elders. When the subject came up in our conversation of the massacre of Palestinians in Sabra and Chatilla this strong-boned, broad-shouldered representative of the villagers turned towards me and said very deliberately, 'We can get more children in one night than the Jews can kill in all their Sabra and Chatillas.' In speaking the words a note of defiance came into his voice, arising out of the very depths of his being, and I was chilled by the realisation that the war between Jews and Arabs is now taking place no longer at the lever of diplomacy, economics and politics. That level is comparatively superficial. The fight is now being fought deep down in the loins of these peoples.

(The consequences of our visit are described on p.186.)

18th November, 1983. Tantur

'Poor sod! Hasn't he suffered enough already?' These were the words that sprang instantly to my mind this evening when Eliphaz crept in to tell me about the reported misbehaviour of Melville. Looking back on that instant reaction I can see that it was not the result of any formal teaching, whether Christian or otherwise, but was simply an expression of the code which had been instinctively bred into me by my ancestral tribe, inhabitants of the wholly working-class Pennine village of Claremount. There, presumably on account of the many misfortunes to which all of us were regularly subject, we learnt to greet news of almost any misfortune to one of our tribe, such as being arrested as drunk and disorderly or being sent to Borstal, with the words, 'Poor sod!'

Eliphaz had clearly inherited a different code. He was making a real meal of Melville's misfortune, putting on a pious face whilst at the same time cunningly insinuating that if I did not get rid of Melville then I was endangering the good name and the future of the Institute. Also, no one ever seems to have taught Eliphaz to 'read' other people, otherwise he would not have gone on and on, wittering about how dreadful it all was; instead he would have seen that I was getting more and more angry with him. In fact I felt a deep urge to hit him and thereby put an end to his charade. But I contented myself, for the moment, with thanking him and telling him and his informant to hold their tongues from now on. I also reminded him that to spread bad news about someone in trouble is a worse sin than anything Melville is supposed to have done.

21st November, 1983

I received a message today from Ma'hadda to say that since our visit fourteen men of the village have been arrested and are now being held in Hebron. Whether the arrests are in consequence of our visit we cannot be sure, but the elders who received us three weeks ago did say that there were two paid informers in the community who were keeping an eye on us and would undoubtedly give a full account of our doings to the Israeli HQ in Hebron.

10th December, 1983. Tantur

People are for ever putting forward formulae which they claim will 'solve the Middle East problem'. By doing so they demonstrate that they do not even begin to understand the situation, one in which the given factors are immeasurably too complex to be contained by any formula whilst the imponderables in it lie beyond imagination.

The most useful thing to do in such situations is to discover some pragmatic litmus test which will enable you to judge whose assessments you can trust and whose you had better ignore. One such test which I use on commentators is to see if they place Begin in the same category as Sharon. I regard those who do so as grossly unperceptive. Much of what Begin does saddens me, but I believe that he is actually a very sensitive man who is struggling to integrate into his Jewish tradition the terrible experiences in Poland and Russia which he describes in his autobiography *The Revolt*. Sharon seems to me a totally different kind of person. His murderous proclivities were first manifested publicly in his merciless killing of Arabs when he was the leader of Unit 101, and they have kept him in the public eye ever since. What absolutely astonishes me is that such a man should occupy an honoured post, as Defence Minister, in the government of a democratic country, which Israel certainly is.

However, the mere presence of such a person in high office is by itself corrupting, just as Nixon's presence at the White House was corrupting for the US in 1969. Some Israelis feel this, of course, even more passionately than I do. I remember Deborah, for instance, startling a group of Jewish men by turning upon them and exclaiming, 'Why doesn't one of you kill Sharon? If somebody had killed Hitler in 1933 we should have been spared a lot of our misery.' But most Jews seem to be mesmerised by the man; and so I am interested to see whether there will be a strong wave of protest against the latest manifestations of his coarse brutality.

I am referring to an article in today's *Jerusalem Post* which is headlined *479 massacred in Beirut, and mostly men, Sharon says*. The article goes on to report that Defence Minister Sharon had told Jewish audiences in

New York that Jews should not bear any guilt over the September massacre in the refugee camps of Sabra and Chatilla. He stressed that 'only a very few women and children were massacred in the camp' – eight women and twelve children, as he later explained. He was speaking at an Israeli Bonds dinner, where the diners pledged to buy $14.5 million in Israeli bonds.

Whilst no one in their right mind would want to affix any guilt upon Jews in general for what the Maronites did in Sabra and Chatilla I must say that I find the occasion as described by the *Jerusalem Post* quite obscene. Did no one, in the name of the Jewish tradition concerning the sanctity of life, stand up at the dinner and protest at the dismissive: 'only a very few women and children were massacred'? 'Only', in the name of God!

I yearn with all my heart for one of my Jewish friends here in Israel, without any external prompting, to stand up like the prophet Amos and denounce that man Sharon as a disgrace to the People of Israel.

16th December, 1983. Tantur

'Once you raise the issue of peace with people you automatically raise the demons inside them' is a saying of my Jesuit friend, Gerry Hughes, of which I yesterday witnessed the truth.

The first demon popped up in the shape of a Christian bishop no more than a minute after Landrum Bolling had concluded his lecture for the opening of our Peace Academy. It was my manner of opening the afternoon's proceedings that triggered the demon's appearance.

What I had done was to share with the invited guests, Jews, Christian, Muslims and agnostics to the number of several hundred, the dilemma of inaugurating anything in a society so dividing as ours is nowadays. By contrast, I said, it would have been comparatively easy for our Roman predecessors on this very same hilltop to have carried out an inauguration that would have been almost universally acceptable in the ancient world. In those days we need have done no more than hire an augur who would have interpreted for us the omens provided by the flight, the singing, the feeding and the entrails of the multitude of birds that live around Tantur, and on the basis of his interpretation the augur would have advised us what path we were to follow. But having invited not only Christians but also Jews, Muslims and agnostics to share in the inauguration it would have been offensive to one lot or another to have begun, *In nomine patris et filii et spiritus sancti,* or *Bismillah-aRahman a Rahim,* or *Baruch ata adonai eleynu.* After quoting these three blessings to illustrate our dilemma I had asked everyone present to join for a minute in the universal sacrament, the sacrament of silence. I had also secretly hoped that those in the gathering whose hearts were in pure silence might thereby receive all the three blessings I had very deliberately and liturgically pronounced, the Latin one, the Arabic one and the Hebrew one.

My eirenical efforts proved in vain. For no sooner were the guests streaming out of the lecture hall towards our reception room than this excitable bishop appeared before me and subjected me to a voluble attack for having sold the pass – 'a Christian institution should always use a Christian ritual, no matter who is present', he almost shouted.

I was rescued from his further excoriation, however, by the press around me of a crowd of well-wishers, one of whom, my friend, Bill Clark, an Israeli conservationist, presented me with a most beautiful box. Because of the crush of people I had no opportunity to examine it more closely, apart from admiring its fine finish. I was still carrying it in my hands a quarter of an hour later as I was passing our coffee room on my way to the reception when I noticed our Muslim friends all sitting there apart from all the rest. Straightaway I realised that they had declined to go on to the reception because wine, the forbidden drink, was laid out for guests in our dining hall and they did not wish to be associated with it. So I decided that I must join them, if only for a short time, in the coffee room.

As I went in to welcome them I noticed that the beautiful box in my hand was a musical one; and so, after the customary greetings, I showed it to the sheikhs for their admiration, instinctively opening it as I did so, not knowing or considering what tune it might play. After only a few notes, however, I realised to my consternation that it was playing the popular Israeli song, *Shalom, shalom, shalom aleikhem*. The Hebrew words are, of course, all about peace but, unfortunately, due to the twists of history, the song in Arab ears sounds like a Jewish war cry. As quick as a flash, and before my Muslim friends had time to pick out the tune, I snapped the box shut, smiled at my guests and asked them to excuse me as I now had to go to receive other guests.

Happily most of our other guests were by now well into the swing of the reception, everyone chatting away in best Jerusalem style, greeting one anther like long lost friends, even though they had met one another half a dozen times at similar receptions during the past month. But even here the occasional demon put in an appearance – in the form, this time, of one Jewish professor who button-holed me and asked me what on earth we teach our scholars at Tantur. I tried to explain to him that we don't programmatically teach them anything since they are senior theologians who learn on their own. But that was no excuse for my remissness. 'One of your scholars', he trumpeted indignantly, 'has been speaking to me of what he calls "the West Bank". Doesn't he realise that there is no such place? It is Judea and Samaria, and has been since the beginning. You should teach them better.'

For myself, after all these years, such encounters are no longer very disturbing; they are par for the course. But just as everyone was beginning to drift away around nine o'clock young Bob, one of the Peace Pilgrims, came up to me looking shocked and hurt. He told me in considerable distress that he had been talking to one of our guests and had referred to 'Palestine'. To his astonishment not even his youth had saved him from a fierce onslaught for having used such a pernicious name. He looked quite dazed, still trying to figure out why peace seemed so much more difficult in Jerusalem than it ever had been on the 12,000 kilometres from Seattle to . . . Palestine? the West Bank? Judea and Samaria? Whatever the name, 'there be demons'.

18th December, 1983. Tantur

If only 'liberals' would more often realise how closed in mind they can be sometimes!

Although I almost always obey the letter of the law governing Catholic practice in regard to *communicatio in sacris* there are occasions when in order to fulfil the spirit of the law I have to undertake certain actions which go beyond the limitations of the letter. For a Catholic *communicatio in sacris* is only permissible in very special circumstances which are normally to be determined by the local bishop. But, of course, the local bishop may be so remote from you that you have no opportunity to consult him. And by 'remote' I mean not only simply physically remote but remote socially as well as in other ways. If the bishop is so remote that you cannot consult him and acquaint him with the special circumstances in which you find yourself then he is not a bishop in the sense envisaged by the early Church. He is a true bishop but in an anomalous position. In such circumstances the faithful Catholic has to act according to his conscience.

In the light of such considerations I was preparing three weeks ago to receive communion at the Eucharist which was to be celebrated by a Lutheran minister. But in the end I did not do so, not because I was cowed by Catholic intransigence but because I was excluded by liberal Lutheran narrowness! The Lutheran minister in question (a most amiable man, incidentally) was discussing with me the declaration he had composed in preparation for the Eucharist the following Sunday when he suddenly grew very angry. He was incensed at those Catholics in Tantur who do not go to receive communion at the hands of Protestant ministers. He went on and on against those people 'who are not prepared to share in the Lord's Supper until they have reached complete agreement on every jot and tittle of doctrine'.

I did not consider it politic at that particular spasm of his anger to remind him that in Jesus' teaching not one jot or tittle of the Torah is to pass away until heaven and earth pass away. Instead I told him that if he estimated Catholic doctrinal hesitations to be so completely insubstantial then he did not understand what the Eucharist is for Catholics. The consequence of which, though I did not say it aloud, is that Catholics could hardly be expected to join in a ritual with someone for whom the meaning of the ritual is so substantially different. The effect of his statement upon me was to make me realise that I could not now receive communion at his hands, as I had hoped to do. He had made me feel unwelcome unless beforehand I would accept that the hesitations of Catholics (and Orthodox and certain Anglican and Lutherans, for that matter) are senseless and even – so the overtones suggested – wicked.

I learnt subsequently that certain Catholics who had gone to communion that day were deeply upset afterwards at the careless manner in which our Lutheran friend had disposed of the remains of the sacred species in the chalice and on the communion plate.

Today's experience was perhaps even sadder because the shock happened at the very last moment.

For a whole variety of considerations that had been exercising me day in and day out I went into chapel this morning feeling that I could in peace and good conscience receive communion from the Protestant celebrant. And I remained happy and at peace until the very moment when we were gathered around the altar. Then, to my astonishment, the celebrant suddenly launched into a mini-homily, criticising those who do not come to communion and asserting that 'anyone who believes in the words of the Lord Jesus ought to come and receive.'

Coming at just the moment when I was so open to the Lord, so unguarded and vulnerable, his words landed in my heart like so many blows from the hands of a bully. I simply froze and could not go through with my intention to receive communion.

Why did that good man suddenly launch into that unfortunate homily? It must be a measure of how wounded he has been by our impossible situation. And the wound suddenly burst.

26th December, 1983. Tantur.

What impressive people there are amongst the Bethlehem Peace Pilgrims! From the very old to the very young.

I have been astonished at the maturity of the youngsters. As, for instance, when one of them, a slim, bespectacled girl was asked at a moment's notice to summarise what the pilgrimage had come to mean for her. Modestly, yet quite composed, she formulated her answer in a few beautifully balanced sentences. In brief, she said that a pilgrim is 'one who asks. We asked for food; and it was given to us. We asked for shelter; and it was given to us. We asked for encouragement; and it was given to us in abundance. And now we are asking God for peace for all the earth . . . and we have faith that peace also will surely be given to us.'

But in outward appearance, at least, the most striking member of the pilgrim group, with his mahogany-coloured face and luxuriant, silken white beard, is Fr George Zabelka. He it was who in 1945 had served on Tinian Island in the Pacific as chaplain to the Allied airmen who went on to drop bombs on Hiroshima and Nagasaki. His observations on the pilgrimage I found specially intriguing.

According to Fr George the country in which they encountered the most stubborn polarisation in the debate about nuclear weapons was England. By contrast in Northern Ireland, in spite of the warlike atmosphere, they found the people to be wonderfully warm and open to discussion of the issue. The country where the populace seemed to have been best educated by their government on nuclear matters was Greece.

But it was after they landed at Haifa and had begun to thread their way through Israel and the West Bank that they walked into a seemingly impenetrable wall, resistant to the witness for peace they had been trying to offer over the course of their 12,000 kilometre pilgrimage. That resistance, constituted by mutual suspicion, hatred, lying and the burning resentment of the Arabs against their oppressors – all these obstacles, Fr George said, meant that 'it is this last stage of our journey through the Holy Land, that has revealed to us the point of it all. For me these last days of our approach to Jerusalem have crystallised what it is all about. It is here, where we have met the greatest resistance to our message of peace, that peace on earth will be born again.'

Unbeknown to himself Fr George was affirming what I had said recently at the inauguration of our Academy of Peace: 'Already, thousands of years ago, the skein of human destiny began to coil itself around the city of Jerusalem, one end being twisted around the city and the other end threatening to entangle the whole earth.' The same sentiment was expressed to me some months ago by Herr Brandt, the German TV producer, who had been making documentaries about Jerusalem and Tantur. I met him near our reception desk one Sunday morning when the place was deserted and rather forlorn looking, though not so forlorn as Herr Brandt looked. He seemed so depressed, in fact, that I thought to cheer him up by inviting him to come to our apartment for a cup of coffee.

He followed me down to our apartment in silence and remained silent for a while as he took his first mouthfuls of coffee. And then, raising his head as if it were leaden with weariness, he said despairingly, *'Hier ist alles vergiftet'* ('Here' – that is, in Jerusalem – 'everything is poisoned'). What had caused him such despair was an incident from the previous day, when he had been trying to get a picture of the status within the Christian community of the Orthodox Church in Jerusalem. In order to do so he had interviewed a Catholic priest, a German, who is well known to be close in spirit to the Orthodox, namely Fr Düssing, as gentle a man as you will meet and amazingly well informed on all questions concerning the Orthodox Church. Typical of his benevolent and clean-hearted approach to life and to his fellow human beings, Fr Düssing had come to revere and love Orthodoxy not through study of Byzantine art or through the mystical teachings of Mount Athos but by way of long harsh years as a prisoner of war in Russia, years of which he speaks with no trace of bitterness but rather with an abiding gratitude for their having brought him into contact with Russians.

It was no more than twenty minutes after conducting the interview with Fr Düssing, sighed Herr Brandt, that a messenger arrived, despatched by a Latin[5] prelate, to protest against Brandt for his taking the views of Fr Düssing as an accurate indicator of the position of the Orthodox Church in Jerusalem. Every one in Jerusalem knows, the message went on, that Fr Düssing sees every deed of the Orthodox through rosy-tinted spectacles. 'Presumably', Herr Brandt said, 'the Latin authorities would have been happier if I had managed to present a person prepared to divulge some scandal about the Orthodox. *Hier ist alles vergiftet.*'

'A golden bowl filled with scorpions' is the Arab description to correspond with Herr Brandt's experience, and I am sure that young Dean McFalls would not quarrel with that description after his own treatment since arriving in this 'City of Peace'. Throughout much of the Peace Pilgrimage Dean has been acting as their spokesperson and seems to have done the job very well – until he found himself in this 'golden bowl', where he is completely out of his depth! When questioned by the local press as to the kind of reception the pilgrims had received between Haifa and Jerusalem from Jews and Arabs he answered very honestly and, as he thought, in a balanced and peaceable fashion. From the way in which he was immediately castigated by both Jews and Arabs and their respective supporters he is beginning to learn that what the rest of the world means by balance and peace bears no relationship to what the words mean in Jerusalem. When I spoke with him today his eyes were the eyes of a man who had just been shell-shocked.

Many of these issues came up this evening when I invited the senior members of the pilgrimage to come to our apartment for a drink. But what intrigued me most was the answer they gave to a question I put to them. I said, 'You have all walked 12,000 kilometres, and you have been received by every kind of person, from the lowest to the highest, including many religious leaders. Could you say which, if any, of those people has most impressed you?'

They all sat silently for a while before beginning to exchange comments. Then all of a sudden they came to an agreement. 'Yes, we were most impressed by the Mayor of Marzobotto. He is a Communist, and Marzobotto is a Communist town south of Bologna.' I have to confess that their answer tickled me: Christian pilgrim reports that it was not a Christian dignatory but a Communist mayor who had most impressed them!

27th December, 1983. Letter to the Tablet

How mysterious is the process by which certain truths dawn upon one! In the past I never took seriously some statements made by my friend Hassan Askari, who teaches at Selly Oak, Birmingham, even though I have the deepest regard for him and his perceptions. It was more than ten years ago that he wrote:

The Palestinian question is neither a Russian question nor an American question. It is neither a socialist nor a capitalist issue . . . The Palestinian question is a question concerning the people of the Book . . . The whole world will either be saved or will perish on account of it . . . The life and death of the human spirit depends upon the way in which the Palestinian question is resolved.

Since I am extremely sceptical of all such eschatological declarations, especially when they are so firmly linked with specific issues, I had thought Professor Askari's pronouncement to be a great exaggeration. But, standing before several hundred Jews, Muslims and Christians and addressing them at the opening of our Peace Academy, as I looked down upon the audience I suddenly became convinced that Hassan is right: the life and death of the human spirit depends upon the way in which the Palestinian question is resolved.

Having been formed in the critical Oxford tradition, however, my mind immediately started to explain my conviction away, on the ground that I was simply on a personal 'high' because so many of my aspirations seemed at that moment to be converging and confirming one another.

Amongst the audience, for instance, were the Bethlehem Peace Pilgrims who had set off on foot on Good Friday, 1982, from the Trident Nuclear Submarine Base at Bangor (near Seattle), the home of the deadliest weapons system on earth. Well before they had set out, in 1981, I had seen a notice of their intended pilgrimage in a newspaper and had written to their initiator, Fr Jack Morris SJ, to offer the pilgrims hospitality at Tantur on the last stage of their journey to Bethlehem. And here they were now, some eighteen months and 7,000 miles later, about twenty of them, weather-beaten and looking deeply drained of energy; yet steadfast, and confirmed in their resolve to make peace.

Also, we had managed, against all the odds, to have available for sale in our auditorium a little booklet entitled

The Possession and Use of Nuclear Weapons in the Light of Torah, Gospel and Sharia. As I explain in my Preface to the booklet the task of finding a rabbi on the one hand and a sheikh on the other prepared to deliver the lectures on which the booklet is based was no easy one – nobody in these parts is eager to take up the nuclear issue because of a general awareness, all the more agonising through being suppressed, that one might thereby touch off the final explosion.

Yet eventually Rabbi Pinhas Peli, of Ben Gurion University, in Beersheva, and Sheikh Muhammad Al Husseini, judge of the Islamic Court, in Jerusalem, generously took the risk. And there the two of them were, sitting in front of me, my Jewish friend and my Muslim friend, come to help inaugurate our Academy of Peace.

So I was seeing realised before my own eyes another of my aspirations, an aspiration that I always associate with my dead friend, the Russian thinker Nikolai Fyodorov. Fyodorov used to say that the restoration of kinship amongst mankind requires that those who do not generally speak to one another should begin to speak with one another. And this was what happened during the reception that went on for several hours after the inaugural lecture: Jews and Arabs, both Muslim and Christian, who would otherwise never have anything to do with one another were together in the same company. I do not say that they all came to love, or even to like, one another, but they did at least begin to recognise one another as human beings and not demons.

And all this was happening by virtue of the Peace Academy which we were inaugurating at Tantur. I had recognised the desirability of it already two years ago. I had felt in those days that none of us had quite woken up to the potentiality of our Institute, unique in the Middle East, as a location for peace making. For, according to international law, we were situated in occupied territory, whereas, according to Israeli law, we belonged in the municipality of Jerusalem. The scholars who have come

198

to us belong to different Christian traditions, whilst the staff has always included Christians, Muslims and Jews. And here now was our international president, Landrum Bolling, explaining to our guests just what had prompted the founding of the Academy of Peace as part of our work.

For him, also, the day represented a climax, since throughout his life as scholar, journalist and fund-raiser, his two main concerns have been peacemaking and the convergence of world faiths. 'The nuclear issue', he said, 'is essentially a moral issue. No nation has the right to use nuclear arms, no matter how just its cause, and set off the kind of global conflagration that would threaten the continuation of life on this planet. That is a declaration on which the adherents of all religious faiths can unite . . .' Moreover, 'we must begin the quest for peace with the cultivation of the individual's search for inner calm, strength, serenity – the peace within.'

The Inter-Faith Academy of Peace will provide a location where scholars of all faiths are to be invited to learn together how to live in peace and to make peace. Some scholars will come for two or three months and others for nine months. As a team they will be responsible for issuing a quarterly bulletin so as to make the results of their studies and experiences available in the market place. From the beginning it is being made clear to scholars that they are not being invited into an ivory tower. Tantur is in the eye of most of the whirlwinds that swirl around the Middle East – 'a high risk venture', as Bolling put it.

28th December, 1983. Tantur

As I was sitting at my desk in the Rector's office early this afternoon I experienced a profound sense of peace. It was one of those ecstatically beautiful days such as Palestine in winter sometimes bestows upon us. The brilliant light of the afternoon sun was flooding over the white stones of the enclosure in which my office is situated. A fresh wind was rippling the surface of the pool which stretches the length of the courtyard and draws one's gaze beyond the high walls of the Institute eastwards towards the tiny Arab village of Umm Tuba, the minaret of its mosque just visible beyond a bend of the hill. Often, sitting at my desk, I hear the call of the muezzin echoing from that minaret across the stony hills around Ramat Rachel and Bethlehem, and ruminate in awe upon the mystery of human existence, thinking how strange it is that within two miles of our modern, American-style way of life there should stand village communities, such as Umm Tuba, the pattern of whose culture is worlds apart from ours and goes back to far more ancient roots.

The enclosed courtyard and the ancient landscape always give me the sense of being protected and at peace. That was particularly true this afternoon since there was no one in the library. All the scholars were out for the day, our Arab domestic staff had all gone home, and quiet prevailed throughout the building. I was looking forward to several hours without interruption during which I could work steadily through the backlog of Institute business that had accumulated on my desk.

Just then the phone rang. It was Geries, our receptionist, to say that someone had arrived at the reception desk, unannounced and without an appointment, and wishing to speak with me. At which moment I could have sworn that the backlog on my desk grinned up at me as if to say, 'You're not going to get rid of us today!' Heavy of heart, I muttered, 'Who is he?' 'He says he is a theologian from Strasbourg', came the reply from Geries, who plies a quiet line of mockery at human absurdity. 'A theologian from Strasbourg'; the phrase sounded like the title of a play on the life of a present-day Martin Bucer who had wandered into the Holy Land, possibly to torture my brain on his forerunner's subject of the Eucharist.

'Bring him across', I said to Geries, at the same time making a mental resolution to welcome this wandering theologian in the manner that St Benedict orders us to receive guests: 'All guests to the monastery should be welcomed as Christ, because He will say, "I was a a stranger and you took me in."'

As so often happens when one fears the worst, the reality, in this case a Strasbourg theologian, proved on the contrary to be quite pleasant. Long-winded he certainly was, but pleasant; and so it was not too difficult to give him my full attention for an hour and a half in spite of the pile of papers staring up at me from my desk. And he himself seemed very contented with his visit, after he had taken a cup of tea, when I accompanied him across our garden to bid him farewell.

But the farewell did not last long – no more, in fact, than two or three minutes. Because I was just on the point of stepping into my office once more when the same man burst through the doors of our administration wing almost convulsed with excitement, and in broken, agitated English gasped something about a young man being hurt. I quickly realised there was no way that the cause of his excitement was going to become clear to me through his incoherent words, and so I told him to show me what was wrong.

It had to be something very urgent because our un-athletic-looking theologian from Strasbourg broke out into a clod-hopping run as he led me along rocky paths towards a rather remote quarter of our grounds. There no words were needed to tell me what was amiss: our Arab worker, Fawzi, had somehow managed to pinion himself between the branch of an olive tree and the seat of the tractor which he had been driving. It was certainly a dramatic sight – Fawzi suspended in silhouette against the pale evening sky and the distant hills of Moab – like some sacrificial victim, with his left arm trapped firmly by a branch of the olive tree and the seat of the tractor neatly slotted against his arched backbone, as if holding him in place for the *coup de grâce*. To make matters worse, two of our Arab employees now rushed up and, in their anguish at Fawzi's cries, began frantically to try to move the tractor, not realising that if they lost control of it on the slope then the tractor would slip and the seat would thrust violently upwards and might break Fawzi's spine.

In that moment I bitterly regretted my inadequate Arabic which left me unable to explain the danger. But fortunately Geries now arrived and translated my warning. Better still, I was able to direct him to send for the paramedics to come immediately from the Husseini Hospital in Beit Jala.

In the meantime Fawzi was getting more and more desperate, having been suspended in this manner for at least half an hour; fearing moreover that he was never again to see his wife and children. And though I tried to reassure him, I was myself worried on account of his left arm, which was now deathly cold due to the lack of circulation. I was frightened that gangrene might soon set in.

We all began to breathe easier again, therefore, when we heard the roar of the para-medics' ambulance along the bottom road some eighty yards below us, followed by the tremendous clanging of a fire brigade bell. At which point something extraordinary happened.

Standing at a bus-stop on the bottom road as the ambulance and the fire brigade roared towards the distant entrance to the Institute was a little group of Arab construction workers. They are to be seen at the same stop every evening waiting to catch the Hebron bus, weary from the long day which sucks them into Israel in the early hours and then disgorges them back on to the West Bank in the evening. Today there were about eight of them standing together at the stop, their eyes turned towards Jerusalem, awaiting their bus. As soon as they heard the alarm bell of the fire brigade and saw the ambulance speeding past they looked round and caught a glimpse of us amongst the olive trees. Within seconds they had all scrambled over our seven foot outer wall, and despite their heavy boots they were positively flying up the slope to where Fawzi was trapped, their eyes blazing with determination to aid whoever was in distress.

Never have I seen a group of men respond so spontaneously and instantly to a cry for help. Even now I do not understand how they managed to get over the wall so quickly – as though, in spite of the weariness in their limbs from the day's labour, some invisible spring-heels enabled them to leap over the wall at one bound. And, of course, they proved invaluable at helping the para-medics to bend the olive branch slowly, to hold the tractor from slipping, and then, very gently, to draw Fawzi out of his trap, almost as though they were delivering a new-born baby.

Back now from the Husseini hospital, relieved that Fawzi's back is not broken nor his arm in danger of gangrene, I wonder again at the fine and incredibly complex web of human relations. Suppose that our theologian from Strasbourg had not called this afternoon I might have spent a peaceful few hours clearing my desk; but then he would not have heard Fawzi's cries, and with darkness and the chill of night setting in, perhaps Fawzi would now be dead, his wife a widow and his children orphans.

31st December, 1983. Tantur

'So and so has flipped.' That is a sentence which Dorothy and I often find ourselves saying to one another rather wearily and with slight exasperation. We do so when one or other of us discovers that a member of our community has 'flipped' from a condition of seeing everything through Jewish eyes to seeing everything through Arab eyes, or vice versa (which happens less frequently).

The usual pattern is that a scholar comes to Tantur with a highly idealised picture of Israel and of Jewish achievement in the land, and with an equally distorted image of Arabs as terrorists. Then they personally experience some harassment by Israelis or else they see the day-to-day oppression endured by Arabs, and they flip – now

Arabs can do no wrong, and Israelis can do nothing right!

Americans, with their simplistic view of the world and their anti-Arab media, are particularly prone to flip. But it can happen to almost anyone – even, in a strange way, to a Jew! I am thinking of the evening when Sarah Rosenblum picked us up in her car to drive us to Bethlehem, where all three of us were to have dinner with some American friends. A Jewish immigrant from South Africa, Sarah had pooh-poohed the suggestion that Bethlehem in the dark was no place for a Jewish person to be visiting. During the course of that evening she made one or two derogatory remarks about 'the Arab mentality', especially their habit of forever bewailing their 'oppression'. Not wanting an argument the rest of us kept quiet. But Sarah received a marvellously apt riposte that same night as we were returning home around eleven o'clock.

By this late hour the Israeli army had established a roadblock on the Jerusalem road, and as we approached it Dorothy and I naturally anticipated that Sarah would slow down and stop. Instead she kept going at the same speed until two soldiers brandished their machine guns at us. They made her stop and ordered her to wind down the car window. 'What the hell do you think you are doing?' they shouted at her and made her reverse back to the line of the road block. She was so shocked that she said very little; I could only conclude she had thought that Jews do not have to take notice of road blocks! Moreover, she had almost certainly not taken it in that the two soldiers were not in fact Jews but were Druse. Some Druse may well be ready to serve in the Israeli army, but that does not mean they love Jews, whom they even enjoy taking down a peg.

Once the short altercation was over Sarah drove on silently for about half a mile and then burst out indignantly, 'This place is getting like South Africa!' God forgive me, but I nearly cracked out laughing to see how she had so quickly changed her tune: the very slightest touch of harassment on one's own skin, and one flips.

A more serious case, however, faced me this afternoon when I returned to find awaiting me two American journalists, a writer and a photographer from the *Middletown Gazette*. They were beside themselves with anger.

Their story was that they had come with a group of fellow-citizens from Middletown, a Jewish group who had collected $75,000 to establish a project in Galilee for which they expect to be able to raise altogether $3 million within the next two years. The Jewish group had offered to pay all the journalists' expenses for the ten-day tour, but the two of them had wisely declined on the ground that they wished to retain their professional independence, a decision for which they were now heartily grateful.

For the first week of their stay in Israel they had been kept very busy going from one Jewish project to another, with all of which they had been most impressed, as they also had been with the Jewish officials, rabbis and media workers to whom they had been introduced. But as the days went by they became increasingly conscious of a niggle at the back of their minds: why was it that the group leader always headed them off when they tried to broach the subject of the Arabs? and especially when they suggested exploring the West Bank? They began to feel that they were being brainwashed when this latter suggestion was always greeted with the words, 'There's no point – so little there to see.' The photographer, Fred, was particularly sensitive on account of an incident on the plane coming over. Sitting next to an Israeli woman he had asked, in the course of their conversation, what was to happen to the Arabs. She replied, 'We should annihilate them.'

So Fred and his colleague, Doug, had cut loose from the party and headed for Jerusalem. This morning they had spent several hours at the memorial to the Holocaust victims at Yad Vashem, and then driven from there straight to the refugee camp at Deheishe, where some 8,000 Arabs live in desperate conditions. As I looked at their faces it was clear that both of them were in a state of shock as a result of both these experiences.

Then they started telling me how the experience of Yad Vashem and of Deheishe seemed to them all of a piece; and they had been reinforced in this impression by the interview they had just concluded with the Arab Mayor of Bethlehem, Elias Freij. He, on learning that they had come straight from Yad Vashem, had commented that, 'The Jews, in their turn, are trying to put a holocaust on us', and had gone on to speak of the 'genocide' of the Palestinian people.

Fred and Doug nearly jumped out of their chairs when they saw my reaction to these statements. 'What on earth does Freij mean?' I exclaimed. 'None of his family have been taken to death camps and executed! In fact, so far as I know, none of them have even been arrested by the Israelis. There is no Treblinka on the West Bank. Arabs are allowed to leave the country if they wish. You are free to go into Deheishe and take photographs and publish them in the world press. There is much oppression on the West Bank, and I see it every day of my life, but the degree of oppression here is light years distant from what happened to the Jews in Europe. It is simply immoral, and no service to anyone, to use terms like "holocaust" and "genocide" in that irresponsible fashion.'

Poor dears! They looked as though my reaction had just given a final turn to the violent tumble-dryer in which they had been tossed about these last ten days, buffeted by Jews, Arabs, Muslims, Christians and now at the hand of this exasperated Englishman. And perhaps there was more yet to come. Fred, the photographer, explained rather plaintively that he had just telephoned his official Israeli contact in Tel Aviv to discover whether on leaving Israel he would have to clear his photographs with a censor. 'Don't worry', his contact said calmly. 'The authorities already know that you have been in Deheishe.'

206

The speed of the Israeli intelligence network had left Fred and Doug open-mouthed and eager to get back to Middletown.

2nd January, 1984. Tantur

In future I am going to ask every appointed celebrant of the Sunday Eucharist to draw up a statement of what, in their faith, they believe is taking place in the worshipping community when they preside at the celebration. Each such statement will be given to every member of our community on the Monday before the Sunday when the Eucharist is to be celebrated. After that whoever comes to communion is not a matter for the celebrant to decide but for each worshipper in his or her own conscience.

2nd February, 1984. Tantur

Arnold phoned this morning to say that he would like to talk with me. He asked if I would go into Jerusalem to meet him in some quiet spot where we could talk undisturbed; so I suggested the garden of Christ Church, near the Jaffa Gate, and that is where we met about eleven o'clock.

He is worn out – and I am not surpised – through his endless showing of *The Work*, a slide show which he asked permission to present to our scholars in October. It is really the story of his life: how as a boy of twelve he was taken to Auschwitz: how at the selection he was sent one way – eventually to survive – and his father sent the other way – into the gas chamber.

Arnold survived through the goodness of older prisoners and his own power of fantasy – he convinced himself that he was really a bird and could have flown out of Auschwitz whenever he chose. After being rescued by the Americans and taken to the U.S. he managed to suppress completely the experience of Auschwitz from his consciousness. He married and had children. Some ten years ago he thought that if he were to have his concentration camp tattoo number erased from his arm that would prove that he had never been in Auschwitz.

At which point the suppressed Auschwitz experience exploded inside him and fragmented his life. He went to pieces: his marriage broke up and his children were estranged from him. He was lost; and realised that he would have to return to Auschwitz to examine the camp registers showing that he indeed had been there. He would then have to pick up the thread and follow it into the present.

When he did that something amazing happened. Like a revelation from God he was brought to see that the Holocaust of which the Jews were the victims is also a foreshadowing of a nuclear holocaust which is to be the fate of the whole human family unless human beings are awakened to the peril. Arnold has a call from God to ensure that the human family does not go blindly into death as so many Jews did. Hence his slide show, *The Work*, is the story of his own life, and a warning to the whole human family.

When I agreed to his showing *The Work* one evening last October I had no idea of the powerful effect it was going to have on the Tantur Community. Normally they are a loquacious group, ready to discuss anything whatsoever at a moment's notice. But after Arnold had finished his presentation that evening in October all of them sat quite still, and silent. After a time I quietly suggested that we should disperse in silence; and we did so, much as worshippers reverently move away from the altar after receiving communion.

These events were going through my mind as Arnold told me of his weariness and asked whether he might come and live with us until he feels better. I also remembered hearing of objections being raised some years ago against a rabbi being lodged for a week at Tantur on the grounds that it is a Christian institution. In the case of Arnold I was not prepared to take any notice of such objections. He is coming here tomorrow.

8th February, 1984. Tantur

I must be very dim to have forgotten the lesson of the 'Carlos' of February, 1982. During the last two years we have held many such gatherings that have proved healing for all of us, but this evening I allowed almost precisely the same mistake to occur as on that previous occasion. What I did then was to allow the tone of the meeting to be set by someone who dismissed the need to carry one another's burdens. This evening I did not prevent our resident comedian from striking the note at the beginning which was to determine the tone for the rest of the 'Carlos'.

Our comedian blew in here a month ago clearly intent upon occupying centre stage and being the life and soul of the party. And on a number of occasions his act has been a real boon to the community by raising spirits when they were drooping. But there is a distinct limit upon the extent to which jokes and fooling around can be invoked as a means of resolving a community's problems. Once they are taken beyond the limit they have the opposite effect: they prove stultifying.

Thinking over our comedian's behaviour I also remembered that he arrived rather late and so missed the opening prayers. Arriving rather late is a habit of his, another of his little tricks to draw attention to himself. His entrance, therefore, caught us all vulnerable, still in a passive attitude from our prayers, and we were therefore easily thrown by his amusing stories about certain bizarre aspects of our buildings. And even though I fairly quickly realised what our comedian was up to and sent out oblique signals to the rest of the group to change the course of the discussion they were too mesmerized by our comedian, already too caught up in his act, to catch on to my signals. I was reminded of the saying, 'We have piped unto you, and ye have not danced; we have mourned unto you, and ye have

209

not lamented.' Instead they followed the Pied Piper – with no great harm, it is true, but perhaps the custom of the 'Carlos' has been devalued for the rest of this academic year.

But what should I have done? Should I have issued a rebuke early on? I could have said, 'Don't be so childish!' but when I did that once I nearly brought down disaster. Also it would have been unfair, because our comedian is a good-hearted person. Yet I have come to see how vital it is in meetings, whether of two or of two hundred people, for the first note to be an appropriate one for the occasion – because it will set the tone for all that follows. Perhaps it is a good convention that no one arriving late is allowed to open proceedings. And it would also help if the leader or moderator of such meetings were briefly to tell the story of previous meetings – 'getting everyone on board', as the Americans so aptly describe the process of making sure that no one is left out kicking and screaming and generating disharmony.

27th February, 1984. Tantur

I know that one should never look for rewards but, at the same time, there would be something wrong with you if you did not feel deeply thankful when they come along. Certainly this evening brought perhaps the most rewarding moment of my whole time at Tantur when our Jewish friend, Arnold, came into our apartment to take his leave. Having been with us for five weeks by now he says that he feels at peace with himself and ready to carry on with his work.

As we sat together drinking tea I realised that Arnold was struggling to get something out which was very important to him, something for which he could not find adequate words. Since he could not manage it he began instead to ask me how much he should pay for his stay with us. The dear man – I knew how little money he has. And his hesitancy moved me to the verge of tears, as I am often moved when I see poor people made aware of their lack of money. That is probably because their lack of money reveals their powerlessness and consequent vulnerability. And for the same reason so many of those sermons I hear on 'the Cross', and on Christianity as 'the way of powerlessness', sound hollow to me because I know that the preacher has money, as well as education and social esteem, and he himself, therefore, is far from powerless.

For one brief moment there was a flicker in Arnold's eyes and a movement of his hands in which I thought I perceived the shadow of his helplessness, years gone by, in the concentration camp. But he relaxed when I laughed and said I could hardly ask a guest to pay us for hospitality! But then I realised that to leave the matter there might only render Arnold's feeling of impotence more acute; and so I said, truthfully enough, that many of our guests made small contributions to our staff fund and he might like to do the same.

But all of this, in any case, was just a form of clearing the way for what he had really come to tell me.

'During the course of my life, Don', Arnold said very deliberately, 'many, many Christians have spoken to me about how much they loved me, and what they intended to do for me. But in every case it eventually became clear that ultimately, somewhere at the back of their minds, they were wanting me to convert – and my being aware of that eliminated everything they had previously said to me or done for me. It was really a way of saying to me, "We don't accept you until and unless you convert. As a Jew you don't really exist for us until you convert."

'But here, at Tantur, for the first time, I feel that I have been completely accepted as I am, by everyone in the community. In the five weeks I have been with you, in the dining hall, the seminar room, on field trips, over coffee, at no time have I ever felt any breath of a suggestion that I should convert. And I want just to thank you for that.'

Soon afterwards Arnold stood up to say 'Good night' and leave our apartment. For my own part I sat without moving for a long time, reflecting on what he had said, my whole being suffused with joy, and with gratitude to the entire community here for having maintained a clean heart towards Arnold during his stay with us.

At the same time I remained puzzled by what seems to be an inner contradiction in my own attitude towards our Jewish brethren. I do not work or pray for their conversion. Yet whenever one of my Jewish friends becomes a Christian I have to acknowledge that joy springs up in my heart, just as it does when I hear of anyone of whatever tradition finding Christ. I know that some Christians of my acquaintance who specialise in Jewish–Christian dialogue would frown upon my joy because they are so fiercely opposed to Jews converting in any circumstances.

But do even those Christians seriously suggest that it would in some way have been better, for instance, if Edith Stein, the brilliant Jewish agnostic philosopher who became a Carmelite nun and died in Auschwitz, had never been converted? Anyone who studies her life must surely recognise that it was through her conversion that she became one of the unquestionably holy people of the twentieth century. Such was the impression she made upon all who met her, as for example the Dutchman who encountered her in the transit camp on the way to Auschwitz:

The one nun who caught my attention immediately and whom I have never forgotten in spite of the many horrible episodes which I have seen, was the woman with a smile that was not a mask but a warm radiance . . . I knew this was truly a great woman. In the hell of Westerbork she lived only a few days, walked among the prisoners, talking and praying like a saint. Yes, that's what she was . . . She spoke in such a humble and clear way that anybody who listened to her was seized. A talk with her was like a voyage into another world.

212

Following a strict interpretation of Jewish law one would have to believe, nevertheless, that Edith Stein, as an apostate from Judaism, has 'lost her part in the world to come'. There has to be something wrong about a law which so condemns a saint.

29th February, 1984. Tantur

One of the saddest and most depressing features of living in the Middle East is the fact that you can so often predict how people are going to react to some event. What makes this experience so sad and depressing is because it seems almost to prove beyond a doubt that no one is prepared for any new initiative or imaginative liberation from inculcated patterns of behaviour.

Some weeks ago, for instance, Dorothy and I were discussing the film *Gandhi,* which we had seen in England, and wondering how it would be received when it was shown in Israel. 'I'll guess', I said to Dorothy. 'The Israelis will really dislike it because they will want not to receive the message of the film. But, at the same time, because of their liberal, democratic heritage they will not want to admit how much they dislike it. So they will criticise it fiercely for any small errors or technical failings that they can point to in order to distract attention from the message.'

Reading the review of *Gandhi* in the *Jerusalem Post* you might have imagined that I had managed to substitute myself for the paper's film critic and had written the review specifically in order to prove the accuracy of my prediction. The reviewer writes exactly what I foresaw.

17th March, 1984. Sinai

During the past week there has been no time to make any entries in this journal because the last seven days have been spent in the Sinai desert engaged in a peace meeting with some hundred or so other persons. There were Jews from Israel and the diaspora and Muslims from all parts of the globe except the West Bank; there were Christians from Israel, Europe and North America as well as a good number of Japanese Buddhists and one Japanese Christian. We had all been enjoined to keep the meeting secret because the Egyptian authorities were nervous lest other Arab states should learn about this conference of Egyptians and Israelis just when Egypt is trying to draw nearer once more to the Arab powers.

And what a kaleidoscope of experience the week has provided, from the first moment on Monday morning when our group assembled early at the Jaffa Gate to make the long journey down past Eilat and on into Egypt.

At the corner of Greek Catholic Street I saw two Arab Christians, one from Nazareth and the other from Haifa. They were standing apart from the rest of the group, which was composed mainly of American and Israeli Jews, most of whom were laughing and joking. The two Arabs were clearly nervous. You could tell that from the rapid puffs they were taking at their cigarettes and by their defensively drawn faces. I guessed that they are unsure of how their consorting with Jews will be looked upon by their fellow Arabs – by those sitting at their stalls around the square, for instance, who are selling pitta bread and falafel and occasionally casting suspicious glances towards this strange gathering.

I strolled over to the two Arabs and quietly let them know that I also am Christian, a Catholic, and this seemed to reassure them and help them to relax – though not sufficiently to persuade them to accompany me when I moved over soon afterwards to join the Jewish group. 'Swie, swie,'[6] I thought.

Once I approached the Jewish group I was immediately recognised and greeted by both friends and strangers, a heart-warming moment on such a chilly morning.

Amongst the group were two men whom I had not previously met but to whom I was immediately attracted.

214

One was a very straight-looking man – straight not only in his physical bearing but also in his speech and facial expression. I later learnt that he is Mordechai Baron, a career soldier of distinction who has recently retired from the Israeli army. The other person was quite different, a gentle, quizzical man who drifted around the edges of the group looking as though his face might break out into a smile at any moment. I heard someone call him Avraham.

It was already mid-afternoon by the time we reached the tiny port of Taba in Egyptian territory on the Gulf of Aquaba. There we changed into trucks for the five-hour drive over the bumpy desert roads that lead up to Sinai. For the following hour upon hour our bones were shaken almost out of their sockets as our Bedouin driver seemed to hit every rock in the desert, and as my ten companions in the back of the truck coughed away on account of the clouds of dust that kept swirling into the truck and choking mouths and noses. I was spared that ordeal because I had brought with me my keffiyeh which I wrapped round my face in best Bedouin fashion to keep out the dust. Nor was that the only unpleasantness from which I was spared by my keffiyeh. For the keffiyeh around my mouth, keeping me silent, provided a satisfactory explanation for some of my companions as to why I was not joining in a conversation that one or two of them were maintaining which was not edifying. What saddened me was not so much the unpleasant feeling of possibly being thought prudish for not joining in the banter but rather the fact that some people setting out on a peace pilgrimage seemed unaware of the strict discipline of mind and heart and tongue which peace work demands.

By the time we rumbled into our camp ground of Abu Zeituna the night was dark with the darkness of the desert, and already most of the conference members had arrived and established themselves in the various tents and had equipped themselves with the blankets and sleeping bags which the organisers had promised us. And within a few

215

minutes most of the companions of our journey had done likewise, except for the man whom I had noticed early that morning at the Jaffa Gate, and who was evidently called Avraham. So the two of us stood waiting around in the centre of the camp site for half an hour or more whilst organisers came and went, all announcing that the tents were full and that there were no sleeping bags for us. Though we each felt somewhat incompetent and foolish to have been left standing there, nevertheless it did give us the opportunity to get to know one another. I, for my part, was delighted to discover that my companion was Avraham Weiner, whose book *9½ mystics*, I have read and re-read, enchanted by its gentle wisdom.

By a further piece of good luck we eventually found ourselves allocated to the same tent, which gave promise of our being able to further the friendship which had begun with our wait in the centre of the camp ground.

The following morning the delegates held a common service of prayer out in the desert – the place was actually a natural bowl formed by the surrounding high ground. At first we felt rather eerie since even as we were praying we could see, silhouetted against the ardent blue sky, the figures of Egyptian soldiers who had been posted there – whether to protect us or keep an eye on us was not explained.

First of all it was our Jewish brethren who prayed; powerfully led by my friend Rabbi Zalman Schachter, they called upon God to lead us on the paths of peace. They were followed by the Christians, then the Japanese Buddhists and then an American Indian, and finally by the Muslims, disciplined as always and in their very postures a sign of the 'straight path'. The sincerity of all the prayers drew each of us into a deep sense of the peace that was descending upon our whole assembly. And then the screaming began!

At first I had no idea where the screaming was coming from, not until I noticed that there was a circle of little black objects situated at intervals in the sand around the man who was praying. Each little black object was about four or five yards distant from the man. I then realised that they were recording instruments meant to record our prayers (as if God could not be trusted to do so!): and the tuning of the instruments themselves was achieved by means of a further series of machines in the hands of various Japanese members of the assembly. And, presumably, these latter had not got their tuning accurately adjusted because all manner of weird shrieks were being emitted from their machines and had now reduced the man who was supposed to be praying into stunned silence.

At this point in the proceedings I hardly dared so much as glance at my companions nearby for fear that I should disgrace myself on this awesome occasion by bursting into laughter at the sight of the disorientated Japanese. They were looking completely startled, trying in their puzzlement to understand what was distressing their gods in the little black boxes so deeply that they were shrieking in this furious manner. The word which flashed through my own mind was that our assembly of ancient religions had been invaded by the gods of technology: these invaders had silenced man and were now busy recording each other's prayers, technological shrieks to render human prayers superfluous.

Happily, however, it is true of human beings that our weakness is also our strength because by one o'clock everyone was both hungry and desperately thirsty. So the machines were switched off, formal prayers ceased and we all trooped back to our camp ground.

But in the next two or three days I came to realise more sharply the significance of Jacob's words at Bethel, 'How terrifying is this place!', meaning not just that the desert is a place of terror, but that any place to which one pilgrimages in search of the holy, and particularly in search of peace, will also inexorably search out one's own impurities.

This truth was borne in upon me by the train of events when we climbed Mount Sinai itself during the night in order to be standing at the summit gazing towards the sun as it rose the next morning over the long ridge eastwards of the Mount. In fact the ascent of the mountain in the pitch blackness went off very well indeed, with almost everyone in our large contingent showing genuine consideration for the less robust of our companions. One or two sturdy characters, it is true, dodged their share of pack-bearing but there were always others ready cheerfully to take up the slack.

But it was the sunrise itself which was to reveal not only the incredible beauty, majesty and awesomeness of Mount Sinai and its neighbouring peaks but, also, by contrast, to show the pettiness of which we human beings are capable even in face of the miracle of the renewal of light. For on the platform overlooking the sheer cliff face to the east of the Mount there were stationed several individuals from different faith communities who during recent days had assumed the role of spiritual masters. And there they were now, surrounded by their disciples, subtly and not so subtly jockeying for position on the platform to ensure that they would be the one on behalf of our peace conference to welcome the sun to a new day.

Standing next to me during this performance were two strangers to our party, United Nations soldiers. They kept repeating, 'I can't believe it!' Meanwhile, my two Arab friends from the Jaffa Gate stole away towards the lee of the mountain in order to sit in the shelter of a rock and enjoy a peaceful smoke. Next, from a sort of cave to our right, there appeared a small group of Christians, all American, who looked very composed and at peace. They told me that they had anticipated the *brouhaha* around the rock platform and had quietly slipped away to hold an almost clandestine service on their own. Their faces reflected the good beginning they had made to the day.

This constant oscillation between edifying behaviour on the one hand and jarring contradiction on the other was maintained after we had eaten our breakfast. Soon after starting to descend the mountain I found myself walking

218

alone a few yards behind one of the most vociferous of our spiritual masters, who was being accompanied by a fervent disciple of his, a Canadian about forty years of age. Since the path was so narrow, steep and rocky, I felt that I could not decently push past the two of them. So for almost an hour I climbed down behind them. And for the whole of that time the spiritual master talked incessantly, except occasionally to answer a question from his egregiously humble disciple. As the master poured out one high-flown banality after another, each received with awe by the disciple, I kept asking myself whether this really was the man whose picture and name I had seen on posters in various parts of the world announcing that no one should miss the chance of hearing the wisdom of this spiritual master. The answer was, 'Yes. He is the one.'

Then once more the pendulum swung back towards reality when I reached the foot of the mountain. There I was resting in the shade beneath the wall of St Catherine's monastery when along came the man whom I had noticed that first morning at the Jaffa Gate, Mordechai Baron. After my encounter with the famous spiritual master there was something very reassuring about the sobriety and modesty of this man. Under my questioning about the Israeli campaign in Sinai during the 1967 war he described without rhetoric how he and Moshe Dayan had been the first Israelis to reach St Catherine's. He recalled with amusement how the two of them had to be hauled up from outside the fortress-like monastery walls, by means of an ancient, rickety lift, in order to parley with the abbot about the disposition of their units.

Mordechai then went on to say that in a sense he did not belong in our religious conference since he is an agnostic but that he was now glad to have come because the experience was opening him up to a dimension of reality which he scarcely heeded in the past. In particular, he ruminated aloud, he had been surprisingly moved on two occasions when he had stepped out of his tent in the middle of the night to go to the toilets and as he was crossing the open

219

square he had seen a group of devout Muslims from the Al-Azhar university standing there, shoulder to shoulder, facing Mecca, together carrying out the prescribed pre-dawn prayers.

I was not surprised that the 'straight path' of Islam, of Muslim discipline, should appeal to this upright soldier since I had myself observed during the proceeding days what a presence those imams from Al-Azhar brought to the conference. They were always calm, confident, never less than dignified in all their behaviour. And at the end of that day the same group was to provide me with the most memorable experience of my stay in Sinai.

It was around eight o'clock that night when I was sitting on an arc-shaped stone bench alongside eight or nine of the imams, in a place somewhat apart from the centre of the camp. Sitting next to me on my left was the sheikh whom in my mind I had denoted as the leader on account of the ease with which he moved through the bustle of this world whilst clearly being centred at the same time in the invisible world. Though he and I had never exchanged a word I was perfectly at ease sitting in silence beside him – as also, it seemed, were two other Christians on my right.

And they, like myself, seemed to know instinctively how to respond when, at a given moment, the sheikh stood up. The rest of the group did likewise without a word being spoken; we Christians followed suit, knowing that we were being invited to join the prayer.

What took place during the course of the next half hour was quite unforgettable. We three Christians were privileged to share in a *dhikr* with the imams from Al-Azhar. In other words, for the space of half an hour we repeated unceasingly the remembrance of God, chanting *la illaha illa lah* ('there is no god but God'). We did so standing and swaying, clasping and unclasping our hands, responding by our every movement, our every chant and our every breath to the rhythmic guidance of the small but authoritative sheikh on my left. In that whole ritual there was no sense of strangeness or embarrassment; but rather,

220

an undercurrent of centring as our leader led us through the chanting, slowly at one time and rapidly at another.

As we chanted my mind and heart seemed to become clearer and clearer, so that even in the midst of the *dhikr* I recognised how false is the assertion that *dhikr* is essentially hypnotic. On the contrary, what happens is that all peripheral, secondary impressions fade into their proper proportions and one's heart is freed to acknowledge the reality of God. And from that experience of *dhikr,* at least, I would think it equally false to speak of the resulting condition as a state akin to drunkenness. Once more I discovered the contrary to be the case. For as our leader gradually slowed down our rhythm and deepened our breathing there was no sense of coming down with a crash after having been on a high. Rather, the end condition was one in which the grip of one's feet upon the earth was firm as never before.

Sadly I have to record that soon after that high point the conference itself showed signs of coming apart at the seams. Whether any of organisers picked up the signs of things falling apart I cannot say. Perhaps it is generally true that the ones who are responsible for running such an event are always so preoccupied in dealing with everyone's immediate needs that they are the last to notice the signs – the same often happens in a family that is in process of breaking up. Yet the signs were unmistakable.

For instance, at night the camp continued to be noisy long after we should all have quietened down; and, correspondingly, more and more people were staying in bed until the sun was riding high in the sky. Then one group, in a fit of desert atavism, proposed that a sheep be slaughtered and roasted to make us a celebratory meal on the last evening – and this in order to crown a conference for peace at which many vegetarians were present! As it happened that last evening almost turned out to be a disaster when one or two people took advantage of the closing session to parade some highly sensitive political issues. Tempers rose and accusations began to fly around the camp-gathering in spite of the brave and patient efforts of the luminous Egyptian doctor who was our chairman, and despite the powerful intervention of an Argentinian rabbi. Their attempts at pacification were vain from the start, in any case, on account of two diverse forces.

The first contrary force took the form of certain of the spiritual masters who spoke many, many words about the need for peace whilst seemingly unaware that they, through their prima donna egotism, had released the very currents of discord that they were now claiming to stem. But more sinister than these misguided spiritual masters was a small but vociferous group gathered round a man who was skilled at playing upon the deep resentments which are inevitably festering in such meetings between traditional enemies. The man intrigued me because he and I had held quite a long conversation two days previously during which it had emerged that he was very sceptical of all religious traditions. So I was left wondering why he had come to a conference called in the name of religion. My encounter with the man left me with the impression that he was not straight and, indeed, that he was here to play some covert game of his own.

However, in the early hours of the next morning, the day of our departure, the unpleasantness of the previous evening seemed to be dispelled as we all embraced one another in moving farewells. There was something particularly poignant for the young Israelis and the young Egyptians who must have wondered at the back of their minds whether the next time they met might be on the battlefield. Also, even whilst our Bedouin drivers rattled our bones up and down in their trucks on the journey to Nuweiba, we were buoyed up at the thought of being able to take a dip in the sea before breakfasting at the beach. The chance of cleaning several days of desert dust from our bodies was certainly enticing.

And for those of us who did plunge into the sea just as the early morning sun began to sparkle over the waves the water of the Gulf of Aquaba proved every bit as refreshing as we had anticipated. But that was the extent of the refreshment which most of the swimmers at Nuweiba received: we emerged from the sea to discover that the landlubbers had finished off almost all the food assigned for breakfast and had left no more than one or two crusts. So much, I thought, for the sense of solidarity engendered by Sinai spirituality!

Still, I can't say that the lack of breakfast worried me much because by this time my main interest lay in studying the behaviour of the group and its members. And that interests was further quickened by an incident which flared up even as the swimmers were chewing away at a few crusts.

It happened that a mangy dog was scrabbling away under one of the picnic benches, searching for food, when a young Israeli Muslim who was sitting at an adjoining bench gave the dog a fierce kick. Instantly, there was a yell – not from the dog but from a middle-aged American Jewish woman standing nearby who was beside herself with rage at the young Arab's action. She berated the young Arab without stop for several minutes and in mounting anger. He, for his part, as well as his two or three Arab friends beside him, sat sullenly throughout the woman's tirade looking at her with murder in their hearts. But they said nothing directly to her; instead they muttered some uncomplementary remarks about her to one another in Arabic.

It was not difficult for spectator to see that here we were witnessing a clash between two cultures: on one side a liberated American woman for whom the humane treatment of animals is part of her enlightened world view, and on the other side a Muslim in whose tradition the dog is an accursed animal. But there was more to it than that. Welling up beneath the woman's defence of the dog one could sense a level of feeling far deeper than she herself was aware of, and in which a real loathing for Arabs was being given full rein.

All in all, then, as we made our long, hot, thirsty journey northwards past the Dead Sea to Jerusalem the days in Sinai had left me with plenty of matters relating to peace on which to reflect. Above all, I can see more clearly than ever that peace work demands a far higher degree of self-discipline, spiritual preparation and self-knowledge than we are generally prepared to face.

25th March, 1984. Tantur

They say that the family is *scola caritatis,* a school of charity, and I have often mused that the cricket ground is, in its own way, a school, not perhaps of charity but of a certain discipline preparing you for *caritas.* This evening, at least, I feel that my long years on the cricket field may have helped to stem internal warfare in this community.

Once again it was the Eucharist around which the animosity centred. Earlier in the week our announced celebrant, Fr Ailred, as gentle, kindly and modest a man as you could wish to meet, had issued the customary declaration which is mandatory upon all celebrants to outline the eucharistic faith and practice which is traditional in his or her own church. And though Ailred's statement was very much the conventional Roman Catholic one that has now been accepted for a couple of years without any sharp reaction I was not surprised that I soon heard murmurings against him. My antennae had early this session picked up stirrings in Tantur of what Goethe named *der Geist der stets verneint,* the spirit of negation, for which reason I was not taken aback by the murmurings.

All the same it was not very pleasant to go into chapel this morning and find almost no non-Catholics present. Clearly a group of scholars had organised a boycott of the Mass.

Poor Fr Ailred! You could see from the expression on his face as he processed towards the altar that his heart went into his boots when he saw the chapel half-empty. He had worked so faithfully at his declaration in an effort to avoid offending anyone. And when it came to the homily I truly regretted that the others were not present, because Ailred spoke such humble, careful words as should, I am sure, have melted the hearts of the boycotters if they had been present. Then agony was piled upon agony when the moment for communion arrived and one or two of the non-Catholics who were present walked out.

Our Sunday Eucharist is invariably followed by a joyful time of real celebration, the common meal to which everyone comes, including wives, husbands and children as well as visitors. But for many of the Catholics the prospect of joining in that meal today, a barbecue in the garden, now seemed unbearable. A number of them went off to their rooms without speaking – torn, as I later learnt, between their wounded feelings and their Christian desire to live at peace with their fellows. They sat silently in their rooms, wondering whether to boycott the meal.

Though I myself scarcely had any other choice but to join the barbecue straight away, I must also acknowledge that doing so took no great effort on my part. Which does not mean that I was not distressed when I crossed into the garden and faced a crowd of people already well into their meat and their wine, not even having had the decency to wait for Mass to end. There was something gross about the scene; so it was at least fitting that no one, it seems, had asked a blessing on the meal.

Still I soon found myself chatting to all and sundry as though nothing untoward had occurred, as though they had all been present at our Sunday Eucharist as usual. And soon the Catholics who had gone to their rooms came and put a brave face on the matter.

What intrigues me now as I examine my motives for behaving as I did, is that the image which served most powerfully as a springboard for my behaviour was not, I believe, a specifically Christian one. It may not even be a very commendable one. What was in my mind as I strolled over this morning to the barbecue crowd, some of whom avoided my gaze, was the image of an opening batsman in a cricket team.

The opening batsman in a cricket team usually has to face the fiercest fast bowling and is often struck painful blows on his thighs, his arms, his head and other tender places. The natural reaction, on being struck, is obviously to wince and start rubbing the bruised spot. But already fifty years ago, in Yorkshire, where I started as an opening batsman, it was drummed into me that you do not wince when struck; and, above all, you do not give the fast bowler the satisfaction of seeing you rub the bruised spot. So I did not say a single word to any of the boycotters about their behaviour. At a certain level I even enjoyed not giving them the satisfaction of seeing that I had so much as noticed their absence.

Which leaves me with a puzzle. I am pretty sure that the misery of those Catholics who went to their rooms arose out of a more Christian source than my feigned insouciance. On the other hand, I am equally sure that if I had behaved as they did we should have soon become locked in internal warfare.

Is cricket, therefore, a necessary *praeparatio evangelica* for Christianity?

16th April, 1984. Tantur

So now I know what St Francis was up to with my friend from Haifa! During the course of her visit to us I was greatly taken by her husband, a quiet, gentle man. He had about him an air which is quite unmistakable, the same air that I have virtually always sensed about men who survived the Japanese prison camps of the Second World War. Obviously you can't put your finger on it, otherwise you would not have to describe it as 'an air'; but it is, indeed, unmistakable. The air about such men has something to do with their having gone further into suffering and the depths both of human cruelty and of fidelity than one ever imagined possible, and yet having emerged still compassionate, gentle human beings. Such people are indelibly marked, as by a sacrament.

And he was one of those people. We learnt that he had spent years in Auschwitz and, on being liberated, was overwhelmed by the need to tell the story of Auschwitz and its victims. So after making his way to Tel Aviv he had straight away established himself in an abandoned concrete bunker and, like some hermit vowed to a secret cult, he had devoted himself night and day to describing the world of Auschwitz. When the books that he wrote appeared in print the Jewish reading public quickly recognised that here was someone truly inspired to give voice to their sufferings. But the identity of that someone was something they could never find out, because he so determinedly and skilfully projected his anonymity.

No one could penetrate his secret – not until my 'nutty' friend from Haifa came along and tracked him down in his bunker. Not only that: after eighteen months of relentlessly wooing him she married him.

But it was in her moment of seeming triumph that her troubles began. Over the course of the next ten years the man from Auschwitz slowly recovered in mind and body, step by step, from the trauma of the concentration camp; but his young wife, on the other hand, descended by a parallel series of steps into a condition of terror comparable to the terror he had known in Auschwitz. That double terror is heartbreakingly described by her in a book which she later wrote, entitled *The Prisoner*. There we learn of the pathetic means by which she attempted to keep her terror at bay; that is, by reaching for food as her saviour. What happened to her in consequence was grotesque.

As a result of eating so much and so frequently she grew incredibly fat, so fat indeed that taxi drivers used to refuse to allow her to ride in their taxis. But each such public humiliation could not shame her into controlling her voracious appetite. She would, for instance, bake a huge chocolate cake in the morning for one of her children's

227

birthday and then eat the whole of it herself by lunch time. This left her time to bake another cake before her two children arrived home from school in the afternoon; hence no one would know the extent of her eating.

The story could well, of course, have had a tragic ending. But, as we learn from her own account of her struggle in *The Prisoner*, that was happily not the case. For by virtue of separating herself from her family and making a year long pilgrimage she finally recovered. The fever left her, and she emerged as the smiling figure who burst through our dining room doors – half an hour late for lunch, it is true, but immediately likeable in spite of everything.

Yet that was by no means the end of the matter, for there remains a further story within that story, which in its turn stood within an earlier story.

For some obscure reason, after reading *The Prisoner*, I felt that it might be meant for Arnold, my Jewish friend who had himself been in Auschwitz as a boy (as I have described earlier on p. 208). So without making a big deal of the matter I handed him a copy of the book, commenting that it might interest him.

My comment, to put it at its very mildest, was an understatement, as I was to learn some weeks later when Arnold telephoned me. He could scarcely contain himself with astonishment at what had happened as a result of my lending him *The Prisoner*.

After he had begun to read the book, so he told me, he started to do something he had never done before. He began to read passages of the book out loud for the benefit of Teresa, the woman he had lived with for a year or two, a most attractive and radiant person who yet had lately been suffering from one unspecifiable ailment after another. Eventually both Teresa and Arnold became so absorbed in the book that they read the whole of it out loud to one another, each taking turns to do so. Slowly they came to realise that the story in the book was their story also: just as Arnold had been recovering from 'Auschwitz fever' so Teresa had by the same token been picking up the infection ever more desperately. But, thanks be to God, their very reading of *The Prisoner* out loud to one another had proved to be a healing process. And though still feeling fragile, as one does after a fever has left one, Teresa was once more the radiant person we had first met. Interestingly enough, the process had also left them both very clear in their minds that they should soon separate for at least a year – no longer under a cloud threatening bitterness but with light hearts and ever deeper love for one another.

The more I reflect upon these intertwined stories the surer I become that there is such an infection as 'Auschwitz fever' from which certain victims of the concentration camps manage to recover, but which other people close to them may at the same time pick up. How these latter people themselves recover is not easy to understand but I am convinced that we do need to understand it, because at the collective level the whole Jewish people has been a victim of the concentration camps and has caught 'Auschwitz fever'. Anyone who chooses to come close to the Jewish people, therefore, exposes himself to the risk of becoming infected, which is why so many high-minded people choose to distance themselves from Israel, pretending that the event of Auschwitz was nothing to do with them. I suspect, however, that their behaviour has less to do with high-mindedness than with a selfish fear of infection.

17th April, 1984. Tantur

Our time at Tantur is the first period of my life that I have spent continuously amongst professional religious, and it has awakened in me a deeper sympathy for them in certain respects. At the moment I am being made particularly aware of the spiritual peril that they run into through their having to use tremendous, mystery-laden words so constantly that they are almost bound to trivialise and banalise the awesome realities to which the words are pointing. If they do not succumb to that temptation then

229

they must become saints – and in order not to succumb they have to become saints.

I say this on account of the number of occasions during these past few weeks when I have heard so many people mouthing 'forgiving' and 'forgiveness' as though it were the easiest thing in the world, talking so glibly as to make my hair stand on end in disbelief.

Dorothy and I were the only lay-folk, for instance, at a house-mass celebrated – and very beautifully celebrated – by Fr Francis. All the scriptural passages appointed to be read at the Mass turned upon forgiveness, about which Fr Francis spoke a few modest but penetrating words before inviting the rest of us to contribute our thoughts on the matter. And almost immediately I grew exasperated at the ease with which all the other religious present slipped instantly into pious ecclesiastical clichés, as though through years of practice it had become second nature to them to side-step every difficulty in forgiving. They seemed to assume that we all know what it means to forgive, whereas in reality we only begin to get a glimpse of what it means after we have been trying our very sincerest to forgive someone. And every time, it seems to me, we fall short of complete forgiveness. Perhaps that is why Jesus tells us that we have to forgive those who offend us seventy times seven. This last phrase is usually explained by the learned as a way of saying 'for ever'; and in one sense they are right, but it is better to stick to Jesus' idiom because 'seventy times seven' makes us begin mentally counting and envisioning the number of occasions, one after another, in long succession, when we shall have to pick ourselves up again after yet another failure to forgive completely. The phrase should also signify to us how much practice we all need at trying to forgive.

Of course that phrase, like every powerful phrase, is particularly susceptible to misunderstanding and I suspect that some of my own abortive struggles to forgive have been flawed by my having imbibed such a misconception of forgiveness as a youngster. In accordance with my misconception forgiving for me was a discrete act – so separate that one could distinguish every such act from every other and actually count the number of them, even adding them up, for instance, to seventy times seven.

The other flaw in my notion of forgiving was to believe that the very generosity of the act would of itself and instantly achieve reconciliation between the alienated parties – and that would be an end of the matter. The matter in dispute had now been dissolved away!

In real life, however, it is not like that, as I have been discovering all over again during the past months. Time after time I have forgiven a person both by word and in my heart, only to find that same person within an hour committing that very same offence one more. Similarly, there have been occasions when I have been forgiven yet have found myself soon afterwards on the point of committing the same offence once again. The matter of the dispute has still been lodged somewhere inside me and is going to take a long time – perhaps seventy times, a lifetime – before it is dissolved.

The conclusion I am bound to come to, therefore, is that when we speak of forgiveness we should have in mind not so much a series of discrete acts (though it is that) as a continuous lifelong condition. There is no moment when one is not in need of forgiveness nor any moment when one does not need to be forgiving.

Everything I have written down so far is all well and good, and I believe that the practice of reflection in this fashion actually does help one to behave better in future. But, of course, these abstract formulations cannot conceal from me the awareness that they are all circling around the quite concrete matter of my relationship with Walter.

I feel it would be a comfort, and would make life easier, if I could tell myself that he and I had obviously been incompatible from the beginning. Because then I could do what the great Buddhist Scholar, Edward Conze, did when he and my friend, Fr Colman, had a fierce dispute at their first encounter. Conze asked Fr Colman what his astrological sign was. And when Conze realised that both of them were Scorpios he said, 'That explains why we shall never get along together.' Except, of course, that once they had realised their 'incompatibility' they got on quite well! But that is not true of Walter and myself. We cannot say that our individual chemistries are incompatible. Admittedly questions were raised in my mind on account of certain traits in his original application to come here as a scholar. Still that is the case with virtually every application form one ever reads.

No. Something went wrong somewhere along the line that has led to the present unease between us. 'Unease', however, is too anodyne a word to describe how I feel on Sundays in chapel when the moment comes for everyone to exchange a sign of peace with every other member of our Christian community gathered around the altar. When Walter and I then greet one another I am sure that both he and I are genuinely sincere in wishing peace to one another. Yet even in that moment I remain aware at one level that in no time whatsoever after the Eucharist is finished he will do something or say something behind my back calculated to undermine me and to make life very difficult for me. His habit of doing so seems to be almost a conditioned reflex, as automatic as the drug addict's reaching for his fix.

However, it is a total waste of energy – as well as being spiritually destructive – for me to draw up inside my head a bill of accusation against Walter, listing all the occasions when he has given me grounds for charging him with betraying me. Is this not a case for applying the ancient Catholic maxim of *lectio benevolentior* ('the more benevolent reading, or interpretation'), according to which, when the behaviour of someone is difficult to comprehend, one adopts the more favourable interpretation of their actions? So when Walter goes behind my back and does or says something that cause me endless trouble, may it not be what he wants to achieve is actually in his eyes for the common good of the community? But he is unable to take me into his confidence. Is this because he does not have the courage to confront me, or because he is afraid for my sake, on the ground that until his scheme comes to successful fruition I shall feel threatened by it?

Have there not in the past, been occasions when I have myself 'gone behind someone's back' in the hope of sparing them some experience or some decision that I believed would prove terribly painful for them? And whenever my subterfuge has been revealed, has my conduct not seemed like an act of betrayal? In any case, I am supposed to have learnt years ago to be very slow to speak of 'betrayal', ever since I fell into a trench during the Second World War.

What happened was one of those incidents that our Zen Buddhist friends often cite as occasions of enlightenment.

At the time we were young infantrymen doing our basic training, and on this particular day Sergeant Major Reid had made us run here, there and everywhere, so that we finished up breathless on a grassy verge where he formed us up in a single rank and allowed us to get our breath back. Once we were composed he called us to attention and then gave the order, 'Two paces backwards . . . march!' Like good soldiers we obeyed his order, took two steps backwards and fell down into a deep trench behind us which we had not noticed – much to the delight of Sergeant Major Reid, who almost doubled up with laughter.

Though I doubt whether he was aware of having done so the Sgt Major had, in fact, subjected at least one member of our section, namely myself, to one of those shocks which Zen masters often cause in their disciples so as to provoke enlightenment or realisation. Because ever since falling into that trench I have realised with complete awareness that we human beings do not have eyes in the back of our heads. That may seem a platitudinous thing to say but it has consequences that are far from platitudinous: it means that when we are trying to move into a correct and just position with regard to someone in front of us, we almost inevitably move into an incorrect or unjust position with regard to someone behind us whom we had not seen – stepping on their toes, for instance.

And when someone steps on our toes we do not generally say to ourselves, 'He did that because he was trying to behave justly towards A or B; and, since he is a finite creature with finite limited vision, he did not see, or foresee, the pain his movements were going to cause me.' Instead we invariably interpret the pain caused as having been willed by the person who caused the pain and therefore we regard him as an enemy, or, in many cases, as a traitor to us.

I am reminded of the psychiatrist in San Francisco who was speaking with a Dominican friend of mine and regretting how little he could really help his clients. 'You know,' he said, 'the people who come to me for help are in the end all of them asking the same basic, fundamental question. They are all saying to me, "Is there somewhere a friend who will not in the final resort betray one?" I would love to be able to say, "Yes. There is." But I cannot do so because I am an agnostic, and only if I believed in God could I say, "Yes". But human beings will always in the end betray.'

What the psychiatrist said is both penetrating and helpful, but I do query his use of the word 'betrayal'. Would it not be more accurate to say that 'human beings will always in the end let one down' – at least in some measure, because we are finite creatures and cannot see all round us? We can never see all the consequences of our actions towards others, or even towards ourselves. This is not to deny, of course, that there are occasions when someone delivers us into evil out of malice or selfishness. But once we adopt the *lectio benevolentior* we find that the percentage of occasions when we feel betrayed diminishes, though, correspondingly, the percentage of occasions when we feel let down increases.

But in both cases we feel hurt, and in order to protect our hurt feelings we react with feelings of our own. After all we are not unfeeling stones but highly sensitive creatures. Nevertheless, if, in reaction, we allow our feelings

234

to dominate us then a dark cloud blinds our eyes and a hard lump lies upon our hearts to block the spirit of truth, which is the Holy Spirit of forgiveness. The Holy Spirit cannot then enter our hearts and cleanse us.

In this seeming impasse I have asked myself, 'What can I do to make the miracle of forgiveness possible?' And, by the grace of God, I have arrived at a conclusion that I am beginning to find really helpful: if one honestly observes the distinctive character of one's reactive feelings and analyses them relentlessly, then the mere desire for truth sustaining that observation and analysis will of itself begin to disperse the darkness over one's eyes and dissolved the lump lying heavy upon one's heart. The only trouble is that the process of observation and analysis may unearth truths about oneself that one would rather not know. As it has done in my own case.

I was shocked to discover that my way of dealing with hurt feelings is by recourse to a corresponding feeling of contempt for those whom I judge to have inflicted the hurt upon me. This salutary discovery would not have been possible, I believe, without the unwitting aid of others. I had never, for instance, forgotten the quiet comment of Archbishop Dwyer of Birmingham when he was meeting a small group of us, university teachers, gathered to appoint a university chaplain. In response to one of our number who was speaking harshly of a candidate the Archbishop said, 'We put ourselves into danger whenever we speak with contempt of another human being.' Whether the man rebuked heard the Archbishop's rebuke I cannot say, but I certainly did. The Archbishop had sensitised a spot within me that since then has always been primed to send out a danger signal whenever I have strayed into contempt.

And I also believe that my discovery owes something to one of the scholars here who, despite being described by a visiting luminary as 'an interfering busybody', has nevertheless helped me. Out of good will, I am sure, this man pointed out to me that when the head of an institution from a height of six feet six inches corrects a much smaller member of the institution, it can be rather frightening. So I should be aware of the effect I could have upon those so far below me in physical stature. At first this explanation of the effect I have sometimes had on people seemed to let me off the hook, but then I thought to myself that I know other people of my height who do not appear to produce the same effect. So there must be some other factor present in my own attitude; and I believe that I have pin-pointed it. It is an attitude of contempt, a habit of raising my head and going silent, as if to say,'How can I be expected to have any dealings with such mean-minded people as these? They are not our sort.'

There was something of that in my attitude towards the religious who were blathering away about forgiveness at the house-mass. I was the only person there who kept silence. And I doubt whether that was a holy silence.

18th Aril, 1984. Tantur

There have been times during recent years when I have been nigh to despair about many spiritual teachers, including some with world-wide reputations. The ones in question, for all their high-sounding books and conferences, often do not know how to behave with that consideration for others which could simply be taken for granted even, say, amongst the rough, scarcely educated brickyard workers in my native Claremount.

The latest of the species, who descended upon us in February, seemed to imagine that the sole *raison d'être* for Tantur was to ensure that his recent book is granted the maximum publicity. Not only that, but he insisted on my taking him to all those important centres of learning in Jerusalem where I have friends in order to show them the book. And typically, when we were invited to lunch at the Biblical College, he further insisted on sitting next to the Dean, whom he clearly tagged both as important and a person of his own intellectual stature. Not once did he turn to the little man sitting on his right, an inconspicuous, rather gnome-like creature named Genia.

Actually it was in its own way rather comic to watch this spiritual teacher rattling away throughout the lunch, trying to impress the Dean whilst all the while totally unaware that the little man sitting on his right is probably the most learned man in the place – as well as being a saint! The Dean himself once said about him, 'of all the men I have ever met he is the one least touched by original sin'!

What joy it was, therefore, today, and a cleansing contrast, to glance around our seminar room and to look upon the faces of so many authentic spiritual teachers who are taking part in our seminar on the *The Peoples of the Book in the Light of Asia*. Sitting very upright at the head of the table, as leader of the seminar, was the noble figure of Dom Bede Griffiths, whose reputation and glamorous appearance had attracted a good number of visitors. At a far corner from him my Jewish Kabbalistic friend, Avraham Weiner, was quietly taking notes, whilst gazing at me from the opposite side of the table was the radiant face of my Seraphic brother, Fr Marco Malagolo. Just to see even one of these blessed men in our company would have been enough for my cup of joy to flow over but there were present others who are similarly spirit-filled if not so easily detected. In particular, sitting next to me was God's special gift to me for this term, Sadhu Ittyarivah.

If ever my devotion to the Icon of Unexpected Joy has wavered in the past it should not do so henceforth, after the appearance of Sadhu Ittyavirah, or Itty, as he asks us to call him. Because when I read his book *Echoing the Father's Love* ten years ago and learnt something about his life I never imagined that I should meet and become friends with this sadhu, about whom numerous articles have been written in religious journals. Not only that, but we discovered that we are of the same age (born in 1923), and that I was once stationed for six months near his native village in Kerala. Moreover – what seemed to make us brothers even more – we had both been members of the task force named 'Zipper' which was being mounted to land in Malaya at the time when the atom bomb brought the War to an end. It delights both of us to wonder at the strange ways of providence by which that young Indian soldier and that young British soldier, sailing unknown to one another across the Indian Ocean in the same convoy nearly forty years ago, should now find their lives converging by manifold ways upon the holy city of Jerusalem.

At the end of the War this son of a poor Kerala family had trained for many years to become a Jesuit priest and was indeed within three months of ordination when he was forcibly struck by the thought, 'India does not need another Jesuit priest. What it needs is a Christian *sadhu* who, like any Hindu holy man, will wander throughout the land witnessing to the love of God, only eating what is given by God's children and sleeping in whatever shelter is offered or else under the open sky.'

For almost thirty years Itty did precisely that and became quite famous in the course of doing so. As a result people were constantly seeking his opinion on every subject under the sun. One day, for example, a group of journalists in Madras heard that his wanderings were soon to bring him to their city and so they went to meet him, 'this vagabond and newspaper boy in the name of God'. They said to him, 'Sadhu, you have traversed mnuch of India and seen every aspect of Indian life, what is the great task facing our country?' Every questions anticipates a certain answer, and in this case the journalists were expecting this holy man to issue some profound statement about the spiritual crisis facing the Indian people. Instead he just gave them his radiant smile and said, 'Food'. Then he continued his wanderings.

Now Itty is no longer a vagabond. He is married, has a little son and received worldly acclaim in 1981 when he shared the Albert Schweitzer Peace Prize along with the great guitarist, Segovia. With the money he received Itty has set up the Schweitzer Institute of Prayer and Research on a modest plot of land near his native village. His motivation for doing so springs from his conviction that modern science has gone astray because scientific research has taken place outside of prayer; and he hopes that science will become more fruitful, more of a blessing for humanity if at least one or two scientists prove ready to spend some time at the tiny Schweitzer Institute. And though most observers dismiss his scheme as wildly quixotic, who is to deny the truth of Itty's intuition in the age of nuclear terror, when pollution produced by man's devilish ingenuity is penetrating earth and sea and sky, and is corrupting not only the bodies of all earth's inhabitants but even the very heart of man?

What for me put the seal on the authenticity of Itty's life and teaching was the explanation he gave to me of why he had abandoned his status of *sadhu* in order to become an ordinary householder. He told me that when he reached his mid-fifties he began to feel his bones aching more and more as a result of his vagabond life. In his approaching old age he felt he was going to need comfort such as he had not known for thirty years. So he decided to get married. He did so, having first sought the advice and consent of his ecclesiastical superior.

This explanation for his change of status was simply given, with no trace of affectation or defensiveness. It completely captivated me. As he spoke I could almost hear, as a sort of counter-echo, how the voices of certain spiritual teachers would have sounded if they had taken a similar step. They would have elevated their action to the status of a prophetic statement or a further stage in their spiritual journey or a return to the original life-style of the *sadhu*. Instead Itty just said that his bones were beginning to ache and that he needed some comfort in his old age.

Of course, anyone who can speak with such simplicity is, in his own person, a prophetic statement.

5th May, 1984. Letter to the Tablet

It is reported that Americans are becoming illiterate: they do not know how to read. The cause usually assigned for this state of affairs is television – and, more recently, the craze for computers.

Whatever may be the truth of this report, it certainly seems that those Americans who determine the policy of the United States in the Middle East are illiterate about this region: they simply cannot 'read' the situation. How otherwise can one explain their imagining that the agreement between Gemayel and the Israelis which they contrived on 17th May, 1983, would last? Even as we watched that signing ceremony on Israeli television a year ago, everyone alongside me was both open-mouthed and wide-eyed with disbelief. The unanimous reaction was accurately summed up by one of our company who exclaimed: 'Without Syria?! They must be crazy. Do they know nothing about the history of this part of the world? Have they no notion of what Syria stands for amongst the Arabs?'

Some days later a different explanation began to gain currency. It was that our first reaction had been incredibly naïve. Of course, so the argument now ran, the Americans never imagined the agreement would last: it was all a clever conspiracy on their part to use Israeli flesh and blood to establish a secure base in southern Lebanon for their anti-Soviet strategy.

I must confess that it was the emergence of this conspiracy theory which began to induce in me a certain sympathy for the Americans. Because how can anyone possibly 'read' a situation when the main ingredient of it is millions of heads full to overflowing with conspiracy theories? Even if the position on the ground were amenable to reason, nevertheless millions of such heads would in any event generate a 'noosphere' characterised by insanity.

It is my fate to try to think straight in such an insane 'noosphere'. For instance, I was lately assured by an Arab friend that the reason I misread Israeli policy was that I had never studied *The Protocols of the Elders of Zion*. (If only my interlocutor knew how many hours I had spent on the demented Nilus and all his works!) For twenty minutes I sat literally speechless whilst it was demonstrated to me that the Russian Revolution of 1917 had been a Jewish conspiracy, that the Jews had later tried to do the same in Germany, but that both these conspiracies were simply a preparation for what they are now doing to the Arabs. Again, at almost the same date, another Arab friend assured me that the bomb which killed so many Israelis in the bus travelling along Sederot Herzl was 'a Jewish provocation'. Neither of these friends is a benighted peasant. Both are highly educated; but what they say is insane.

However, education seems to have nothing to do with it. After all, my Jewish friend Chaim is tremendously learned. But he similarly upbraided me, in this instance for my respect towards Islam. He explained that Islam had twice tried to conquer Europe by military means but had been defeated on each occasion; at Poitiers in 731 and at Vienna in 1683. Now a third attempt was being made, this time by ilfiltration; and Christian dupes like myself were aiding and abetting the conspiracy. But even Chaim was not so way out as was the spokesman for Jewish settlers in the occupied territories who insisted that the bombs placed below Arab buses and timed to explode just when they would be full of Arab men, women and children were 'a provocation'.

Why do otherwise sensible and intelligent people try to wriggle out of what they must recognise to be the truth? Only yesterday I heard on *Kol Israel* a long and tortuous semantic exercise designed to prove that a terrorist underground movement in the occupied territories was 'not really an underground movement'. Similarly not long ago, an entire seminar, replete with university professors, was devoted to drawing a distinction between 'terrorists' and 'freedom fighters'. Yet it was perfectly clear that the whole object of this elaborate exercise was to permit the participants to claim in good conscience that their own side were freedom fighters whilst the other side were terrorists.

This question of trying to read a situation has again been nagging at my mind, especially since yesterday evening when a seemingly insignificant incident set me doubting my ability to read what was happening under my very own nose.

I was in a group of Arab Christians watching the Israeli television news when one item showed Gary Hart, the American Democratic contender for his party's nomination addressing an audience of American Jews. Speaking with melodramatic emphasis Hart declared: 'Every penny spent in the defence of Israel is a penny spent in the defence of the United States', a statement which naturally – as intended – drew thunderous applause from his audience. I glanced at the others watching with me to note their reactions and was surprised to see them all start laughing and pointing towards the image of Senator Hart as if the mantle of Charlie Chaplin had fallen about him. 'What extraordinarily good-natured people they are', I thought to myself. 'Here is a politician who in brazen pursuit of power is prepared to say almost anything regardless of the effects of what he says upon the fate and daily lives of these ordinary, decent people; and yet they do not get angry and curse him. They just laugh and laugh.

But during today I have been asking myself whether I was mistaken. Was there not a certain note of hysteria and despair in their laughter, a sign that they feel themselves to be such pawns in struggles for power in

distant lands that they cannot take any politician whatsoever seriously? And the truth is that I do not know
which of my readings of that incident – if either – is
correct.

It is only a few weeks since the bloody climax to the
hijacking of the Egged bus on the Tel Aviv to Ashkelon
route, and yet the details of it and of the human beings
caught in the drama of that Thursday night are already
becoming blurred in most of our minds. Too much happens in the modern world for us to take it in.

But for some reason I continue to be haunted by the
thought of Irit Portugez. Irit was the nineteen-year-old
woman soldier killed along with the hijackers. She was
on her way home that night to Moshav Cochav Michael,
doubtless going on leave in order to celebrate *Shabbat*
with her family. As with families all over the world, they
would already have been anticipating with joy the return
of their daughter. So I have continued to picture Irit as
one of those thousands of girl soldiers one sees in Israel,
usually so neat and trim and innocent-looking – you cannot make a woman look a tough, uncompromising soldier
in the way that you can with a man. The ones I have
encountered have been uniformly pleasant and kind and
helpful.

And apparently the hijackers also were young, and
scarcely ruthless enough to be successful terrorists – at
one point they stopped the bus in order to allow a pregnant woman to get off. The passengers themselves later
said that the four Arabs treated them well.

There also remains in my memory another image of
that night. Ze'ev Bukshenshpan, an Israel Defence Force
combat medic who was a passenger on the bus, and himself
only twenty-six, proved to be the hero of the occasions
by the way he cared for the wounded. And aiding him
were Irit and Jamal, the latter one of the hijackers, a
youngster still in his teens, who helped Ze'ev by holding
a flashlight while Ze'ev was inserting a plasma needle into

one of the wounded. That moment now stands in my mind like a scene from one of Rembrandt's night pictures – the three young people bending over the wounded man, their features etched against the darkness by the light of the torch which Jamal was holding. For a moment the three of them were held together, bent not upon destroying but upon saving life. Yet within hours Irit and Jamal had been blasted into eternity, whereas Ze'ev, by a different fate, lives on to marry the woman he loves. May he have long life and see his children's children.

The truth about what happened on that fateful evening was suppressed by the Israeli authorities. Photographs were banned by the censors because they showed two of the hijackers being led away from the bus, alive and on their own two feet. The photographs contradicted the first official story that all the hijackers were killed in the storming of the bus. Then an Israeli newspaper was suspended for taking up the *New York Times*' revelation that the two hijackers who survived the storming of the bus had been killed by their captors.

Subsequently three members of the Israeli internal security service, Shin Bet, were dismissed for having leaked the truth about the incident.

A saddening feature about the reporting of this tragedy was that the local Arab newspaper never spoke of Irit Portugez or Ze'ev Buskshenshpan any more than the Jewish newspaper named Subdi, Majdi or Jamal, who for them remained anonymous. The enemy must never be allowed to be a human being.

Nearly all our visitors who come to stay with us for any length of time eventually ask the same question: 'How on earth do people manage to remain sane in the midst of all the tension and craziness of this place?'

To this question there are many answers: such, for instance, as the shining example of all the holy people in our tension-riddled city. One day I hope to write about them. But there is an even simpler answer which, sadly, is beyond the experience of almost everyone outside Israel. I am speaking of the Sabbath. Of the Sabbath it is eminently true to say, 'Taste and see that it is good', for unless you taste it you cannot appreciate its goodness.

And you may taste it in the most unlikely places. After all, Netanya is a Mediterranean holiday centre where you would expect to encounter the usual noise of the modern entertainment world – anything but the quiet of the Sabbath. Yet when we arrived there at lunch-time on Friday, you could already feel the town settling steadily into the silence of the holy day. The volume of traffic had gradually diminished: the shops were closing their doors; and even the pedestrians were beginning to move more slowly, their voices quieter as they greeted one another, '*Shabbat Shalom*'. By the time the sun was setting over the Mediterranean the beach was unpeopled and those of us sitting on benches or strolling along the tree-lined sea front were beginning to breath more unhurriedly, scenting the fragrance of *Shabbat*.

When I looked up towards the hotel where we were staying, there, to my joy, I saw that the common room was now lit up and filled with my Jewish fellow guests dressed in their prayer shawls and wearing their yarmulkas. At that moment it seemed completely right and proper for them to be davening* on behalf also of those of us outside – except that I did not feel to be outside, because I was being embraced within the light to lighten the Gentiles.

A strange thought then entered my head: how I wish that the spiritually starving youngsters from Liverpool, Newcastle, Stoke and other cities might taste the sweetness of the Sabbath! Because then they might again see goodness. But England no longer knows 'the mystery of the Sabbath . . . the table wreathed with precious mystery. Deep and hidden, beyond the reach of the word.' So her hungry children never taste Sabbath and cannot, therefore, see goodness.

* a form of prayer characterised by swaying of the body.

8th May, 1984. Tantur

Yet another twist to the saga of *koinonia!* After numerous failures over the past three years I managed to persuade an Orthodox scholar to come and live at Tantur for a term. Since Vladimir, the scholar in question, is Russian Orthodox and belongs to the Moscow Patriarchate his coming here did not cause the complications with the Orthodox Patriarch of Jerusalem that, say, an Orthodox from Greece might have caused – Vladimir is a Swiss citizen.

Vladimir's presence has been a great joy to all of us and he has communicated to us some of his own enthusiasm for the riches of the Russian Orthodox tradition. In particular he gave us such glowing accounts of the Russian celebration of Easter that a number of scholars asked whether they might accompany him to the Easter service this year.

Only now have I been told the sickening story of what happened when they went.

When the moment came for communion Vladimir went up to receive, but the priest in front of whom he stood questioned him, 'Are you Orthodox?' 'Yes', answered Vladimir. 'To whom did you make your confession?' In response Vladimir named the priest, only to be told, 'I have never heard of him.' At which the celebrant passed on. And Vladimir had to return, heavy-hearted, to take his place beside his dismayed Tantur friends.

Certain Westerners, inevitably, will in future listen to glowing accounts of Russian Orthodox Easter with some reserve.

20th May, 1984. Tantur

Tonight I feel as though an enormous load has been lifted from both my head and my heart. What happened this evening at dinner was enough to make you believe in God and goodness.

At no meal in which I have partaken since coming to Tantur have I felt a stronger current of unfeigned good

246

will, fellowship and holy joy in each other's company than I experienced this evening. All five of us at our table joined easily in the conversation, which was at one time concerned with social affairs and another time devoted to theological issues, always serious but also humorous with lots of relaxed laughter. Above all, the current of feeling around the table was one of warmth and trust.

Only towards the very end of the meal did I suddenly realise that the four men sharing this heart-warming occasion with me were precisely the same four whom I had once characterised in my mind previously as 'malcontents'. And a few minutes later, as we were bidding each other 'Good night and sleep well', I found myself reflecting, 'Well, if you had told me three months ago that these four could be in such harmony with me and would be showing such respect and affection for me personally I would never never have believed you.'

In those days an accidental discovery had left me shaking with anger against them, though perhaps my anger arose less from their conduct than from that of the misguided character who indirectly transmitted to me the caustic remarks about my running of the Institute which he had elicited from them. For although I could tell without any difficulty, on account of both the nature and the tone of each complaint, which of them had said what, nevertheless the whole circumstance surrounding the incident was so messy that if I had confronted each of them individually our relations would have been strained for the rest of our time together.

So, instead, I decided to take to heart the criticisms levelled at myself as honestly as I could manage but, above all, to regard my knowledge of their criticisms as privileged, as having been given in trust to someone, and therefore I was under an obligation not to take advantage of it. In the last few months that has not been easy. After all, it is now almost fifty years since I discovered an ability within myself to hit people off with a phrase;

and it would have been easy enough for me to finish off each of these four with a polite but deadly gesture of characterisation.

I hope that my determination not to indulge my ability owed at least something to the inspiration of the Holy Spirit but I am bound wrily to recognise that my Yorkshire sense of economy also had a bearing on it. After all, for nigh on forty years I had been investing precious energy into curbing a fatal capacity for hitting off people with a word who have crossed me. Was I now going to blue in that lifetime's investment just for the satisfaction of hurting someone who had hurt me? 'Not likely!' said the thrifty Yorkshireman inside me.

But that motive of economy alone would not have been enough to maintain my resolution in face of the many subsequent moments of temptation to break it. The factor that gave most weight to my resolve illustrates the benefits of having affirmed one's beliefs and opinions in the public forum so clearly that one cannot stifle them in the private forum situated within oneself. In this case, having so often and so firmly voiced the need to control one's tongue, I kept hearing some of my own words whenever I faced temptation: 'As the Buddhists teach, "Learn, whenever you are on the point of speaking, to swallow your own words. If you can't swallow them, how can you except others to do so?"' 'Becoming holy is not at all complicated. All we have to do is what St James tells us: control our tongues, and then everything else in our life will fall into place.' Or, those golden words attributed to St Seraphim of Sarov, 'Keep away from the spilling of speech. Instead of condemning others, strive to reach inner peace. Keep silent, refrain from judgement. This will raise you above the deadly arrows of slander, insult, outrage, and will shield your glowing hearts against the evil that creeps around.'

But perhaps it is something that I have read rather than anything I have said which has in a manner stunned me into silence – by the power of its conviction drawn from a thousand years old tradition. That is, the book entitled *Guard Your Tongue*,[7] a practical guide to avoiding derogatory speech based on the teachings of a Polish rabbi, Chofetz Chayim. Until I had studied Chofetz Chayim's compendium on the myriad ways in which one can sin through *leshon hora* (one's tongue of evil) I had never realised how much of our everyday conversation is corrupted through derogatory speech. Here one learns to appreciate the great strength of the rabbinic tradition in that it does not allow one to escape into generalities but rather rubs one's nose in the concrete details of human behaviour. As, for example, if a person with whom you are conversing on the telephone insists on relating derogatory information you should rebuke him even if the derogatory information is true. If this is not possible you must find an excuse to hang up, saying 'Excuse me, something has just come up' (i.e. the derogatory information) and break off the conversation. No wonder that some rabbis go so far as to say that tale-bearing is even more sinful than the cardinal sins of murder, adultery and idolatry. And no wonder that it is a Jewish saint, James, who compares the evil tongue to the very tiniest spark which sets a huge stack of timber on fire, just as the tongue can send up a whole community in flames.

It is thanks to all these teachers, Chofetz Chayim, St Seraphim, St James and our Buddhist friends that I have managed to traverse these past few months without offending against the 'malcontents'. Let that be a warning not to fall into the fashionable pose of scorning teaching in the name of experience. True teachers illuminate the path ahead of us so that we become aware of pitfalls and do not strike our feet against a stone, neither scandalised nor scandalising.

I am still breathing with relief, moreover, through becoming aware of what a close shave it was – just one hard word from me these last few months and that wonderful atmosphere at dinner this evening would have been quite impossible.

30th May, 1984. Tantur

Even as it was happening you could sense that tonight's encounter at Hebrew University between Professor Leibowicz and Professor Emile Fackenheim was to be historic, and that it would be talked about for a long time to come. For the four of us from Tantur who were present it was a particular privilege to be there since we were the only Christians in the lecture hall. This meant that the fifty or so Jewish professors and students in the hall were hardly conscious of us. Consequently our Jewish brethren argued very openly with one another and expressed themselves in a way that people only feel free to do when no one but family is present – as, for instance, Leibowicz did when referring to Christianity as 'the enemy of Judaism'.

The impetus for this historic confrontation was provided by the publication of Fackenheim's latest book *To Mend the World,* a work in which Fackenheim reaffirms how vitally important it is for Jews to remain faithful to their traditions, and especially for the centrality henceforth in Jewish religious thought of the Holocaust and the State of Israel.

In his introduction to the discussion it was again the Holocaust and the State of Israel which Fackenheim emphasised, along with his well-known assertion that every Jew must be faithful to his traditions so as not to give Hitler a 'posthumous victory'.

When Leibowicz stood up to reply his approach to the pulpitum was grave and dramatic, not without a touch of the histrionic. His bald head topped by a skull cap, his face pale with age and study, this prophet of Israel leaned his right elbow on the pulpitum and placed the long, bony fingers of his right hand against his cheek. Then slowly, as if wearied by the folly of his fellow human beings, he declared, 'If I had read Professor Fackenheim's book

250

before accepting the invitation to come here and discuss it, I would never have agree to do so. The book is totally alien to my way of thinking and has nothing to do with Judaism, in my understanding of Judaism.'

I had never heard a discussion between two academics to be initiated in such an uncompromising, aggressive fashion. Hence my sympathies went out immediately to the discomforted Fackenheim, in spite of the fact that I have in the past been scandalised by the way in which he seems to me to distort history for polemical purposes.

At the same time I was utterly fascinated at the manner in which Leibowicz relentlessly pursued the logic of his own position. 'Faith', he said, 'is not a conclusion from empirical data; it has nothing to do with experience. It is a decision. It is *mitzvah* in this miserable world.' He went on to say that there is no religious meaning to be found in the Holocaust, nor does he attach any religious significance to the existence of the State of Israel (even though he himself worked to establish the State) because there is no meaning in history. God is beyond history; he is beyond space and time; therefore to look for a Messiah in history is a form of idolatry. Which is why 'Christianity is the enemy of Judaism'.

To all of which Fackenheim had no reply. How can you reply to any such fundamentalist who, in effect, begins by declaring that there is no ground for discussion and that nothing you say will affect his fundamental position? Once you grant Leibowicz's narrow view of logic then he was the victor of the evening and Fackenheim was revealed to be confused. Nevertheless, our little group of Christians felt close to Fackenheim – though he might not have been pleased to learn it – because as one of my friends afterwards summed it up, 'at least his confusions are Christian confusions'.

But for me the reward for attending the debate did not emerge from the intellectual encounter but from an incident that occurred when we were leaving the hall as some desultory wrangling was still in progress. Just as I was passing the back rows of the audience my glance fell upon Mrs Pnina Peli, Mrs Fackenheim and Moshe Greenberg. I smiled at them and they smiled back and I received from them such a warm feeling, a feeling of real friendship, a sense that these Jewish friends have become such an important part of my life. That is a reality which no theological differences can obscure, much less destroy.

22nd August, 1984. Nairobi

A wise man has said, 'The soul is not a fixed entity. It is a movement that begins whenever a man experiences the psychological pain of contradiction.' That is an observation which gives me a good deal of consolation because in the past I have felt my acute sense of contradiction to be an affliction. Though I have only detected the source of it in recent years, yet for most of my life I have experienced a pain such as our wise friend is referring to. But now I have become aware that in my own case what causes the pain is any contradiction between words that are spoken and the voice in which they are spoken. I hear false notes in a person's voice in much the same manner, I suppose, as a trained musician is painfully aware of false notes in the playing of a piece of music or the singing of a song. A false note in a voice scratches across my heart like sandpaper, especially if the voice is my own.

In any case this gift – or affliction, whichever it is – does act as a rough indicator of the kind of company in which I find myself. This in turn places me in the dilemma of wondering whether I should respond to the actual words that someone has spoken, in which I hear falsity, or to some reality which the words are disguising. If I respond to the former then I am allowing myself to be drawn into the falsity; but if I respond to the latter it causes embarrassment in the company present who do not want to be made aware of the contradiction, since they themselves are colluding in it. Sometimes, at least, I believe one ought to speak to the reality, especially when one is amongst the English for whom embarrassment is a weapon which they have spent long years perfecting.

Those were some of my thoughts both during and after the journey we made by car to Ben Gurion airport *en route* for a meeting in Nairobi of the World Conference of Religions for Peace. It was a Protestant minister from the US whom we had agreed to pick up in Jerusalem who prompted them. He did not commend himself to any of us, in the first place, by keeping us waiting for half an hour and then offering a weak apology in the most off-hand fashion. But that was excusable compared with the way in which, with no previous acquaintance, he proceeded to harangue us with one item of ecclesiastical gossip after another, and to bad-mouth every person his waspish mind lit upon, for some of whom I have deep respect.

I have rarely heard a voice so near to sounding totally false, and it left me asking myself, 'Is this how one makes one's spiritual preparation for a peace conference?'

Fortunately for me he must have decided by the time we climbed on to the plane that I was not a worthy recipient of his gossip and so he attached himself to Mrs Nasrullah, who is worthy, being a prominent figure in the World Council of Churches. It was also my good luck to be seated next to my friend, Rabbi Jack Cohen, a wry, humorous, sceptical man. He and I did not talk much because, since he is a good Jew, he was not going to lose the opportunity provided by our long flight to add to the sum of his learning. So he immersed himself in a large, learned and abstract Hebrew tractate which he had brought with him. Sitting in silence beside my Jewish friend intent upon his learned book proved to be wonderfully peaceful. From several rows behind us I occasionally caught the sound of the waspish Protestant minister's protesting voice. The contrast between my Jewish neighbour and my fellow-Christian

253

struck me as intriguing, an appropriate preparation for a peace conference directed towards transcending religious boundaries.

That evening, as the plane took us closer to Nairobi, the meaning of boundaries presented itself to me again but in a different sphere.

For hour after hour, as we flew over the plateau of southern Ethiopia and north-east Kenya we were looking out of the plane windows across endless vistas of flat, grey earth occasionally dotted with shrubs and trees. Soon I began to get a breath of what is meant by the phrase 'the magic of Africa'. It is the sense of space and timelessness which induces one to breathe ever more slowly and deeply, slipping into a primal rhythm, the rhythm that was in the dream time when both animals and men moved across the face of the earth at the speed of their own walking. In those days there were no machines, and there were no boundaries. For our conference this was a sobering thought: scarcely more than a century ago there were no frontiers throughout the whole of this seemingly endless continent of Africa, an age when men and animals traversed these planes on foot, crossing forests and rivers unshackled.

As the plane alighted upon the runway at Nairobi airport I noticed several armoured cars on either side of the runway accompanying the plane into the airport itself. The armoured cars were crammed with armed soldiers.

23rd August, 1984. Nairobi

What an exhausting day this has been! From ten-thirty in the morning until after seven in the evening, with a short break for lunch, several hundreds of us sat patiently in the astonishingly plush Kenyatta Conference Centre listening to endless repetitious speeches, some of them very pompous.

However, half-way through the hot, airless afternoon I told myself that in order for any human gathering to be successful it has to enact certain ceremonies wherein there needs to be a touch of magnificence. And, granted human nature, that magnificence will inevitably turn sometimes into pomposity. So you just have to put up with it if you want the gathering to be successful.

At the same time you could feel so much good will and patience amongst the hundreds of mute peace pilgrims who continued dutifully to applaud the repetitious speeches that the Spirit of God was bound eventually to inspire someone to raise the spirits of the audience. That did indeed happen when the ninety-year-old Hindu sage, Divenkar, spoke spontaneously from his heart and so touched our own hearts. It happened even more obviously when a youngish Catholic priest of the liberation theology school from Chile was called to the microphone. Not only did he invoke the Spirit, he was filled with the Spirit as he described his work amongst the poor and oppressed of his native land. But, best of all, he actually moved us – in the basic, literal sense of the word! He called upon us to stand up from our seats and all together sing *Kumbaya,* a swinging spiritual that is ideal for loosening up stiff, middle class intellectuals. All at once the conference had come to life; so we were able to leave the Kenyatta Conference Centre in a cheery mood.

On our way back by bus to our own conference campus north of the city we drove past many opulent residences outside of which armed guards were stationed to protect their rich masters. Some of these rich masters had been present in the Kenyatta Conference Centre where they had joined in exhorting us to make an option for the poor.

31st August, 1984. Tantur

Looking back upon the Peace Conference it is borne in upon me once more how vital the spiritual dimension is for all of us who aspire to work for peace, yet how little regard is paid to spiritual discipline at so many of these meetings. It is as though we doff our hats to the Spirit at the beginning and then say, 'Now let us put that aside and get on with the serious business.'

I am thinking particularly of last Friday. We had been asked to fast for part of the day as an expression of our solidarity with the oppressed people of South Africa, and to meet in the main forum for common prayer at half-past midday. Already we had been informed of the presence amongst us of Graham Stanton, an Anglican priest, who had been imprisoned in South Africa by the Botha regime and had only been released a day or two previously. He was to speak at the meeting.

As it turned out there were only half a dozen people present by the time appointed, including Stanton himself, clearly a very sensitive man who had about him that same indefinable air of having touched something ultimate which one invariably finds amongst the survivors of the Japanese POW camps of the Second World War. He waited patiently, along with the rest of us, for more members of the conference to arrive. A few did so. But the attendance was still sparse even three-quarters of an hour later, at which time it was decided to wait no longer but to begin the service of intercession.

Similarly, the organisers of the conference had encouraged members to take part in a meditation session in the evenings at nine-thirty, the sessions to be led by a different person on each occasion in accordance with the various traditions represented amongs us. In the event the number of meditators never rose above one in fifty of the conference members.

And in one area at least of our work you could trace the destructive effect of this neglect of spiritual discipline in much the same way as you can trace the path of poisoned blood in a limb whose immunisation capacity has been undermined. This area was that of the Middle East workshop where some twenty-five of us spent two whole days in the same room thrashing out the issue of peacemaking in the Middle East. There were present Jews from Israel, the US and Canada; Christians from the US, Britain, Canada, Israel and the Philippines, as well as Muslims from Egypt, Pakistan, Iran and the Sudan.

There were some elevating moments during those tense two days, above all when three women managed to slice a path through the macho rhetoric that was clogging the room up. One of the women came from the West Bank, a Christian; the second, Jewish, came from Israel, whilst the third was a Muslim from Lebanon. They stood together for a period in a mutual embrace that cleansed the atmosphere for a time. The image of those three is memorable.

But there were some very bad experiences as well, especially when interventions were made by the Iranians, spokesmen for Ayatollah Khomeini, who had muscled in on the conference. Their terrifying mentality was revealed when they were asked to comment on the accusation that many people in Iran are being persecuted on account of their religion. The Iranians' answer was even more stunning than the questioner had anticipated. The reply came, 'There is no persecution or discrimination against Jews, Christians and Zoroastrians, the peoples of the book. They are all allowed to fight in the war and are all buried in martyrs' cemeteries.' Not only those words but also the faces from which the words emerged, hard as if set in stone, made me think of Cromwell and his Ironsides – as did their emotionless voices when a Jewish participant exclaimed, 'So you are planning to capture Jerusalem and destroy the Jews in Israel?' Tonelessly they replied, 'It will not be necessary for us to do so – God will do so in order to punish you.'

But the behaviour of the Khomeini followers was not the most disturbing aspect of the Middle East workshop. After all they had marched into the meeting unbidden and we scarcely expected better of them. Far more difficult to comprehend and justify is what happened to the six or seven Jewish members of the workshop.

Almost from the first minute that we gathered in that stuffy room the Jews present were subjected to a stream of accusations from other members of the group on account of the oppression practised upon the Palestinians by the Zionist State of Israel. Coming at the very beginning this expression of hostility raised the tension within the room to such a height that henceforth, no matter what subject we might ostensibly be discussing, everyone knew in their nerve endings that the iniquities of Israel were likely to break in upon our discussions at any second.

The result was what anyone with even a grain of intelligence could have predicted: the Jews felt themselves cornered since they were being made to feel personally responsible for every iniquitous policy practised by the State of Israel. Naturally, in reaction they displayed the less amiable features of their own personalities.

To watch all this happening almost reduced me to despair. Nevertheless I tried to deter the most persistent accusers by catching them at a coffee break and retailing to them the story of the French zoo whose directors affixed a notice to the cage of one of the animals. The notice read, *Cet animal est très méchant. Quand on l'attaque il se défend.* ('This animal is very wicked. When you attack it, it defends itself.') I was hoping that the story might induce them at least to modify their own behaviour; but there was precious little evidence that it had done so.

Their attitude, in fact, brought to mind again the classical teaching that stupidity is not simply the result of some mechanical or technical error, but is rather the consequence of some self-induced moral obtuseness. They appeared unable to see that our Jewish colleagues, by the very fact of joining in such a peace conference, had shown themselves prepared to face criticism from their right-wing fellow-citizens in Israel who were likely to accuse them of 'consorting with the enemy'. Indeed some of these Jews had already suffered obloquy for standing up in defence of the rights of West Bank Arabs. And now, as a reward for defending West Bank Arabs, they were being attacked

258

by other Arabs! It is hardly surprising that after two days they themselves began to sound like members of the Israeli right-wing Likud party.

1st September, 1984. Letter to the Tablet
on Conviviality

The deep resonance of the word only struck me as I was sitting, away from home, in the corner of a grubby foodstall on a back street of Larnaca. Beside me a cheery-looking Cypriot workman was eating his boiled eggs and drinking his beer with unselfconscious gusto. I also was glad of the beer after the hot morning wandering around this quarter of the town. In particular my mind was filled with images of various mosques which l had seen, now abandoned and decaying but still dignified by the nobility of their minarets. But what haunted me even more was the realisation that in this quarter of the town both Greek and Turkish Cypriots must once have lived cheek by jowl; and no matter what tensions and animosities they may have experienced, nevertheless in some measure they had practised conviviality. Whereas now, some ten years after the ideologues had their way, there were no Turkish Cypriots in this part of the island, just as there are no Greek Cypriots in the northern part. So today neither Turks nor Greeks have the least chance any longer to practise conviviality.

'Con-vivere', I thought to myself. What a wonderful word! To live-with others. Could there be any greater grace than the grace to live with others?

Of course they had quarrelled throughout the centuries, these Greek and Turkish neighbours. But at the same time they had seen one another celebrating the birth of children; they had watched, and even shared in, one another's marriage feasts; and at a death in the community they had been touched by the others' mourning. They had at least known that the others were human beings and not

259

demons. But now they never see one another. They are as invisible as demons, and therefore they can demonise one another.

I was reminded of an earlier day in Jerusalem, when I had walked into the home of some friends who lived in the Old City. They had greeted me warmly and asked: 'Where have you been, Donald?' 'Over in West Jerusalem', I replied, brightly enough. There was a silence: West Jerusalem is Jewish. Eventually one of my friends said: 'Oh! We never go there now.' 'Why not?' 'Because we find it so uncongenial.'

It so happened that I had spent quite some time in Jerusalem that morning sitting on a bench in the open space below the Great Synagogue named Liberty Bell Gardens, watching scores of young children playing on the grass and hiding in the bushes – some of them handicapped children carefully tended by their teachers. They all seemed so happy! And there was joy in my heart as I watched them; until suddenly, like a hammer blow, the thought struck me that a generation ago these same children, utterly delightful, absorbed in their games, would have been herded off in cattle trucks to die in gas chambers simply because they were Jewish.

Sparked by that vivid memory, I said to my friends: 'In that case, perhaps it would be a good idea for you to make a point of going into West Jerusalem at least once a week. Just sit on a bench or at a café table and watch the people going about their everyday tasks, and you will soon begin to feel for them as human beings. What you are doing now is to keep away from the people of West Jerusalem so that you are then in a position to demonise them.'

Of course I realised why my friends adopted their position: they had seen their Arab neighbours ill-treated; they knew only too well the difference between the facilities given to Jewish children and those available for Arab children. But when all that is said, and much more in the same vein, does not my joy in the security of those Jewish children afford some chance, however slim, of conviviality? Whereas practising apartheid, standing at a distance, only exacerbates ideological differences.

Strangely enough, there are some who stand at a distance for seemingly good reasons. A number of my liberal Jewish friends in Israel, for instance, including a leading writer, absolutely refuse to enter the West Bank whilst the West Bank is under Israeli occupation because, so they say, even to pass through that area at present would risk placing themselves, as Jews, in the ranks of the oppressors. But should my writer friend not take that risk in order to be able to convey to his readers the feel of everyday life on the West Bank? Because, as it is, Israelis in general – even liberal ones – have almost no sense of what life is like for a people who yet live only a few miles away.

A much greater risk was taken lately by our Arab staff. They joined us on an outing into Israel, to the beach at Netanya. For them it was most daring because they always fear what might happen to them in Israel – that they might be arrested, for example, and vanish forever into an Israeli prison. One or two of the older amongst them, moreover, had never in all their years ventured to the coast. But in the company of us Europeans and Americans they seemed to feel protected.

And they were greatly rewarded not only by the pleasures of the beach but even more by moments of real conviviality.

At first our Israeli neighbours on the beach looked very surprised to see some thirty Arabs accompanied by one or two Westerners settling themselves on the sands with numerous large hampers of food and drink. Indeed a few of them, when they saw our hampers all set out, assumed that the food and drink was for sale and hesitantly came across to try to buy some of it – to the merriment of Jews and Arabs alike when their mistake was discovered.

But perhaps the *pièce de résistance* occurred when some of the younger Arab women in our party switched on a transistor and spontaneously broke into dancing. There were smiles all round; and from then on, for the rest of the day, the atmosphere was easy and friendly.

But both the worst and the best was yet to come. In the evening, just as we were preparing to board our bus and go up again to Jerusalem, our cook Da'oud was suddenly taken ill, wracked in great pain. Realising that it might be very serious, I ordered our driver to head northwards immediately to a hospital which, as it turned out, is situated in an area wholly populated by Orthodox Jews. This became obvious to me as soon as Yakoub and I started shepherding Da'oud through the emergency waiting room. Because that afternoon it was serving as the ante-natal clinic and was full of manifestly pregnant women dressed in Orthodox fashion and being attended to by doctors and attendants all of whom were wearing kippas. Women, doctors and attendants understandably looked startled at the sight of the writhing Da'oud being propelled along by a hefty, heavily-moustachioed Arab and a tall, beard Westerner. However, the doctors quickly recovered and rose to the emergency.

Two hours later, we were able to help Da'oud back onto the bus, a much relieved man – just as we ourselves were now much wiser by whatever wisdom accrues to one through sitting patiently and quietly for two hours surrounded by pregnant Orthodox Jewish women – a wisdom which I felt to be considerable.

Yet the best, as I said, was still to come. On arriving back at Tantur, and before alighting from the bus, we prayed a prayer of gratitude to God for the wonderful day we had shared together, and last of all thanked him for the kindness and skill of the Jewish doctors who had restored Da'oud to us. It was a sincere, heartfelt prayer, a perfect ending to our outing.

'And another thing', as Yakoub said the next morning at coffee time as he dramatically recited the great deeds of yesterday for anyone who would listen. 'And another thing', he repeated in his thunderous voice. 'They only charged us 4,000 shekels. On the West Bank that would have cost us 16,000 – no! 20,000 shekels!' For some reason this perpendicular drop from the sublime to the shekel was too much for his audience, with the result that they almost fell off their chairs with laugher. Palestinian Arabs have such a ready sense of humour.

Of course I am aware, more than I dare say, that the Jewish–Arab conflict is not be camouflaged by stories such as I retail here. But even in conflict one flash of conviviality is worth more than a whole generation of apartheid, whether physical or ideological.

22nd September, 1984. Tantur

There are occasions, living in this land, when you are made to feel as though you are a character in some corny spy story.

All I wanted to do, in the first place, was something you might have thought perfectly simple and straightforward. Seven years ago I gave a series of lectures to a class in Bethlehem University after which the students engaged me in a lengthy debate. I had spoken of Gandhi's *satyagraha*, the way of non-violence and they had told me that it was foolish idealism.

They told me of how, in 1967, the Jordanian artillery positioned on the heights eastwards of Tantur had shelled the Jewish forces in Jerusalem for two whole days but had not managed to kill a single person, whereas 'the Jewish tanks took up position near Ramat Rachel and shelled Bethlehem for only forty minutes but they killed so many people in that short time that the Jordanians surrendered Bethlehem.'

I remained silent for quite a while as the students waited for my response to what they deemed an irrefutable argument. Eventually I said quietly, 'You mean to say you admire the Jews so much that you wish to imitate them? to become like them?' I must have touched a raw nerve because they grew very angry with me.

263

In light of that experience it seemed to me some months back that the only way to present non-violence as a feasible alternative for Palestinians was to introduce the subject obliquely, in an indirect fashion. And the film *Gandhi* presented a God-given means of doing so: I would watch the film in the company of Bethlehem University students and then we would all discuss it together afterwards.

That seemed simple enough. But not in this land! In the first place the Israeli authorities are not allowing the film to be shown in cinemas in the occupied territories. In the second place, the students at Bethlehem University are very suspicious about what lies behind my suggestion. And, finally, my various aides keep turning up with video versions of the film which are hopeless – either the sound is garbled or the picture is blurred or bits are missing. Moreover, when I start to show signs of impatience at this pantomime they become conspiratorial and hint that getting a video of *Gandhi* is almost a secret service operation – you have to smuggle it across the Allenby Bridge in peril of arrest by the Shin Beit. I don't believe the half of it.

17th October, 1984. Letter to the Tablet

As the time for my departure from Tantur approaches, and with it the end of this series of extracts from my Jerusalem journal, I realise that during the past four years I may well have failed to communicate the impact on our everyday lives of events that take place actually within sight of our Institute. So this month, instead of trying to reflect upon the entries in my journal so as to extract a general theme from them, I decided simply to record in all their abruptness certain events of this sort and show how they have struck us – or, rather, how we have stubbed our toes on them.

As, for instance, happened when I drew the bedroom curtains the morning not long after my return from my visit to Nairobi. Some 600 yards away, across the valley towards the hilltop settlement of Gilo, there was now an enormous heap of rubble where previously had stood a two-storey family·house. And strewn about the hillside below the rubble were uprooted olive trees and almond trees from which the family had drawn their living.

I walked up the hill later that day to discover what had happened, and was able to piece together a confusing story from the broken English of Muhanna, a sturdy middle-aged man who had lived in the house along with his simple brother Mahfouz and his eighty-five-old father, Salman Saleb Arab. The old man, all his days a land-worker, had lived in the house for over fifty years until one morning recently. On that morning a group of men brandishing guns had arrived with a bulldozer; they had thrown everything out of the house – furniture, clothes, appliances and the rest – and within half an hour had reduced the Arab house to rubble. The family were left to sleep out under the open sky beside their ruined home until the Red Cross provided them with a tent. But even that had been torn down by the time I arrived.

Who were the members of this group that had behaved so barbarously? 'Settlers', said Muhanna. I understood why he said that, because West Bank Arabs always assume that civilians toting guns are Jewish settlers, but I doubted whether that was the case. The settlers may be ruthless, but this was not their style. And my doubts proved to be well-founded: the men in question had been hired by a wealthy Jew who lives in Los Angeles and who claims that he is the owner of the land.

But even in the gloom of such miserable happenings, human beings can be sources of astonishing illumination. Sitting there on his heap, like the Patriarch Job, the old man calmly smoked a cigarette, lifted his hands towards the heavens and said, 'It is the will of God.' And the vigorous Muhanna, though more excited, also showed no bitterness. 'God is good', he said. 'There is room for us all, Jews and Muslims and Christians.'

Yet the incident most calculated to dumbfound a Western mind was to occur several days later. Whilst Dorothy, my wife, and I sat with the family on some rickety old boxes, two agents of the contractor drew up in their car. As they were walking across the rubble towards us, they began to look sheepish at the unexpected sight of two Westerners sitting there. But whereas I gazed stonily at them, our Arab friends did not.'*Ahlan, wa sahlan*', they called out – 'Welcome, welcome'. 'This is overdoing traditional Arab hospitality', I said to myself. But more was to come. The contractors later asked a neighbouring European family if they might leave the notorious bulldozer for safety on their land. Indignantly, the Europeans refused – but the Arabs themselves allowed the bulldozer to stand on their property.

And there were other good moments which showed that although this part of the world may sometimes seem like the Wild West, nevertheless Israel remains a democracy, in spite of all the strains upon it. My wife, for instance, wrote a letter to the *Jerusalem Post* about our neighbours' plight which prompted a compassionate freelance reporter to publish a full-length article upon the incident. And nothing could have been prompter than the response of Teddy Kollek, one of the great city mayors of this century, when I informed him of what had happened. Immediately he sent along Amir Heshin, his adviser on Arab affairs, to investigate. He, on seeing the condition of the Arabs, straightaway bought food for them out of his own pocket. And I have no doubt that justice of some sort will now be achieved.

In the meantime, there had taken place the drama at our gatehouse. It was Sunday morning and our skilful handyman, Yakoub, was sitting on his porch drinking coffee with that air of leisured satisfaction which in itself is already a vote of confidence in God. Suddenly he heard cries of alarm just beyond the gate and rushed out to see what was happening. There he saw three Israeli soldiers running away from a smoking truck whilst a fourth was gripping the absurdly inadequate fire extinguisher provided in an attempt to prevent the vehicle from going up in flames.

266

Instantly Yakoub dashed back into his house, seized a proper fire extinguisher and within minutes had the smoke quelled and the danger of an explosion averted.

The terrified soldiers hardly knew how to believe their luck. They had been driving to Hebron from the Allenby Bridge on the Jordan when something had gone wrong with the truck's petrol system. Now they realised that they might all have gone up in flames. But what were they to make of this Arab who had saved the day? Especially after he invited them into his home to have some coffee and cakes and to telephone their commanding officer at the Allenby Bridge to come and make a report on the accident?

When he told me all this next day, Yakoub was bubbling with laughter as he described how the Israeli soldiers had hesitated before accepting his invitation – they clearly thought he might be a 'terrorist'. However, they calmed down after spending a few hours drinking his coffee until the arrival of their commanding officer, who was even more fulsome than they in his thanks to Yakoub.

'That's all very well, you being a hero, Yakoub,' I said, 'but who is going to replace our fire extinguisher?' 'They will, professor. I told them it was not mine, but the Institute's. And,' he continued with a sly smile, 'perhaps they will also send us a spare one. And,' slyer still, 'perhaps they will even give me a note to say that in future Yakoub must not be kept waiting at the Allenby Bridge when I am going to Amman?' I shouldn't bet on it, Yakoub.

During this same period we had been hearing the sound of drums beating and a crowd singing for several nights. The sound came from the courtyard of the hostel in the care of the Salvatorian Fathers from Lebanon which is situated about 200 yards south of us, on the rocky path towards Bethlehem where the local people say that Joseph, Mary and the donkey travelled. On Wednesday afternoon, as she was walking past the hostel, Dorothy discovered the source of the singing and drum-beating. It came from some thirty or forty people of all ages from Lebanon who were making merry in the courtyard.

For a few minutes Dorothy stood watching, enjoying the occasion but declining the repeated invitations to join in the dancing. Then, before she knew what was happening, an enormously fat and jolly Lebanese woman seized her by the arm and swept her into the company of the dancers, all of whom began clapping to encourage their new recruit.

She whirled around with them for a quarter of an hour but then excused herself as she had to go into Bethlehem. Still out of breath but smiling to herself, she was startled a hundred yards later to find herself confronted by an Israeli soldier carrying a machine gun slung across his chest. It was the stark contrast within such a short distance between the merriment and the machine gun which made her jump. The young soldier, however, was extremely pleasant and kindly; he realised how he had given her a fright and went out of his way to assure her there was nothing to worry about – 'Just some trouble in Deheishe.'

Deheishe is a camp of some 8,000 refugees which lies about two kilometres south of us on the Hebron road. Its name is known to many in Israel because the inhabitants of the camp are often in conflict with the Jewish settlers who have to pass by Deheishe on their way to their settlement overlooking Hebron. For us at Tantur the camp is more than a name; it is part of our everyday awareness since, apart from anything else, our gardener lives there. He often comes to work on a donkey. Whenever I see this, I remember how the Institute has available a Peugeot, a Volkswagen and a Fiat. And I am reminded of Jesus. Many days our gardener cannot come, because his camp has been placed under curfew.

'The trouble in Deheishe' that day had centred around the racist member of the Israeli parliament, Rabbi Kahane. Kahane, who advocates expelling all Arabs from Israel and the West Bank, had gone into the camp accompanied by military officers, soldiers and journalists. He had conducted afternoon prayers in face of the camp mosque and had declared, 'I will show these dogs that just as *they* can wander about Tel Aviv, so *I* can move about here.'

Reflecting on all the other incidents from *il piccolo mundo di Tantur* recounted here, I can find some sign of redemption. But for Kahane in Deheishe I can find none.

23rd October, 1984. Tantur

I have not been very successful in trying to bring the Christian members of our Arab staff into the worship life of the community. Soon after I took over as Rector I was dismayed to discover that when the community was ferried into Jerusalem each year to take part in Christian Unity services it was customary for the expatriates (scholars and monks) to go into the services but for our drivers, Sami and Yakoub, to remain outside until the service was over. So the foreign Christians went in and the native Christians remained outside! Which provided an ironic comment on a community dedicated, as we are, to the search for Christian unity.

At first I was inclined to rail within my own mind at the colonialist attitude on the part of the expatriates towards the local Christians which this customary behaviour exemplified. And doubtless there was some justification for my railing; but since those days I have come to realise that the Arab Christians have their own way of dealing with such situations. Although for expatriates to say that the Arabs themselves prefer the customary way is only an unwitting way of acknowledging the Arabs have been cowed by colonialism. Indeed they have. Nevertheless, that is by no means the whole story: the Arabs have shown that when they deem a situation sufficiently serious they are quite capable of taking over the reins and guiding events in the direction that they consider proper, as they proved at Lane's funeral.

And they are infinitely better than us at celebrating funerals; perhaps because in their lowliness and poverty they are nearer than we are to nothingness and death, and are therefore more serious about life. I certainly felt the full power of their seriousness one morning two months ago when I went into Bethlehem to take part in the funeral service for Carlos' mother in the Church of the Nativity (Carlos being one of our two night guards).

In best Arab fashion they had been very vague about the time at which the funeral procession was supposed to come into church, whether at ten o'clock or ten-thirty. So, in order not to be late, I arrived at ten o'clock, only to find almost no one there. But that in the event proved to be a blessing because amongst the patient people of Bethlehem waiting is itself a mode of communion. Their capacity for waiting has shown itself over thousands of years as they have watched one after another of their conquerors come and go whilst they themselves have quietly survived. And all that grinding history is written on the faces of these men and women as they come into church, cross themselves and then sit quietly, looking straight ahead towards the altar. Their faces are weather-beaten from the burning sun of summer and the fierce winds of winter that do indeed beat upon Bethlehem. All the faces are heavily lined, the men with thick moustaches and generally a stubble of beard. And all of them, men and women, are wearing cheap, worn clothes and much-mended shoes. But their apparent drabness is defied and overcome by the proud and skilful way in which their head-dress is set, the traditional keffiyeh, patterned in both red and grey. Their faces are extraordinarily beautiful, reminiscent of the sort of beauty that one also finds amongst the Irish of Connemara.

After the service only the men accompany the coffin to the graveyard, the women going apart to prepare the funeral meal. So I was one of about fifty men who made our way through the traffic of Manger Square and up Milk Grotto Street. It was there that I was moved to tears when I gazed over the heads of my companions as they filled the whole width of Milk Grotto Street between the open shops on one side and the high walls on the other, moving along like some powerful river. Unhurried, they moved in unison in spite of some of the older men occasionally stumbling; and everywhere you could see the heads bowed in sorrow, the shoulders bent from years of toil and at every step the keffiyehs rising and falling like the waves of the sea. In that moment the funeral procession symbolised for me almost everything there is to say about our human condition: the agony of a creature doomed to know death, the hope that springs from knowing poverty, and the capacity for compassion which binds us into one.

And how well, how instinctively, these Arabs of Bethlehem know the way that ceremony should be accomplished. Without hesitation and with no need for books or an orchestrating priest or official they knew when to stop to allow the close relatives to go forward, in what order to present their condolences to the line of chief mourners and in what manner to take their leave so as to bring that part of the ceremony to a close with dignity and due order.

I believe it was the funeral of Carlos' mother that drew him and me close together, just as his fellow night-guard, Akel, and I had already been drawn together by my sharing Akel's sorrow over the death of his new-born child.

And now, almost every night, we meet for a short space of time and commune with one another – though I think Akel and Carlos would show a proper hesitation about using the high-sounding word 'commune'. But that is what really happens when they come up to the roof each night in the course of their guard duties and often find me walking up and down under the vast night sky of Judea. Even on a moonless night they are able to pick out my figure in the darkness and greet me, '*Kif Halak, doctur?*'

Usually we speak for no more than five or ten minutes, but in that time I seem to learn far more than I generally learn from the seminars of the day just gone. And I dearly hope that I shall never forget what they said last night, each speaking in turn, antiphonally supporting one another:

'Why do men lie to one another, *doctur*?'
'Because they forget about death.'
'There is only one moment when men recognise truth.'
'That is when they stand at the grave-side looking down.'
'Then they walk away.'
'And twenty yards later they forget the truth.'
'They begin to lie again.'

As Akel and Carlos intoned these truths, like two sides of a choir responding to one another, I gazed at their strongly-boned faces silhouetted against the faint lights of Bethlehem and remembered how often I had seen such men as these being treated by Western tourists as though they were uneducated and therefore ignorant. Will the educated never learn that truth only comes through hardship?

14th November, 1984. Tantur

I have waited in vain for a voice to be raised in Israel against that statement, 'only a very few women and children were massacred', made by Sharon. It may well be that my friends in the peace movement have become weary of denouncing Sharon. But now I await again for someone to denounce Sharon's lawyer who is representing Sharon in his action against *Time* magazine. According to today's *Jerusalem Post*, the lawyer, Milton Gould, maintained that 'many of the approximately 500 killed in Sabra and Shatilla were terrorists' and, again, that only about fifteen women and fifteen children were among the dead.

272

I wonder if women and children would be so lightly dispatched if they were the wives and children of Gould and Sharon?

6th December, 1984. Tantur

Last night I kept being wakened by the noise of the fierce wind that was whistling around these bleak hills. And each time I awoke I found myself thinking of the Arabs in their tent on the hillside opposite. I have told them so often that they can come and live in Tantur if the weather gets too bad, but Muhanna and his father are very reluctant to do so. I know that some of their reluctance is due to their fear lest once they leave their tent empty it will be interpreted as a sign that they have given up the struggle, and a signal to Shawli and his toughs to take over their land. However, there is another factor at work. Ever since I showed Muhanna the room in Tantur where I thought his father might be comfortable I have been aware that Muhanna is uneasy; he senses that some members of the Tantur community at all levels are opposed to his father coming to stay in our buildings. One or two of those opponents are frightened that the pilfering from the Institute which they practise might get revealed – as if I didn't know about it! But there are others whose reasons are more despicable.

However, I felt that I had to go up the hill this morning to urge the Arabs to think again about coming in, otherwise I am afraid Salman might die. I was even more afraid when I did go up and I crawled into his tent, because at first I couldn't make out whether what lay on the camp bed was simply a pile of clothes or whether Salman lay hidden amidst them. And when eventually I did discover him and gently roused him the cries he gave were like the mewing of a helpless kitten before its eyes are yet open. Of course, his eyes, already almost sightless, gave him no light in the darkness of the tent and so he clung on to my hands with his own hands, still so firm and muscular, whilst clasping his rosary beads between thumb and forefinger. The old

273

man and I sat together like that for some considerable time, he swaying backwards and forwards slightly as he praised and gave thanks to God, and myself trying in the Spirit to stay close to the movement of Salman's spirit.

But then I heard a movement outside the tent and Muhanna appeared, the tough skin of his face and hands seemingly unaffected by the harsh winds. When I went out to speak with him he was as explosive as ever, ready to take on all opponents. He recited for me a list of dignitaries and officials from whom he had in vain sought help, Christian, Jewish, Muslim, to fight his case. As though chanting a litany he intoned of one after another: 'Mayor X say he has no money! Hah!', at which he gave a great roar of contempt, 'King Y! He has no money!' – an even more mirthful roar!

Finally he repeated his litany of contempt, naming each of the misers and saying after each one, 'He think he is big man. No big man.' He ended by saying decisively, 'No man big . . . only God', and then, in a wonderful flash of afterthought, 'and my father'. Thinking of the bundle of clothes inside the tent I suspected that Muhanna's afterthought came straight from God Himself.

10th December, 1984. Tantur

From where inside ourselves do certain words or deeds suddenly erupt? They astonish us just as much as they astonish others.

Today the committee was discussing whether it would be prudent of the Institute to take in our unhoused Arab friends up the hill. The general feeling was that it would be unwise of us to do so and when the other members were waiting for me to agree I suddenly heard the words, '*Kutum hogia*! Finish! If they wish to come they are welcome.'

And then I realised that it was I who had emitted that authoritative Urdu exclamation which puts an end to any further discussion of the issue. It is, perhaps, forty years

274

ago since I last used the phrase, since I was a soldier in India, in fact. *Kutum hogia* must have exploded out of the gulf between the suffering of the Arabs and the easy speeches flowing from us who only yesterday had been standing in chapel piously singing 'Whatsoever you do to the least of my brethren, that you do unto me.'

12th December, 1984. Tantur

So in the end the *Gandhi* scheme did not work, in spite of all the racking of brains and searching of hearts on the part of myself and Eddie Kaufmann. Eddie, a professor at Hebrew University, produced an even better idea than my own: he would bring a select group of Jewish students from Hebrew University to Tantur to watch the film and discuss it; I would invite a similar group – say, about eight or nine Arabs from Bethlehem University to do the same. Then we would try to persuade both groups to meet at Tantur for a meal and to discuss their various responses to the person and message of Gandhi. By doing so we hoped that the Arab and Jewish students might find some common ground and might even discover that on some issues certain Jews agreed with certain Arabs rather than with their 'own side', and vice versa.

Well, they certainly found common ground, all right, but not the common ground which Eddie and I had anticipated or hoped for. The Jewish students who watched the film said afterwards that it had no relevance to their situation because 'Gandhi in his non-violent campaign was dealing with the British, who can sometimes be reasonable, but we have to face the Arabs with whom you cannot reason.' The Arab response, when it came, was like a reverse echo of the Jewish statement. They said, 'Gandhi's non-violence may have worked with the British, who have some sense of decency, but it would never work with the Jews, who are merciless.' After which no one could be blamed for thinking, 'That is that! There is no point in taking this charade any further.' However, Eddie

275

and I have at least learnt that if you are going to undertake the work of reconciliation you simply cannot say 'That is enough! I am giving up.' And by some miracle a group of eight or nine Jewish students and a similar – though more reluctant – group of Arab students did agree to come to Tantur and share a meal together and afterwards to share their thoughts about the film (much of which, by this time, I felt to know by heart!).

When the appointed day came round the Jewish students duly arrived in good time for lunch and we all waited for the Arab contingent to come. However, time went by and went by, but no Arab students came; and we all grew more anxious about the enterprise, until eventually the telephone rang. An Arab student was on the line.

What else would you expect in this country, but that our efforts had been rendered vain at the last minute? The student's message was that the Israeli military had erected road blocks on the way from Ramallah, so the students from there could not get through. As a result they had phoned their colleagues in Bethlehem who, out of solidarity with the Ramallah students, would not now be coming to Tantur.

By this time lunch was somewhat overcooked, like the country, but we made the best of it.

There is an intriguing footnote to the whole Gandhi episode. I was sitting around drinking coffee with the Arab students after we had first watched the film when one of them made an amazing observation. He said, 'You know, we Arab men could never follow a Gandhi. We are so macho that we could not respect a man who makes a principle of non-violence. But we might follow a woman Gandhi – a strong woman like Um Fahum.'[8]

26th December, 1984. Tantur

What a marvellous evening we had last night, in spite of there not being very many people in the house, and in spite of our not having organised any celebrations!

In fact a capacity for such spontaneous celebration may well be the distinctive sign of an authentic community. And spontaneous it certainly was! We were all sitting around the music room chatting amiably, though in a slightly desultory fashion, when Ed began to play some lively tunes on the piano. The mercurial Sara immediately turned to Simha and said, 'Simha, now we are celebrating Christmas in a Christian community, so you must dance with me.' Since Sara has been unsuccessfully inviting her husband Simha to dance with her for almost fifty years, ever since they arrived in Palestine as Jewish immigrants from Poland, she can hardly have believed that Simha was going to change his tune at this late stage, when they are already both in their seventies. But it is a tribute to Sara's unending zest for life that one could still hear in her voice a note of hope, as if from a teenage girl.

'I will dance with you, Sara', said Simha in his slow, patient manner of speaking – and then, after a pause, he gave her the answer he has been giving to her for decades – 'when there is peace between Jews and Arabs.'

On seeing Sara's exasperation I took hold of her hand and drew her into the middle of the room. And in no time the two of us were whirling around and across the room in a form of dance invented on the spot. And not only Sara and myself; because for the next half hour Alexa and Joseph and Mike and Robin and several others swept around, changing partners and improvising steps as Ed at the piano skilfully interwove tune upon tune. Sara's eyes, always unusually brilliant for a seventy-two-year-old, were like Hallowe'en sparklers by the time we eventually sat down.

After the party I kept thanking God that our first Jewish scholar at Tantur has been Simha. I knew nothing about him three years ago when Richard happened to say to me, 'Simha Flapan is the best man I have ever met in my life', and soon afterwards Raphael independently made virtually the same comment. Believing, as I do, with my Sufi friends, that life does not offer us arguments but signs for which we have to be on the watch, I decided then and there that I was meant to see more of this Simha Flapan. I have since learnt that Simha was brought up in a Polish town as one of the town's very few Jews. His family were not observant but secular and socialist, and he has told me that he never experienced any anti-Semitism there. After immigrating to Palestine in 1930 he became very active in MAPAM (the United Workers Party), working especially for understanding between Jews and Arabs. In 1957, at the prompting of Martin Buber, he founded and edited *New Outlook*, a radical monthly journal devoted to Middle East issues, and so he has been working tirelessly for peace in the Middle East for some forty years. It amazes us all that in spite of almost daily set-backs Simha never shows the least trace of becoming down-hearted. He has all the traditional socialist virtues.

For months I had no idea how alien Tantur must have seemed at first to Sara when Simha agreed that they should live here for eight months. Apparently, last August, after they had inspected the apartment allotted to them, they were on the bus back to Tel Aviv when Sara turned to Simha and exclaimed, 'Simha! After all these years, now in my old age you take me to live in a monastery! It is too much!' With much raising of her eyebrows and exclamations of disbelief Sara told us this story three weeks ago when Dorothy and I were taking coffee in their apartment. What had prompted her to do so was the fact that Fr Joe O'Connor, the Jesuit, and Fr Hank Beninati, the Maryknoller,[9] had called in for half an hour to say 'Goodbye' before they return to the US. And as they were on the point of leaving Sara had flung her arms round each of them in turn and given each of them a loving embrace, which they had returned equally warmly.

Once the door had closed behind them Sara stood for a few seconds as if dumbstruck and then, her eyes seeming to open wider with every word, she said in astonishment, 'I would never have believed it! I come to love Roman Catholic priests and put my arms around them! If you had said that to me six months ago I would have laughed at you and said you must be crazy.' She added, 'This is the best community I have lived in during my life.'

Simha smiled at this but said nothing, though I believe I could guess the phrase that was in his head, a favourite phrase of his: 'As always, Sara, you exaggerate.' For Simha is through and through a political animal, and for him it is the political insights afforded by his time at Tantur for which he is specially grateful. In particular he says that for all the years he has spent in Tel Aviv trying to persuade his fellow Jews to understand the Arabs of the West Bank, nevertheless he himself had never appreciated what it must be like to be an Arab on the West Bank until he had spent these months amongst us. Here he has seen with his own eyes the daily harassment to which Arabs are subjected and he has heard with his own ears the injustices and miseries which the Arab in the street has to endure – and has heard it not from the lips of intellectuals in conferences but from the lips of ordinary men and women who have little interest in politics. Living here has changed his sense of the situation in a way that could never have happened whilst he was living in Tel Aviv.

In another respect also he has been changed: much to his own surprise he has come to understand and sympathise with those Israeli soldiers who are responsible for order on the West Bank. That happened only a few days ago.

The occasion arose out of my having invited several Israeli officers and soldiers, both male and female, to come and have lunch with us. When Simha and Sara heard that a group of Israeli soldiers would be at lunch with us I think they were rather shocked at first – as though we were adopting the role of collaborators, like the Vichyite French under the Nazis or the Judenrat in Eastern Europe. In fact they did say at first that they would not come in to lunch that day. However, when I pointed out to them that as they were almost the only fluent Hebrew speakers in Tantur they would be in the best position to help me act as a good host, they kindly agreed to come.

And what a revelation that was for them! I placed them next to the two most senior officers at one table whilst I engaged the junior members of the party at a different table. Naturally I kept glancing in their direction with some anxiety, but soon I relaxed on seeing that all four of them were talking earnestly and good humouredly – and without pause! So much so that the four of them continued their conversation long after the rest of the community had finished lunch and drifted along to the coffee room.

But eventually the two officers glanced at their watches and suddenly realised how long they had stayed talking. No time for coffee! So up they sprang, quickly collected their forces and bade us all a friendly farewell.

When I took Simha and Sara along to the coffee room they were aglow with gratitude for having had the opportunity to discuss so freely and at length with some of the military men who are responsible for maintaining law and order on the West Bank. They were really astonished to discover what enlightened views these soldiers had on many issues. And they were impressed, above all, by the soldiers' intelligent and sympathetic analysis of the position of the West Bank Arabs. 'They have a much better judgement of the situation', said Simha, 'than the politicians in the Knesset whose orders they have to carry out.' And when he said that I could not help wondering to myself whether this may not have been the very first opportunity for these two Peace Now activists, Simha and Sara, to have had a really human discussion with military men, a type which they perceive as alien. If so, that is certainly a plus to Tantur's account.

And yet I wonder if any of these incidents with Simha and Sara will remain as vivid before my mind's eye in future years as one which occurred three Sundays ago. The incident sprouted a form of comicality that seems to flourish on theological territory.

For several weeks I had been pestered with school-marmish notes from Henry, one of our scholars, who objects to our singing the doxology as the blessing for our Sunday lunch. He considers it very reprehensible that we invoke Father, Son and Holy Spirit when there are Jewish guests present. (Why do so many Americans insist on sending 'memoranda' instead of just coming and having a word with me? It is in every sense a noxious habit because once someone has committed themselves to paper they then feel they have to stick to it with a stubbornness that would be dissolved in a warm face-to-face discussion. Also, I have to confess that I was a bit irritated at being instructed on Jewish–Christian relations by someone who was not even born when I was already wrestling with the matter.)

In any case three Sundays ago no sooner had we all – or almost all! – finished singing the doxology when Henry indignantly rushed across to the table where Simha and Sara were standing and apologised profusely to them for the bad manners of the community in singing the doxology despite their presence.

Even from a distance, and hemmed around by scholars intent upon their meat roast, I was able to observe Simha's reaction. He was completely nonplussed by Henry's excited address to him. What he does not seem to have known is that Simha is just about as secular as a human being can get – not in a fiercely anti-religious fashion, but in the way of someone for whom words such as 'god' or 'gods' or 'saviour' belong in a foreign language which is used mainly by reactionaries and fanatics – although, it is true, a few of his friends do occasionally employ it.

So he gently assured Henry that he and Sara were not in the least offended by the doxology and were all the time enjoying the opportunity to observe the customs of Christians. All of this he told me afterwards with a little wry smile, leaving me with the impression that, like some field anthropologist, he would be most disappointed if the tribe amongst whom he was living and whose manners he was studying should in any way truncate their customs out of a mistaken regard for him.

281

Indeed, he assured me that as a result of living in Tantur his curiosity about religion had been aroused and he was even thinking that if he had time he might at some future date investigate the Jewish religion to which his ancestors belonged but of which he knows nothing.

1st February, 1985. Tantur

It was a great blessing to have begun keeping a journal all those years ago. The practice now seems to have become fashionable with people who are 'into spirituality'. And good luck to them and their mentors. Nevertheless I am grateful that I found the way into the habit on my own spontaneously, which is why I have refrained from reading any instructions concerning the practice, out of fear that I might spoil the spontaneity. What I have found most valuable about it over the years is the way in which a journal gradually reveals the distinctive threads out of which one's own life is meant to be woven. For instance, I was amazed, not long ago, to discover from my very first journal that already by the age of fifteen I was gnawing away at the distinction between a mystery and a problem, and at the need for myth in the attempt to express experience.

And the experience during the past month of having Fr Enomiya-Lasalle living here beside us has revealed to me a thread of desire that has been running strongly throughout my life without my ever having seen its continuity until now. For a seemingly unrelated purpose I picked up one of my ancient journals and began to peruse it. There, to my astonishment, I noticed how strong and persistent in its pages has been the longing for transparency. And then it dawned on me that it was only in the light of Fr Enomiya-Lasalle that I was now seeing the truth of it. That lovely old man came into my life at exactly the right moment. I am not at all sure that I could have received what he has to teach me at an earlier period of my life, and later might have been too late.

Nor was I immediately aware, when we first met, what a profound impression he was to leave upon me. Apart from the fact that I am tired of 'spiritual masters' who jet around the world and frequently land on my doorstep, I had many years ago read Fr Enomiya's book, *Zen. The Way to Enlightenment*, and had not felt myself specially enlightened at the end of it. On the other hand, you must be able to learn something from a Catholic of Huguenot ancestry, born in Westphalia, who was wounded as a young soldier in the First World War, became a Jesuit, founded a settlement in the Tokyo slums for the care of the destitute and was within one kilometre of the spot where the first atom bomb dropped on to Hiroshima. Since which date he has become a Japanese citizen, received the freedom of Hiroshima and graduated as a Zen master. Moreover he continues to go round the world at the age of eighty-six, teaching Zen meditation in Spain, Germany, Italy and who knows where else – fulfilling a programme that might kill off a man half his age,

Yet although it only took a few days to realise that there was something very remarkable in this small, slight, boyish-looking, humorous, courteous character who had landed amongst us, I could not focus on what that something was until the occasion of his lecture three weeks ago entitled 'The Way of Zen. The Way of Christ'. My dim-wittedness was overcome not by what he said but by just one gesture.

Perched upon the elevated platform in our lecture hall I introduced him to our learned audience drawn from all quarters of Jerusalem, which included Christian prelates and professors and rabbis of various sorts as well as one or two Zen *aficionados*. Accordingly Fr Enomiya stood up at the pulpitum to deliver his lecture; and after talking for a few minutes commented that one should not make the full lotus position into a *sine qua non* for the practice of meditation. 'All the same', he continued, 'it is well for all of you to know how to take up the position.' Forthwith, before the startled gaze of our audience, this old man of eighty-six nipped up on to the table at which I was sitting and took up the full lotus position. At this point, from my seat of privilege, gazing down the length of the hall, I saw row upon row of eyes nearly popping out of heads attached to the shoulders of Jerusalem dignitaries who are not accustomed to informality at any time, least of all during an academic lecture.

However, after explaining several points about the full lotus position Fr Enomiya slid down from the table, returned to the pulpitum and went on with his lecture as calmly as before.

The striking feature for me of that incident was the completely natural way in which he did what he felt he needed to do. For him it was simple: no embarrassment, no hesitation, no trace of playing to the gallery; in a word, the action of a free man. And since that day there have been so many similar incidents which I have been observing with growing attention and gratitude.

Just to give one other example. At the dinner table one evening a scholar was holding forth who knows that Fr Enomiya has incurred the severe censure of the Pope's favourite theologian, Hans Urs von Balthasar. Von Balthasar maintains that Enomiya is undermining Catholic faith by adopting Zen practices, which carry the taint of Buddhism. Our voluble scholar quoted one particularly critical statement about Enomiya attributed to von Balthasar and then turned to Fr Enomiya and, in a challenging voice, stated, 'He did say that about you, didn't he, Fr Enomiya?' Without any trace of anger, indeed with a little smile, Fr Enomiya said, 'Yes, I believe so.' He did not say one word more but simply got on with his eating. The scholar's question was clearly intended to sow mischief both here and abroad, and the rest of us at table were silently waiting to hear what Fr Enomiya was about to say in defence of himself or in criticism of von Balthasar. But he did nothing of the sort. He had answered the question; the matter was now at rest, so he applied himself to eating the grilled fish on his plate with proper Zen concentration and gusto.

The seal was put upon my conviction that we had here a truly transparent human being yesterday afternoon when it came to discussing the financial reckoning for his time amongst us. That could have been very tricky and complicated because of calculating how much of his air fare we should cover (since he was also visiting other institutions in Europe), how much we should pay for him for his lecture and how much he owed us for the food and lodging of himself and his companions. In the event I have never known any such transaction pass more quickly and more smoothly, and to the complete satisfaction of both parties. From which I am inclined to conclude that the ultimate test of transparency – indeed, of spirituality in general – is money; that is, whether we are straight about money.

How often does one encounter people prepared to disclose their political or religious beliefs, their family background, sexual relationships and every other aspect of their lives, but as soon as it comes to their money they shut up like a clam! In so doing they reveal where their treasure is: 'where your treasure is, there is your heart also' – in money.

The signs of a transparent human being, therefore, are simplicity and freedom. They only appear in someone when that person gets beyond vanity and beyond fear.

27th February, 1985. Tantur

Although it was a burial which has made this day so memorable, nevertheless Ruth's burial was an occasion of joy and, above all, it brought a sense of fulfilment.

We could never have guessed, when we met Ruth and Günther in 1982, that the two of them were going to become so dear to us, nor that I should be called upon to play such a part in the events of today. My first sight of Günther in 1982 was shocking, even somewhat

285

unnerving. At the Rest Centre on Mount Carmel where we were staying I could hardly believe that there was life in the skeleton-like figure I saw sitting at the dinner table to which Dorothy and I had been assigned. It was his eyes which first riveted my attention before I even noticed the corpse-like pallor of his face and the skull bone that was almost surfacing through the skin: Günther's eyes looked as though they were about to leave their sockets in a spasm of terror. Some unimaginably terrifying experience had left their wild traces upon him. And yet when he began to speak his voice was reverent and gentle and sure, so that you immediately knew him to be a man who had actually overcome terror and despair.

And so it proved when, over the course of our ever deepening friendship, we learnt the story of Günther and Ruth.

It was in the days when that sinister black cloud had not yet completely blotted out civilisation in Germany. It was during the year 1934, in Hamburg. Though Ruth was slightly younger than Günther they were both pupils in the same class at the Gymnasium. And one day the two of them arrived late at the door of their classroom – separately, but at the same moment; and both of them were out of breath through having had to hurry. They grinned ruefully at one another and each asked the other whether they should go late into class or slip out of school together and sit in a sunny park nearby to await the next class.

So Günther and Ruth sat in the park telling each other their stories, as adolescents have done throughout the ages. And from then on they were in love with one another – he an orphan from an artistic Social Democratic family and Ruth, a Jewish girl from one of those cultured German Jewish homes where the members seemed to breathe literature and music and art.

For almost a year they knew the joy of sharing the ecstasy and agony of growing up in that world poised

286

between hope for a new ordering of society and despair at the rising barbarism around them.

And then Ruth's family emigrated to Palestine, settling in the beautiful coastal city of Haifa at the northern limit of the Carmel mountains. There Ruth was cut off from news of Günther, first by the Nazi restrictions and then by the Second World War. And there she also drifted into a marriage with a man who proved to be both selfish and cruel. When this man eventually divorced Ruth she was left to care for her two sons, who grew up to be both handsome and clever. Sadly for her, however, the eldest of them was killed in Israel's war of 1967 against the Arab states. And, perhaps even more painful, her brilliant younger son not only quit the country on account of Israel's unbearable chauvinism, but was then seduced into following the false guru, Rajneesh of Poona in India.

But many times, during the years between, Ruth's heart had turned towards the memory of the young man with whom she had been in love in her girlhood days. She often asked herself what had happened to him, and this question exercised her so insistently that she decided to try to find out: she inserted a notice in a German newspaper asking if anyone could give her news of her old school friend, Günther Lys.

In view of the cataclysm that had overwhelmed Germany thirty years previously Ruth had not been specially hopeful that her enquiries would bear fruit. But to her delight they did; she managed to contact Günther. And what, in the meantime, had the cataclysm done to him?

Since he was a Social Democrat by conviction, and a pacifist to boot, it was only to be expected that Günther's path in Nazi Germany had proved to be a thorny one. As he later told me, he had always refused to say, '*Heil Hitler!*', commenting humorously that '*Guten Tag* is good enough for anyone.' What precisely happened to him between the outbreak of war in 1939 and Germany's surrender in 1945 we never discussed beyond the fact that he spent virtually the whole war in concentration camps. From Ruth I further gathered that Günther had been tortured and had been subjected to various medical experiments. Typically the book which he published anonymously concerning his years in the concentration camp is very modest, even undramatic in the sense that he always seems to be pointing towards certain currents of humanity and wisdom flowing beneath the terrible outer happenings that are deeper and more abiding than the inhumanity. Also he made a film entitled, *One day in a concentration camp*, to which he even gave certain humorous touches since, as he once explained to me, 'no matter how terrible a situation may be for human beings, there is always a chance of something happening which they will find humorous.'

Such was the man for whom Ruth sat waiting in the airport at Tel Aviv after thirty years of separation. Her decision to invite this now unknown figure from her past to come and visit her had provoked scepticism amongst nearly all her friends. 'As soon as he sees you he will realise the folly of your meeting again', said one of them. 'He will catch the very next plane back to Germany.'

But the wiseacres were proved wrong. For, as Günther told me, 'The moment we saw each other, even after all those years and even though now we were both old, we knew that this was how it should have been always. And ever since it was wonderful.' From Ruth I learnt that she had said to Günther as they left the airport lounge, 'Here is where we wait for the bus to Haifa.' 'A bus', said Günther. 'Why wait? Let us take a taxi.' 'Oh no!' replied Ruth. 'They are so expensive.' 'So what? We have already wasted too many years of our life. We will take a taxi so that the two of us can be alone.' And so they did; and they sat in the back of the taxi, just the two of them, holding hands, all the way to Ruth's flat in Haifa.

Whenever I have been with Ruth and Günther I have felt so much at one with them in spite of their 'not being believers', to quote Ruth's own phrase. Once, indeed, she said to me with unquestioning confidence that I would not

288

take it amiss, 'Religion can serve as a crutch for those who do not have Goethe and Beethoven and Mahler . . .' But, strangely enough, she did turn to me for help when her own heart became more and more broken over the behaviour of her younger son. And, in a sense, she has turned to me again from beyond death.

Last year, on Passover eve, she had yet another of her painful conversations with her son by telephone, after which she put down the phone, turned to Günther and murmured, 'I shall not survive this night.' Nor did she. Her heart was truly broken, and was dead by morning.

Shortly afterwards Günther was explaining to us that Ruth had left her body to the Hadassah Hospital in Jerusalem for medical research purposes and that her remains would become available for burial in a year's time. And that, he said, was a cause of concern to him because Ruth had insisted very strongly that she did not want any rabbi to say prayers over her remains when they were being interred – because she could not abide the narrow-mindedness of religious Jews. Moreover she asked him to see that she was laid to rest in a graveyard where Jews and Christians and Muslims and unbelievers could all be buried together. Granted the all-pervading fanatism of the religious in Israel, how on earth was poor Günther to find such a spot? There was no such spot in Israel, he was sure; and so he asked me if I could find a place where we might bury Ruth's remains in accordance with her last wishes.

In between all my other tasks I have searched high and low during the past twelve months for a solution to Günther's dilemma, but as this year's Passover drew near without any success I began to feel rather desperate, envisaging an awful moment when we would collect Ruth's remains but have to stand with them helpless, having nowhere to lay them to rest. What on earth would we do with them?

By the grace of God, however, almost at the last minute, we found the perfect place, a place that would furthermore

289

symbolise Ruth's desire for all human beings of whatever persuasion to find peace together at the last. And from that discovery onwards the whole action of burying Ruth's remains worked perfectly, moving through every difficulty with the smoothness of some ancient, well-practised ritual, from the moment yesterday when I asked the help of Yakoub and Abu Jihad until the end of the funeral meal in our apartment where we all warmed our chilled bones with whiskey.

I needed Yakoub, my Christian friend, and Abu Jihad, my Muslim friend, to help me to prepare the grave because the weather had been stormy and bitterly cold, and the bottom of the grave was deep in water. They are strong fellows and know how to handle picks and shovels, how to deal with such eventualities. And I found it deeply moving to see how readily they responded to my request for help. Their immediate unspoken understanding of the occasion reminded me of the words spoken at the Introit for the Mass: 'I will go to the altar of God.' It was just as though my Arab friends were Mass servers, responding by declaring their readiness also to go to the altar of God.

Abu Jihad, in particular, without any fuss, conveyed by his every gesture a profound sense of the liturgical needs of the occasion. It may seem contrived for me so to describe his response since Abu Jihad and I would on the surface appear to have little in common. Driven from his native village by Jews over thirty years ago into a refugee camp, he still lives in that same camp where he has brought up fourteen children. Many of his children work abroad, some as doctors. The ones that I know are a credit both to him and to the straight path of Islam. But Abu Jihad and I have been greeting one another each morning for several years now in a liturgical fashion: '*Sabah el Kher, ya Sheekh*', '*Sabah e Nur, Doktur. Kif halak?*' '*Mabsut el hamdo' l' illah, Kif inte?*' '*Ana mabsut, nushkur Allah.*'[10] We never say more; nor could we, because my knowledge of Arabic is as scant as his knowledge of English. But from those few economical words, repeated each morning, an understanding has arisen between us, a respect for each other's dignity grounded in our reverence for God.

Hence there was no ill ease or hesitation between us after we eventually made our way over the soggy, clay ground to the grave and Abu Jihad for a moment assumed a hierarchical role superior to my own. With the confidence and assurance of an experienced priest of burials he jumped down into the grave in order to place stones in position so as to raise the coffin above the water. And from down in the depths he controlled the labours of the rest of us like a priest shepherding altar boys. As he stood there in his rough clothes and gum boots I thought of the Jewish saying, 'I learnt holiness from the very limbs of my teacher.'

Once his handiwork was done, and after I had spoken appropriate words, Abu Jihad gracefully withdrew, once more into a minor hierarchical role. Standing by my side and looking down in the heaped grave he said in a low voice, almost whispering, 'That is the way of all human beings, Doctor, the way of us all.'

But what were the 'appropriate words'? On the previous occasion – when I conducted funeral prayers for Mary Rudolf in Santa Cruz – at least Mary and her friends were in some sense believers, and so it had been possible for me to fulfil the priestly role: that is, to speak to God on behalf of the mourners and to the mourners on behalf of God. But now, out of loyalty to Ruth's wishes, I could not do the same. Instead I addressed Ruth as one still living amongst us. At first when I pronounced her name boldly and directly I sensed a tremor run through those gathered around her coffin, as though they had not expected her to be present. But almost immediately it seemed perfectly natural, both to them and to me, that we should be thanking Ruth for her life of goodness and loving-kindness.

As we were slowly picking our way through the mud, out of the cemetery, Günther gently took my arm and, his eyes wider than ever, said in his hoarse voice, 'Every word you spoke, Donald, seemed to come out of my own heart.'

6th March, 1985. Tantur

We had a very bad time indeed today – so many people grinding away at their hidden agendas. But whereas I myself can afford to be philosophical these days about such matters since I am soon to leave, my colleague, Francisco, is in no such position. And he certainly showed no inclination to be philosophical late this afternoon after everyone else had left the seminar room. Always clinging, in spite of his scepticism, to a rather winning hope that Christian clerics, professors and religious will prove to be better than the average citizen, his fierce comments upon them are a symptom of his dreams being shattered.

In an effort to stem the torrent of excoriation that Francisco was pouring out upon the religious breed in general I said to him rather diffidently, 'But there have been some religious people here who were for real.' At which he suddenly stopped, paused for a minute looking pensive, and then his eyes brightened, his voice softened and with a smile he said, 'Yes. Whenever I get like this I need only to think of one person who has been here this year – Itty – and he redeems the whole thing.'

My heart leapt for joy at hearing those words. I had known that a number of people had looked askance at Itty's contributions to our seminars on the grounds that he was 'theologically unsophisticated'. Francisco's statement was a recognition that some people can reach you without theological stepping-stones, because they know how to swim.

16th March, 1985. Tantur

Once more, having spent a lifetime trying to explain matters by way of words, I discover that it is the events of life itself rather than words that lead to clarification. I am thinking of recent events surrounding our Shepherd's Hut. They have done more to illuminate for me an aspect of a certain Protestant mentality than all the books on Protestantism that I have studied or the lectures I have listened to.

What set off the train of events was the impending departure over a year ago of our librarian, Brother Bartomeu, as a result of which I had to search for someone to replace him. Since we needed someone with linguistic and theological skills similar to Bartomeu's the search proved difficult and even began to seem hopeless until Fr Peter mentioned the name of Brother Gabriel.

Brother Gabriel was a most learned Frenchman, a Jesuit of Jewish extraction, who had received permission from his superiors to pursue the hermit life out in the Judean desert, in the remote wadi of Ein Fara. According to my friend, Fr Peter, he was an excellent librarian and Peter suggested that he might be willing to come and direct our Institute library if only we could set up a hermitage for him within our grounds. At first that sounded to be a way-out idea until I suddenly thought of our Shepherd's Hut. Although the Hut (actually a stone structure) was at that time almost buried in a blanket of nettles and looked as though it was scarcely more than a heap of rubble, I decided at least to examine it and give the old building a chance of renewed life.

When I did so one morning of bright wintery sunshine it was as if the Shepherd's Hut itself responded and opened itself up to me to reveal its beauty. I noticed for the first time how snugly it rested in a quiet corner of our grounds, hidden so deeply both by the folds of the land and by the olive trees that some scholars have been known to spend a whole year in the Institute without ever discovering its existence. Its stonework blends comfortably into the rocky ground about it, and its proportions are so harmonious as to set one into an attitude of prayer the moment one enters. Standing outside you look directly across the Judean desert towards the mountains of Moab in the far distance, whilst once inside the play of light and shade from the windows induces a feeling of being safe and at peace. Further, towards the rear of the hut, almost invisible, there are a few steps leading down to a cave, in themselves an invitation to penetrate even deeper through the heart of the cave into the cave of one's own heart. With its earthen floor so beautifully dry and its thick walls to protect one from the rain, the wind and the burning sun, our Shepherd's Hut was itself waiting to be adopted as a place of prayer.

And that is how I described it in the letter I sent to Brother Gabriel offering him the Shepherds's Hut as his hermitage if he would agree to come and serve as our librarian. But he never received my message. Two days after I had dispatched the letter the dear man's body was discovered at the base of the cliffs in Ein Fara, directly below the cave on the cliff face which served as his hermitage. Apparently he had slipped and fallen to his death.

Saddened as I was at the news of the good man's death, my thoughts scarcely ever turned again towards the Shepherd's Hut until one bright sunny winter's morning when my path took me near it and my heart was suddenly moved, almost as though Brother Gabriel was touching me in order to tell me something. Straight away I realised that, as an act of *pietas* towards him, I was being called to restore the Shepherd's Hut: it was meant to become a place set apart for silence and meditation and prayer. I straight away shared my vision for the hut with my colleague Tony, our administrator, who in no time was working out the details of our project.

Confirmation of the vision's authenticity was given to us soon afterwards by the four young Muslim workmen to whom we entrusted the work of restoration. Without words, intuitively, they caught on to the vision we had of the Hut's purpose. All those four workmen live in the wretched Deheishe refugee camp nearby, and yet, in spite of the squalor in the camp, and the continual harassment they have to endure from Jewish soldiers, those young men remain unbowed. And they undertook the work with a sensitivity and respect for what they were about. During the months that followed they were always ready to listen intelligently to our proposals for the interior fashioning of the hut, and they would often put forward suggestions of their own which almost always proved to be just what was needed. And all these exchanges they carried out with the quiet dignity of men who have been formed with a sense for the sacred.

So it did my heart good to see the bright gladness in their eyes when I thanked them and congratulated them on having worked so hard that the hut was all finished and beautifully appointed by 20th February, Ash Wednesday. That was the day we had chosen to celebrate the inauguration of the Hut.

And how powerful was that experience of Ash Wednesday! A little before eight o'clock, in the darkness of the night, we picked our way over the rocky ground south of our main building, stumbling along, holding on to one another, in the direction of the Shepherd's Hut. By the light of our torches we managed to carry safely all the equipment needed for the Eucharist and the distribution of the ashes. For a good part of the way we also carried Jill, who suffers from multiple sclerosis. And perhaps it was the carrying of Jill which released the current of healing that palpably flowed through the whole community during the subsequent hours. Whatever may be the explanation, everyone present sensed the sacredness and solemnity of that moment when the Shepherd's Hut was being consecrated to a new life in the light of the still flames of the candles as Lloyd celebrated the Eucharist according to the Anglican rite, and as the Roman Catholic priests then passed around reverently from one to another of the faithful who were standing with bowed heads, and signed them on their foreheads with the Cross of ashes. It was enough to move you to tears to hear the quiet responses of everyone as they were asked to remember in their prayers those who had contributed to the blessedness of this special moment in this special place: amongst them the shepherds who for two hundred years had sheltered here; Brother Gabriel, whose death was the inspiration for our restoration; and our Muslim brethren from Deheishe whose skilful workmanship was even then being highlighted by the radiance from the candles.

In all the years I have lived here I have never known a moment of such healing as the one we experienced the night of Ash Wednesday.

Yet now I hear that after I leave Tantur the Shepherd's Hut is to be made available for a commercial re-enactment of the Last Supper.

I was stunned when rumours of these plans came to my ears but now I have come round to seeing them as a sign of a great gulf between an extreme Protestant view of the world and the Catholic or Orthodox view. For the former the sacred is not that which in Hebrew is described as *kadosh,* set apart, the sign amongst Jews of holiness. There is little stress upon the fact that in the order of the sacred there are places set apart for the glory of God; that there are times set apart for special prayers; and there are people set apart for special service – vessels set apart, vestments set apart, signs of the sacred.

Likewise there are special blessings for places, times and people, as we know from the woman who is blessed among women; for, as David Jones sang, 'She that loves place, time, demarcation, hearth, kin, enclosure, site, differentiated cult, though she is but one mother of us all: one earth brings us all forth, one womb receives us all, yet to each she is other, named of some other . . .' And in a further poem David gives voice to his fear that these special places might be reduced

> to a common level
> till everything presuming difference
> and all the sweet remembered demarcations

       wither
    to the touch of us
       and know the fact of empire.

17th March, 1985. Tantur

Often one recognises one's priorities not by sitting down
and working them out but by reflecting on one's behaviour
and, through reflection, coming to recognise one's priorities. An instance of that process was the way Dorothy and
I tried to make sure that all the official farewell ceremonies
of today were not going to prevent us from saying good-
bye properly to Salman Arab. Immediately after an early
breakfast we went up the hill to the exposed spot where
in his tent he has endured all the fierce rain storms, gales,
snow and cold of this winter.

As we approached his tent we were greeted by several
rounds of loud, staccato barking on the part of the dog
which he has recently acquired. But the dog quietened
down; and having made our way through the rubble to
the tent, we peered inside. We saw that he was not lying
huddled on his camp bed as he has been doing throughout
the whole of the winter. He was not there, and the tent
seemed ominously empty. For a moment a sharp fear came
over me that perhaps he had been taken ill and had gone
to hospital, or even that he had died during the last few
days. But then I glanced around the hill top and saw him,
about twenty yards distant. In his blindness and deafness
unaware of our presence, he was crouching beside a rock,
defecating. Hanging down clearly outlined against the
white rock, I could see the old man's genitals. In his naked-
ness and vulnerability he stood for me as a symbol of the
frail creatures that we human being are. I was reminded
of the words spoken to Edgar by King Lear on the heath,
the night of the storm: 'unaccomodated man is no more
but such a poor, bare, forked animal as thou art.'

And yet, after we had waited quietly for him to finish
cleaning himself and I went over to him to take him by

the arm and lead him back to his tent and he realised who we were, I, in turn, realised that Shakespeare's troubled humanism shatters on the rock of Islam. The old man has never lost his dignity throughout all his trials. Not for a moment has there been even the slightest hint from him of a plea for pity. And when the moment came for us to say our final goodbye he blessed us with complete composure, assuring us that the recording angel had quite literally written down every kindness that we had done towards him.

As we walked away from the dear old man, to whom I now felt so close, I could not help asking myself a question that went through me like a sword: how many of us on the hill opposite, in the Institute of Tantur, who talk day in and day out about God and spirituality, have enough faith to have endured what he has endured, without bitterness or animosity or any questioning of the will of God?

19th March, 1985. On the Flight from Tel Aviv to Manchester

Although we have now gone through it so many times we still find ourselves bewildered and emotionally drained by the whole process of bidding farewell to a place where one has lived very intensely amongst others also living intensely and where one has made deep friendships not only with individuals but also with the peoples who dwell in the land and, indeed, with the landscape itself.

Sitting here in the plane, recollecting the appreciation and love which has been shown towards us during these weeks of farewell, there are two occasions which keep presenting themselves before my mind's eye. The first was at the Rainbow Group two weeks ago. Before the programme for the evening began of this Jewish–Christian group the chairman, my friend Rabbi Jack Cohen, surprised me by asking me to stand up so that he could wish me well on behalf of the Rainbow. Having done so very warmly he came over to me and presented me with two Israeli coins. One of them, he explained, was to help me on my journey outwards; and I was to be allowed, according to the traditional custom, to spend it. The other I was to keep to sustain me when I returned to Israel. It symbolises the heartfelt desire of the members of the Rainbow Group that I should one day come back to the land. Only a brief ritual, one may think – even trivial – but I found it moving and meaningful.

The second occasion was more emotional, as befits an Arab happening. It took place last Saturday morning.

Without any need to discuss the matter Dorothy and I and our Arab staff decided independently that we and they wanted to bid each other farewell on our own, just the Arabs and ourselves, with no Americans or Europeans present.

The Arabs of this district, even after all the centuries of foreign incursions and the floods of tourists, still retain an instinct for how to conduct themselves according to the occasion. In other words, they have maintained a culture, in contrast with representatives of modern secularised cities who do not know how to behave. On Saturday morning this meant that all of them, cooks, handymen, receptionists and office workers, were sitting around our music room waiting to greet us in what I can only describe as a hierarchic fashion. The order in which they were sitting and the manner in which they held themselves were reminiscent of the somewhat solemn attitudes adopted in church. One knew, without having to be told, which of them would take the lead in making a speech, who would translate, and who would make the presentation of whatever lay within the large parcel resting on a side table.

Since I knew that I would be expected to say more than a few words on such an occasion this solemn atmosphere constituted a slight problem for me: how could I speak in a dignified fashion whilst at the same time lightening the atmosphere which threatened to become oppressive? I thought I had solved the problem reasonably well with a few humorous reminiscences that I made towards the end of my ten-minute response to Issa's address – until the very last sentence, when I turned towards Dorothy to ask her to say a word of gratitude.

That did it! The cheerful smile on my face vanished when I looked into Dorothy's face; her eyes were filled with tears and her voice was choking as she began to express her affection for all of them. She had hardly got a sentence out before she was unmistakably weeping; and that set me off, and many of the Arabs present also began to weep.

In a way it was marvellous, a truly Arab occasion with plenty of speeches and many demonstrations of emotion leading to a welcome catharsis, finishing up with everyone sitting around, restored to cheerfulness, unashamedly tucking into the coffee and the mountains of cake.

6th April, 1985. Letter to the Tablet

Dear friend,

Here it is now night on the Mount of Olives, where I have come as the most propitious place from which to respond to your request that I should send you a final letter on the eve of my departure from the Holy City. I have chosen to come here because this Mount of Olives has never ceased to be a place of mystery for me. So I wanted to discover if I could somehow penetrate into its mystery by remaining here alone in the silence and the darkness, peering over the Kidron Valley towards the Old City of Jerusalem. Because I knew before – and know even more forcibly now – that the mystery of this place is the mystery of Jesus, the man with whom mankind can never come to terms.

For no matter how many times or in how many ways mankind may strive to capture Jesus, whether in words or in painting or music or any other mode, he always escapes. The Gospel says about Jesus's home town crowd's attempt to fling him over the cliff: 'but passing through the midst of them he went away' – and still to this day he cannot be grasped, although now he will never go away. Of course there are many people who wish he would. Some of them have written learned books to show that he never even existed; others have written equally learned books to prove that he was no more than a Galilean rabbi; yet others have tried to reduce him to the rank of a mere prophet. But it is no good. After all those words and all those arguments and definitive statements, this ever more mysterious Jesus remains, gazing steadily at each one of us.

And I know of no place where that steady gaze is more inescapable than at the altar within what the Latins call the Holy Sepulchre, and what the Orthodox more truthfully name 'the Life-giving Tomb'. Over that altar there is set an icon surrounded by a metal casing. And perhaps it is from the metal casing that the unflinching eyes of Jesus catch a certain glint of sternness as if to remind us that this man is not to be trifled with. Having seen it all, yet he did not flinch. Those eyes are saying, 'Behold man! Now you know what it takes to be a man.'

And here, on the Mount of Olives looking down upon Gethsemane, you can more readily envisage what it took in those days to be a real man in the earthiest sense. I am sure you remember, dear friend, the day that we stood here and pondered together on the nitty-gritty details of those days after Palm Sunday when Jesus lived on this very patch of the hill where we were then standing. His feet must have been bruised, for you cannot walk through the Judean desert barefoot or in sandals without constantly striking your feet against rocks and stones and pebbles. Probably his skin was cracked; and likely enough he had fleas on him from riding the donkey. He and his disciples had sweated on the long pull up from Jericho; they must have all smelt of dried sweat since there were no showers in those days and no daily changes of clothes. And we asked ourselves how did they manage to clean themselves after emptying their bowels, since toilet paper and water closets were not yet invented? In the way still favoured by the Bedouin?

People who live distant from the Mount of Olives may hold such considerations to be irrelevant. But they are far from irrelevant if you wish to stand in the sandals and enter into the mind of the man Jesus, this northern provincial of Galilean accent, as he sat on the Mount of Olives and gazed across at that sky-scraping Temple, which was the centre not only of bloody sacrifice in the name of religion but was also the treasury, the centre of money-power, and of Israel's men of learning. And hard by, in uneasy alliance, stood that terrifying symbol of military power, the Antonia fortress of the occupying Romans.

As he looked across the Kidron Valley towards all that concentration of power – religious, financial, intellectual, political, military – the man from Galilee must have wondered sometimes whether he had gone clean out of his mind to confront such a concentration and take it upon himself by Spirit alone to destroy every part of its edifice even to the foundations, so that for all ages there would remain of it not one stone upon a stone. And most agonising of all, he would have to do it alone. Because he, who knew what was in men's hearts, knew that his own disciples would desert him and deny him, and that he would die transfixed between earth and heaven, seemingly rejected by both men and God. No wonder that he trembled, and shook so much that despite the cold night air his sweat fell upon the ground like great drops of blood.

These are some of the thoughts which for the hundredth time went through my mind yesterday as I sat on a wall reading the Gospel narratives of the Passion. The sun was warm, but underneath, as so often in these harsh Judean hills, there blew a chill wind from the north, really biting. So not surprisingly there happened what constantly happens in this land as one reads the Scriptures: the meaning of the words seemed to stand up from the page and strike me between the eyes, like a blow from the fist of a heavy-handed labourer, leaving its meaning ringing in my skull.

For the Passion narratives are extremely primitive, all about money, bread and blood, about hunger and thirst. Just read them again, thinking of what I say and you will discover, even in your London flat, that what I say is true. Think, for example, of the widow's mite, the ejection of the money-changers, the price of the jar of alabaster, the purse kept by Judas, the thirty pieces of silver. 'Money and blood', I thought to myself yesterday after I noticed a rivulet of blood running in the gutter at the side of the road as I was walking back from the Mount to Bethphage. Looking to discover where the blood came from, I saw a group of children gathered in a garage around a man who had just slaughtered a sheep which he held in his left hand whilst with his right hand he brandished a large knife. The man was sacrificing a sheep because his new house was now finished and the next day his son was to marry and bring in his new bride. Once the blood was outpoured God would not begrudge him his wealth and his houses, so the man thought.

As for thirst, the Judean desert impressed the deeper meaning of that upon me once more two days ago. Not long after sunrise I set off to walk through the desert on my own and I spent the whole day alone until sunset. The only people I spoke to were two Bedouin shepherds whom I came upon at midday. They invited me to share their wonderfully refreshing sugary tea which they had boiled between some stones. Soon afterwards I ran out of water. And as I clambered up and down the wadis in the burning sun, I could feel my whole body becoming dried up and withered. For the last two or three hours of the day, my mouth was completely parched and I could think of nothing except water. Then I found a piece of orange peel which I gratefully chewed. What I experienced for an hour or two is everyday life for millions of our fellow creatures.

As for bread and hunger, they are symbolised for me in this land by the Musrara. The Musrara you may remember as that open space between the rather splendid hostel of Notre Dame and Nablus Road. It is there that crowds of workless Arab men gather each day at first light in the hope that someone will hire them and enable them to put bread into their own mouths and into the mouths of their wives and children or of their aged mothers and fathers.

On no single occasion nowadays do I travel through the Musrara without thinking of Jesus's parable of those labourers who were standing idle in the market place because no one had hired them. Often it is not at the eleventh hour but after twelve that I go past them all; and by that time certain of them, both young and old, are sitting silently on their haunches by the roadside. From their eyes you can see that they have now abandoned hope of work and bread for the day. I remember with special vividness one day when we swept past them in the Institute car on our way to a full dress occasion in the Anglican cathedral, the consecration of a new bishop. And throughout the beautiful liturgy in the cathedral my spirit was unceasingly troubled by the thought that before coming to seek his presence in the cathedral Jesus had meant us to seek his presence amongst the poor men whom no one had hired.

Knowing that here I am simply echoing the feelings expressed by Mary, the mother of Jesus, in her prophetic Magnificat, I am led to tell you that what my sojourn in this land has changed as much as anything else is my image of Mary. In previous years that could hardly have been any other than what I have received through Piero della Francesca's paintings or Gerard Manley Hopkins' poems

304

or Gounod's music – the image of some dreamy, ethereal young lady untouched by everyday toil.

But since that time I have met the peasant women of Galilee. So now the image that comes spontaneously to my mind is of a woman with strong hands, sinewy through much work; and of a face whose skin is rough from exposure to the sun and the wind; of feet that are broad-spread through climbing the hills around Nazareth barefoot; but above all, of eyes that are steady and a mouth that is firm through enduring the sorrows of the refugee, the poor and the oppressed.

On reading the above, my good friend, I can see you frowning and asking yourself whether my stress upon the earthiness of Mary and of Jesus may not be leading me – and for the first time – to ignore the heavenliness of Jesus. But do not fear. I realise more each day that the hidden and secret wisdom which we have received is about what no eye has seen nor ear heard nor the heart of man conceived, and that if we are to penetrate ever deeper into the deep things of God we have to be led by the Holy Spirit. It is simply that through contact with this land we learn that we can only search everything, even the deep things of God, once we allow everything in our own lives and indeed of all creatures to be measured by the mystery of this man Jesus.

How truly he is the mystery at the heart of all mysteries burst upon me three weeks ago beside the Sea of Galilee. The weather at the time was stormier and colder in Tiberias than has been known for a generation. The waves on the sea itself were sweeping in violently and crashing over the promenade as we struggled against the fierce wind towards the little church of St Peter. Once inside we found a haphazard congregation numbering no more than seven or eight persons. The priest, seemingly of eastern origin, made his way painfully through the rite of Mass in a mixture of Latin, pidgin English and what seemed like broken Italian. Everything pointed to a most unpropitious occasion,

305

Then came a moment of truth, when the priest raised the host at the elevation. 'This is my body.' In an instant I realised with complete conviction that the body being raised was the same body who had indeed sailed the sea just outside nearly 2,000 years ago; who had calmed that same sea one night when it had been stormy, as now. He is the body whom we can only come to know through the sufferings of our own body, through attending to the sufferings of other bodies, and through sharing bread. That is why the man Jesus will for ever remain the mystery of mysteries whom nobody can fathom.

Peace and love, Donald

An ancient Irish prayer

Mo theora ucse forsin Rig
intan noscairiub frim chri;
nimraib dorat i coibsi,
nimraib nama,
nimraib ni.

(Three wishes I ask of the King
when I shall part from my body:
may I have nothing to confess,
may I have no enemy,
may I have nothing.)

Notes

1. A book I wrote which was first published in 1981 by Darton Longman & Todd.
2. I pursued my enquiries later and came to the conclusion that the story was not true.
3. Bishop of Guildford (1922–1982) who was a Tantur scholar from January until May, 1982.
4. A Hebrew name, meaning 'Banner of the Nations'. It is a *moshav* (or land community) established near Haifa, mainly through the inspiration of Dutch Reformed Christians, as a witness to Christian solidarity with the Jewish people and an act of repentance for Christian persecution of Jews over the centuries.
5. Roman Catholics in the Holy Land are generally referred to as 'Latins'.
6. A common Arabic saying. It means 'slowly, slowly'.
7. Jerusalem, 1975.
8. Um Fahum was an almost legendary Egyptian singer whose voice was listened to with reverence by all the Arab peoples of the Middle East. People who could not agree on any other single issue would agree that Um Fahum was the voice of the Arab soul.
9. Fr Joe and Fr Hank were the organisers of renewal courses for Maryknoll priests which took place at Tantur from 1981 to 1985. Although the courses themselves were not the business of Tantur, the Maryknollers joined in many aspects of our community life. I have never met a finer bunch of men. They made all the difference.
10. 'Morning good, O sheikh.' 'Morning of light, Doctor. How are you?' 'I am well, glory to God. And you?' 'I also am well, thanks be to God.'

INDEX OF NAMES